BETWEEN DREAM AND NATURE:
ESSAYS ON UTOPIA AND DYSTOPIA

DQR Studies in Literature 2

Edited by

F.G.A.M. Aarts / J. Bakker / C.C. Barfoot / M. Buning /
G. Janssens / W.J. Meys

Subseries to Costerus. New Series Vol. 61

BETWEEN DREAM AND NATURE:
ESSAYS ON UTOPIA AND DYSTOPIA

Edited by
Dominic Baker-Smith and C.C. Barfoot

AMSTERDAM 1987

The editors and the publisher would like to thank the Victoria and Albert Museum, London, for permission to reproduce *Sir Thomas More and his Family* (p. 116), and the Nationalmuseum, Stockholm, for Jan Massys' *Venus Cytherea* (p. 124). The illustration on p. 14 is taken from the frontispiece of the first edition of *Utopia*, Louvain, 1516.

The paper on which this book is printed meets the requirements of "ISO 9706:1994, Information and documentation - Paper for documents - Requirements for permanence".

Transferred to digital printing 2006
ISBN-10: 90-6203-959-6
ISBN-13: 978-90-6203-959-3
©Editions Rodopi B.V., Amsterdam 1987
Printed in the Netherlands

TABLE OF CONTENTS

INTRODUCTION

The papers printed in this volume are a selection from those given at a conference held by the English Seminar of the University of Amsterdam in September 1984 on the theme "Utopia and Dystopia". The idea for such a conference, sparked off by a generous proposal from the British Council, was inevitably linked to Orwell's *Nineteen Eighty-Four*; but it was our hope that it would prove useful to treat Orwell within a wider tradition of political fantasy and to consider some out of the range of imaginary projections which made his novel possible. It is clear that many contributors to this volume have used the occasion of the Amsterdam conference to view their own presiding interests in a utopian light. Not every piece published here takes utopia as its natural starting point (although this may be somewhat disguised in the presentation or the writing) but rather reveals how many different scholarly or literary preoccupations may be shown to border upon or be revealingly associated with utopian themes.

Quite apart from the intellectual benefits of such an approach it turned out to be a welcome alternative to obsessive chatter about Orwell which marked the opening months of the *annus terribilis*. By September everyone was glad to broaden the perspective and put *Nineteen Eighty-Four* in a context. For one thing this brought attention back to the novel as a literary text rather than some kind of threatening prophecy. Nonetheless, that brief and distracting coincidence of fictional and calendar time did serve to highlight the strange relationship found in all utopian (and dystopian) writing between an imagined world and the familiar theatre of human experience. This is not quite the same as the relationship between literature and politics — though that issue is raised as well — but touches on the complex way in which the imagined world is still so linked to our "real" world as to suggest the possibility of movement between the two. It is almost a definition of a utopian work that it should be contagious, that is to say designed to infect our reading of our world.

This problematic relationship is noticeable in the interesting interaction between literary and historical concerns in the papers we have printed. The same dispute which has marked recent discussion of Thomas More's *Utopia* has its relevance for the whole genre. While literary critics have emphasized the ambiguity of the dialogue, the uncertain status of the interlocutors and the consequent invisibility of authorial intention, political historians have noted its place in a tradition of social analysis and read its communism as More's considered judgement on the evils of nascent capitalism. Thus the conference provided a convenient opportunity to bring together contrasted approaches, revealing in the process some unexpected connections and patterns of development.

As will be clear from the papers which follow, it proved difficult to make any sharp distinction between utopia and millenium. From its inception the utopian tradition has been entangled with schemes and symbols of religious renewal, most strikingly so in the seventeenth-century examples considered here. The future can only be guessed in terms which may transcend present in- adequacies yet which build on present aspirations. The critical point in any utopian fiction will be this contact between dream and nature, which may be why, as John Dixon Hunt suggests, the garden is so consistently linked to utopian contexts.

In this respect one cumulative feature of the papers is the evidence they provide of the interplay of broad historical or ideological factors with the rhetorical patterning of utopian works. One could summarize it in the formula that optimism promotes literalism. In other words, the more hopeful the prescription the more direct the message. By way of contrast, More's Utopians and Swift's Houyhnhnms offer models of wholly rational behaviour which are cut off from human experience by complexities of narrative structure which make the interpretive antics of the critics a paradigm of man's fallen state.

It is the pessimists, among whom we can include Orwell, who present us with the problems. The pessimism conveyed in the defeat of Winston Smith may be slightly qualified, as Bernard Bergonzi suggests, by the "slow and difficult business"of rendering down Shakespeare, Milton and Swift into Newspeak. In this respect Orwell, like More and Swift, is a humanist; even if we allow for the fact that he misread Swift, nevertheless he shared with his predecessors their awareness of literature as a moral witness to human nature, one which gives due prominence to the irrational forces in man. Whatever one makes of More's ideal polity, the fact remains that it allows precious little scope for individual moral struggle, and the same can be said of Swift's equine world. That is why both Utopians and Houyhnhnms have a highly problematic relation to human nature as it is commonly found. An ambiguous narrative handling of the "ideal" element marks off *Utopia* and *Gulliver's Travels* from those hopeful projections which aim — from Bacon to Darwin — to elevate mankind by environmental reform. In the latter the contentious issue no longer lies in man's moral nature but in social liberation or scientific advance. Yet Bacon saw science as a means to heal the effects of the Fall, and the myth of that first, lost garden haunts utopian literature. As Marijke Rudnik points out, the liberation of woman from a male dominated society is still presented as a model for the regeneration of a fallen mankind.

It could be argued that the emergence of a feminine point of view is one of the most significant developments in the history of the genre, offering more than a new system or a new technology. Conceivably Thomas More would have admired George Eliot's portrait of Savonarola in *Romola*; her account of the passionate reformer trapped in the corruptions of power has a pathos and even a dignity far beyond the imaginative range of prescriptive utopias. Here the most marked contrast would seem to be Shaw who, as John Peereboom argues, uses his hope for the radical improvement of man (in spite of the inadequacy of the electorate) as an evasion of darker perceptions. Reviewing a revival of *Androcles and the Lion* some years ago, Harold Hobson observed that the trouble with Shaw was that he knew all of the answers and none of the questions. To us in the 1980s it seems that the questions are more compelling; too many of the answers have been tried. This explains why our approach to utopias is almost invariably ironical or interiorized.

Sidney and Beatrice Webb, those heirs of nineteenth-century optimism, saw in Soviet Russia a new civilisation; possibly they saw it in terms of William Morris's *News from Nowhere*, the final chapter of which is headed "The Beginning of the New Life".

4

Myths of the new order, whether brought about by angels or revolutionaries, all aim to give a transcendence to the affairs of daily life. Morris betrays the formula in his description of the new spirit which follows on the revolution:

> More akin to our way of looking at life was the spirit of the Middle Ages, to whom heaven and the life of the next world was such a reality, that it became to them a part of the life upon the earth; which accordingly they loved and adorned, in spite of the ascetic doctrines of their formal creed, which bade them contemn it (Penguin edn, 1984, p. 298).

After Stalin, and the compromises of Euro-communism, this new spirit seems very remote. Even that New World which stirred More's imagination is now the Third World, a mirror image of our problems and our social guilt. It might seem reasonable to suppose that the fable of social improvement is out of fashion. Yet the lasting interest of all utopian writing lies not so much in its capacity to engineer a new type of humanity as in its aptitude for dramatising that central human dilemma of having both an imagination and a will that fails to support it. It is perhaps because we do not believe in utopias that we need utopian literature; it has, after all, a deeper purpose than social efficiency — it can restore a sense of being human. John Passmore, in *The Perfectibility of Man*, ends his comprehensive account of human schemes for self-improvement with the cautious opinion that, "Men, almost certainly, are capable of more than they have ever so far achieved. But what they achieve ... will be a consequence of their remaining anxious, passionate, discontented human beings"(London, 1970, p. 326). As this collection goes to show, it is within these bounds that utopias really do their work.

Amsterdam   Dominic Baker-Smith

THE ESCAPE FROM THE CAVE: THOMAS MORE AND THE VISION OF UTOPIA

When, in 1474, Marsilio Ficino completed his *Theologia Platonica*, he presented a manuscript of the work to his patron Lorenzo de' Medici, "Il Magnifico". This beautiful manuscript, still preserved in the Laurentian Library in Florence, opens with a dedicatory letter in which Ficino justifies his endeavour. Clearly he expected some criticism of the way in which his title yoked together theology and Plato, and he tries to meet it in advance. It was scarcely a new debate, but the relation between natural reason and Christian revelation takes on a new urgency in the Renaissance when the culture of pagan antiquity is increasingly recommended as a means of social and moral reform. It was under the influence of Ficino's "Sancte Socrates" that Erasmus made his celebrated, or notorious, suggestion that the great pagan moralists were moved by some divine power.[1] In his letter to Lorenzo Ficino makes two points of interest to us now. First of all he praises Plato, on the authority of St Augustine, for teaching the existence of God and the immortality of the soul; secondly he praises Lorenzo for realizing that ideal platonic combination of philosophy and political authority.[2] Since I am talking about Thomas More's *Utopia* you may recognize that the two items of religious faith which Ficino attributes to Plato are shared by More's Utopians, while the combination of philosophy with political power is a crucial issue in that debate concerning political involvement which must be the basis on which any authentic interpretation of More's book will rest. That spectre of the platonic ruler haunted the Renaissance, and if you are strongly impressed by the compliment to Lorenzo it will be a healthy corrective to realize that a similar insinuation was made about Henry VIII.

1. *Convivium Religiosum, Opera Omnia*, Leiden, 1703-6, I, 682A-683E.
2. Marsile Ficin, *Théologie Platonicienne*, ed. R. Marcel, Paris, 1964, I, p. 37.

Libellus vere aureus nec

MINVS SALVTARIS QVAM FESTI-
uus de optimo reip. statu, deqz noua Insula Vtopia
authore clariffimo viro Thoma Moro inclytæ
ciuitatis Londinenfis ciue & vicecomite cu-
ra M. Petri Aegidii Antuerpiéfis, & arte
Theodorici Martini Aluftenfis, Ty
pographi almæ Louanienfium
Academiæ nunc primum
accuratiffime edi
tus.¦.

Et dono Rev. Vir.
J. Smith de Wisbech. 1717

Cum gratia z priuilegio.

1516
·/·

Lib. Konnoll.

A word is born: the title-page of the first edition of *Utopia*, Thierry Martens, Louvain 1516.

In his recent study of English utopian writings of the sixteenth
and seventeenth centuries,[3] J.C. Davis proposes five basic modes
of ideal society: utopia, millennium, arcadia, cockaygne and the
perfect moral commonwealth. The attempt is stimulating rather
than successful. One might usefully appeal here to Wallace
Stevens' observation that "Eventually an imaginary world is
entirely without interest"; usefully, that is, if we take "imaginary"
to mean a fantasy world, devoid of the rigour of practical
reference. Certainly that rules out Cockaygne, even if that is the
nearest to Utopia most of us get. Arcadia, with its premise of an
harmonious natural environment, is really a form of nostalgia for
a pre-lapsarian Golden Age, with a minimum of political
machinery. The so-called Ideal Moral Commonwealth, which
attempts to perfect existing social structures by means of individual education and moral formation (on the pattern of Sir
Thomas Elyot's *Governor*) seems too banal to merit a separate
category, and that leaves us with two modes — the utopian and the
millenarian. These can be distinguished by the utopian tendency to
a realistic estimate of human behaviour (i.e. the concern is with
social control), while the millenarian expectation is for an historical intervention which will alter the entire social calculus, nothing
less than the Second Coming which will radically transform
human society and the terms on which it operates.

It will be interesting to see how these categories stand up in the
course of this conference, but I have to admit to a certain
dissatisfaction with them. The different emphases need clarifica-
tion, but I am not convinced that we can make such a tidy
dissection. What has happened, I believe, is that a series of
political categories (using the word quite loosely) has been imposed on a mode of imaginative fiction. Again, I am using the
word fiction rather loosely, because the Hebrew prophets (whom
Davis places, rather oddly, under Arcadia) write fiction, though
they have a very real reference. The point is that millenarian texts
tend to operate figuratively. A land flowing with milk and honey is
not a pastoral fantasy; the pastoral element is there to point to an
unimaginable (because unrestricted) divine intervention. It does

3. J.C. Davis, *Utopia and the Ideal Society: A Study of English Utopian
Writing, 1516-1700*, Cambridge, 1981.

seem to me an important point, too, that utopian writing cannot be subsumed under political theory. The decision to operate through a fiction may suggest the inadequacy of the political concepts available, and a consequent desire to extend and refine those concepts by means of an imaginative exploration. To opt for fiction may indicate an intention to subvert established theory and with it the reader's conventional attitudes.

At the centre of all utopian writing is a concern with the mediating process between ideal forms and the inadequate provisions of experience. As a result the utopian mode hovers uncertainly between literary and socio-political concerns. Whether we are more concerned with the imaginative genesis or the practical limitations of a utopian text — whether, in other words, we are playing at being literary critics or political theorists — still our particular emphasis has to do with a transaction between imaginative vision and practical intelligence. The critic should be unusually alert to practical criteria, and the theorist should be unusually alert to the play of imaginary forms. Whether it is utopia or dystopia that we are considering, the separation from fantasy is absolute: both imply a reference back to the world of concrete acts and familiar experience which fantasy excludes. The central feature of utopian writing is the effort to reconcile ideal possibilities with the recalcitrance of the known. Even in the case of dystopian writing it is that emphasis on the obstinate features of a known world which suggests desirable alternatives — one reason why utopia and satire are so closely related.

One reason why utopian and millenarian modes seem hard to hold apart is that utopias tend to have a "historical" foundation. Someone starts them. The whole complex system of checks and restraints which is More's island of Utopia could only exist because King Utopus had the arbitrary power and the political vision to set the mechanism in motion. The millenarian significance attached to Oliver Cromwell, even by such a subtle and sophisticated observer as Andrew Marvell,[4] is a reminder that political advance and sacred history were not distinct categories to the pre-Enlightenment mind. In fact the search for that platonic combination which Ficino admired in Lorenzo de'Medici was as

4. For example in "The First Anniversary of the Government, 1655".

marked in the Ancient World as in the Renaissance. If we take More's actual title, *De Optimo Reipublicae Statu* (though having made the effort I shall now fall back on the conventional *Utopia*), then his work immediately slips into that category of works *De Republica*. However, More uses fiction to achieve his purposes. What of the others? I propose to look at two seminal works well known to More, Plato's *Republic* and Cicero's *De Republica*. Both are in a sense fictional in that, like More's book, they adopt the structure of a dialogue together with a specific physical setting. Then both Plato and Cicero make use of allegorical elements which take us right outside the restrictions of political theory.

Cicero's *De Republica* was written during a period of enforced political inaction which ended in 51 B.C. It was a period which he devoted to legal work and to the popularization of Greek thought in a series of philosophical dialogues. This choice of medium is significant, reflecting in structural form his scepticism about the possibility of formulating final truths. While the *De Republica* was known to Augustine it was lost to the Middle Ages and only fragments have been recovered. But until 1820, when Angelo Mai discovered a further section in a Vatican palimpsest, the only part known was that allegorical sequence preserved within Macrobius' commentary called the *Somnium Scipionis*, Scipio's Dream. Thanks to Macrobius' popularity and his careful discussion of *somnia*, Cicero's text became the ancestor of all medieval dream poems. Scipio's account of his dream, which stands out in the quasi-naturalistic dialogue which presumably made up the bulk of the *De Republica*, is an attempt to provide a more satisfactory answer to the problem posed in Plato's *Republic* by the so-called Myth of Er which closes that work. Er, a Pamphylian soldier killed in battle, returns to life after twelve days and gives an account of his experiences in the after-life. It is a fairly simple, if crude, device by which Plato uses an allegorical scheme of post-mortem judgement to provide the necessary moral link between the realm of pure Ideas and the political arena. In this way the Pythagorean belief in judgement of the dead is a means to promote political judgement on earth. This was, again, one of the key tenets of the Utopians who refused public office to anyone who did not believe that after this life "vices are ordained to be punished and virtue rewarded".[5]

The function of the *Somnium* was to suggest a metaphysical sanction for the idea of the perfect comonwealth. It was an attempt to face the epistemological question, how do you establish a link between the ideal model and the brute reality? The fabric of the allegory is predictable enough: after a conversation about his dead grandfather, the great Africanus, Scipio sleeps and is carried up to the heavens where the spirit of his grandfather initiates him into authentic, eternal, values. What is so typically Roman about Cicero's fable is its practical focus on public affairs. Man is presented as God's vicegerent on earth, a duty which extends to the establishment of political communities. Nothing on earth is more pleasing than social groups founded on the rule of law. The harmony of the spheres, which Africanus reveals to his grandson, is mediated to human consciousness by three classes of men: sages who cultivate "divina studia", those "docti homines" who recreate heavenly music with stringed instruments, and those who establish and preserve social communities by imitation of heavenly order.[6] Thus ethics, the arts and government are three channels by which an ideal order can filter into human activities.

The common theme which surfaces in Plato's and Cicero's myths, and which is still present in later utopian exercises, is a Pythagorean vision of cosmic harmony. Pythagoreanism has been described as "une métaphore ... tenace et repandue";[7] leaving aside arguments as to whether Pythagoreans were forbidden to eat beans, we can see that this key metaphor of a celestial model for human affairs is the ancestor of Utopia. The Hebrew prophets, on the other hand, look to a future in which utopian conditions are themselves a metaphor for divine intervention and a transformation of the terms of life:

> Then shall the lame man leape as an Hart, and the tongue of the dumbe sing; for in the wildernes shall waters breake out, and streames in the desert. (Isaiah xxxv, 6)

5. *Utopia*, eds. Edward Surtz, S.J. and J.H. Hexter, New Haven, 1965, pp. 221-223. Further references are to this edition.

6. *Somnium Scipionis* ed. A. Ronconi, Florence, 1961, III, 1; V, 2.

7. J. Carcopino, *La Basilique Pythagoricienne de la Porte Majeure*, Paris, 1926, p. 270.

It is more than irrigation that Isaiah has in mind. Nevertheless, the common ground of utopians and millenarians is that both have an eye on the consumer or the extra-textual response. Even the prophet wants to have an impact *Now*. In whatever device the utopian fiction may be packaged — a voice from the dead, a dream vision, a Lucianic excursion to the underworld — the critical thing is its engagement with the reader's non-utopian experience. In the abstract utopian and millenarian modes may be distinct, but it hardly surprising that in history they frequently overlap. Even if social order is only a metaphor for divine intervention there is always the sneaking thought that social order might speed up the process. Both modes want to convert the reader. Once converted, though, the reader shares the author's perplexity, how to make it happen? For the snag about Utopia is that it is a collective condition, not a private moral resolution. How do you generate the collective from the individual? The lynchpin of the utopian argument is the platonic philosopher-king, because only in such a person are those qualities which Ficino admired in Lorenzo to be found: the association of wisdom with power. It is the combination which makes possible the legend of Utopus, but remains as elusive as the combination of wealth and taste.

Let us now look at the credentials of More's informant about the remarkable isle of Utopia, Raphael Hythlodaeus. At the opening of the work More goes to some trouble to establish a link with Plato's *Republic*; the narrative begins after Mass in the great port of Antwerp even as Plato opens his fiction after a religious festival at Piraeus. The narrator, More's own *persona*, is struck by the figure of the stranger, "a man of advanced years, with sunburnt countenance and long beard and cloak hanging carelessly from his shoulder". He appears to be a ship's captain, but Peter Giles mysteriously implies that he is no common seaman, "for his sailing has not been like that of Palinaurus but that of Ulysses, or rather of Plato". We seem to be talking about journeys of the mind as we progress from a drowsy helmsman, through the *viator* figure of Ulysses to the metaphysical seeker, Plato himself. We learn that this Raphael has visited the New World with Vespucci and set out on further travels which included the visit to Utopia. But there are two particular features I want to stress, the fact that he has passed on his patrimony to his brothers so as to be free to travel, and his

absolute refusal to enter royal service, even though he is urged to
on account of his special experience. Since it is the fictional More
— "Morus" we can call him — who urges him, this refusal is all
the more remarkable for its reminiscence of a man the real More
had closely studied: Giovanni Pico della Mirandola. Perhaps it was
Colet who guided More to the life of Pico by his nephew
Gianfrancesco Pico; in any case Pico, the brilliant scholar and
associate of Ficino, who had died in 1494 aged thirty-one, is an
example certainly, but also a warning. Savonarola spoke severely
of him for failing to enter the religious life, and More had just
decided against the Carthusians. So Pico was an ambiguous figure
for More, and the English translation of *The Life of John Picus Erle
of Myrandula* which he prepared cut the biographical detail to
focus on the tension between learning and godliness.[8] Given this
selective approach it is all the more striking that More includes
Pico's sale of his patrimony for a nominal price to his nephew and
gives a translation of a letter in which Pico, writing in 1492,
adamantly refuses to enter the service of a prince. His correspondent had suggested that Pico could thus use his studies to
general advantage, and had regretted the divorce between
philosophy and courts. In reply Pico insists on the freedom of the
philosopher, adding that practical application of this sort turns
learning into merchandise.

The encounter between Morus and Raphael goes over exactly
the same ground, Morus taking the line of Pico's correspondent
and Raphael using Pico's own petulant arguments. The opening
pages of *Utopia* recreate certain tensions that the author had
experienced more than a decade before; significantly, they also
reveal the platonic traveller, Raphael, in an uncertain light. His
own fierce integrity is preserved, but at the price of any transaction
between philosophy and politics.

If we consider this figure of Raphael, the outsider, the man set
apart by an experience beyond the ordinary, then it is useful to
look back to Plato's specific treatment of this problem of social
transformation, the Cave Myth in *The Republic*. There are reasonable grounds for doing so since Erasmus not only alludes to the

8. Alastair Fox, *Thomas More: History and Providence*, Oxford, 1982,
p. 29.

myth in the *Encomium Moriae* (1511) but in the 1515 edition of the *Adagia*, another work which More seems to echo in *Utopia*, Erasmus makes the Cave central to his discussion of social reform: those who remain in the cave and accept the shadows thrown on the wall as reality are content with conventional values. Those who escape from their fetters and learn to perceive the real objects which throw the shadows are those who can disengage from the accepted *mores* of society and penetrate to an authentic source of value. But Plato's myth is not concerned only with this ascent to true vision; it is equally concerned with the problem of return. A man who has ascended to the source of light is alienated. He can no longer tolerate the conventional ways of other men, and the return to the cave blinds him; he is like the inspired fool at the end of the *Encomium Moriae*. Plato is realistic about this:

> Now if he should be required to contend with these perpetual prisoners in "evaluating" these shadows while his vision was still dim and before his eyes were accustomed to the dark ... would he not provoke laughter, and would it not be said of him that he had returned from his journey aloft with his eyes ruined and that it was not worthwhile even to attempt the ascent. And if it were possible to lay hands on and to kill the man who tried to release them and lead them up, would they not kill him?[9]

This total failure of ideal vision to penetrate the conventional world is precisely what disturbs Raphael; what gain will there be in serving a prince if no one will listen to him, let alone understand him?

The significance of this dilemma in *Utopia* becomes much clearer if we analyse its literary structure. At the centre of the fiction is the experience of an ideal commonwealth, a rational system where thanks to the absence of private property, institutional life controls private affairs and all forms of irresponsible pleasure are eradicated. Yet this detailed account of the Utopian system is not the simple blueprint for social stability and justice which it is often assumed to be. Set around Raphael's description of the island are a series of narrative devices which seriously adjust our response to this strange island. It is even possible to resurrect

---

9. *Republic*, 517a, tr. Paul Shorey in *The Collected Dialogues of Plato*, Princeton, 1973.

the likely process of composition in such a way as to clarify this controlling frame in which Raphael's description is set. The core section on Utopia was the first part of the work to be completed, during More's enforced leisure on a diplomatic mission to Bruges and Antwerp during 1515. He also wrote at this time the introductory pages which set up the fiction of a dialogue in an Antwerp garden. But the actual container for the account of Utopia is the extended argument between Morus and Raphael which runs through the whole of Book I and surfaces at the very end of Book II. It was completed in London the following year when More, on the verge of a permanent appointment to the King's Council, was concerned with advice to princes. Thus our view of the island is coloured by the dispute, and in particular by Raphael's condemnation of all coventional politics. Then, set outside the actual text, but still part of the "book" in an inclusive Renaissance sense, are the dedicatory letters and the letters from admiring friends. These establish a kind of game situation in which our reality, the historical, mundane reality of our lives, becomes entangled with elements of the fiction. If Raphael draws an absolute line between Utopia and Europe, the line between the fiction and "reality" is far less clear cut.

To illustrate what I mean, let us take the Letters which accompany the text. These are written by More himself, by Erasmus, Guillaume Budé, Peter Giles (who also plays a part in the fiction), Jerome Busleyden, all actual friends of Thomas More, though one should add a set of verses on Utopia supposedly by Raphael's nephew. This is typical of the strategy by which fiction and reality are interwoven. In Giles's letter to Busleyden the location of the island is discussed:

> While Raphael was speaking on the subject one of More's servants had come up to him to whisper something or other in his ear. I was therefore listening all the more intently when one of our company who had, I suppose, caught cold on shipboard, coughed so loudly that I lost some phrases of what Raphael said. I shall not rest, however, till I have full information on this point so that I shall be able to tell you exactly not only the location of the island but even the longitude and latitude — provided our friend Hytholodaeus be alive and safe.[10]

10. *Utopia,* p. 23.

But in the succeeding letter from More to Giles More is worried as to the exact length of the bridge in the Utopian capital Amaurotum; he cannot be certain whether it is five hundred or three hundred paces. He, too, is anxious to fix the precise location of the island since a theologian of his acquaintance is planning to travel there and evangelize the Utopians. In a final letter, printed after the text, More again tells Giles of his irritation at suggestions that the work is a fiction: if it were, surely people can imagine that he would have made a better job of it. They have only to check with Raphael, who was last heard of in March in Portugal.

The blurring of the demarcation between fiction and the ordinary world is a constant feature of utopian writing. In a mode which is so fundamentally concerned with the relation between imagined and experienced worlds, where the force of the imagined world lies in its apparent power to infiltrate the ordinary world, any tampering with the frontiers of the probable is likely to have an odd effect, to whisk the reader off, like Alice through the Looking-Glass, to some privileged participation in the imaginary world. It is clear that More, well-trained in the arts of rhetoric, had a very sophisticated awareness of author-reader relations and was able to exploit them as teasingly as Raphael. This in itself should warn us about too literal an approach to his wonderful island.

Once we advance beyond the outer layer, the quasi-historical world of More and his correspondents, we come up against the narrative frame provided by the conversation in that Antwerp garden. As I suggested before, our view of the utopian polity is influenced by this frame which has as its central theme the encounter between philosophy and practical politics, the problem of the escape from the Cave. If you have seen the real forms, if you have travelled to an ideal polity, what do you do on your return? Do you, as Morus suggests, get involved in the imperfect politics of the Cave — at the risk of misunderstanding or worse — or do you follow Pico and Raphael and keep your hands and thoughts clean? In the course of Book I Raphael provides two anecdotes to support his case, the supposedly "historical" visit to Cardinal Morton's household (where More himself had been a page) and an imaginary account of the French royal council in session. The latter is a satirical exposure of power politics in the tradition of Erasmus' adage "Scarabeus aquilam quaerit". Who can introduce the language of moral philosophy into such corrupt discourse? Can it serve any purpose? There are, suggests Raphael, plenty of books available already.

The Morton episode is slightly more complex. Against the prevailing view that the only way to deter thieves is to hang them Raphael argues that the deterrent does not work, that man is not entitled to take life for such an issue as property, and that account should be taken of the social conditions that led to theft. He describes the benevolent system of penal servitude found among the Polylerites, a mythical nation in Persia. His views are vigorously opposed by all present, except for Cardinal Morton who silences the opposition and listens thoughtfully to Raphael, whereupon everyone else hurriedly praises his novel ideas. Morton, again, is a historical figure, well known to More in his youth, who followed a perilous political career until the Tudor accession, and died full of honours as Archbishop of Canterbury in 1500. He is, indeed, that same Morton who, as Bishop of Ely, is sent by Shakespeare's Richard III to fetch some strawberries while Hastings' doom is sealed. In other words, as a figure from the darkest phase of the Wars of the Roses, he represents the political survivor, the man who can adapt yet retain a basic loyalty to principle without being too ponderous about it. More had served as a page in Morton's household, was indeed his protégé, and presents him in *Utopia* in a favourable light. He, alone, does listen to Raphael and weighs his argument without prejudice.

The ironical fact is that Raphael fails to note the significance of Morton's response. He denies any possibility of mediation between his ideal vision and the sordid compromises of political dealing. The key to this narrative frame which surrounds the island of Utopia is the exchange between Raphael and Morus at the close of Book I. Morus attacks Raphael's negative view; it is his fault if he presents his ideas in such a way that they have no effect. "In the private conversation of close friends this academic philosophy ('haec philosophia scholastica') is not without charm, but in the councils of kings ... there is no room for these notions".[11] Raphael's philosophy, then, is "scholastica"; what Morus proposes is "alia philosophia civilior", "which knows its stage, adapts itself to the play in hand, and performs its role neatly and appropriately". It is interesting that More should use an image

11. *ibid.*, p. 99.

from drama (as he does in *Richard III*) to suggest political behaviour; instinctively, it seems, he read life in terms of role-playing. The basic argument, however, is one of rhetorical decorum; you pitch your argument to fit your audience. Raphael's obsession with his private revelation, the polity of *Utopia*, fails to recognize Morton's open-mindedness, and fails completely to link the golden and the brazen worlds. I use Sidney's terms on purpose, since, despite his own reservations about *Utopia*, his argument in the *Defence of Poetry* is rooted in the same concerns that More shares. That is, indeed, the central obsession of the Renaissance: how to connect ideal forms with actual life. And it was invariably to the persuasive powers of art that men turned to solve the dilemma. Raphael is no more helpful than Pico at resolving matters.

The island of Utopia strikes modern readers as austere, and its debt to monastic regimes, especially to the Carthusians among whom More had once lived, is clear enough. Private moral choice is almost eliminated by collective pressures, simply there is no privacy — glass walls have reached us from Utopia *via* Geneva. In other words acts of will are almost unknown; individual responsibility for good or evil is removed. In this respect there is something millenarian about Utopia; as Morus remarks about the sorry state of Europe, "it is impossible that all should be well unless all men were good, a situation which I do not expect for a great many years to come".[12] I have a strong suspicion that Utopia should be viewed with Savonarola's godly Florence in mind, when under the pressure of the Dominican's apocalyptic preaching the city became, at least for a while, a prototype Geneva. More probably knew Gianfrancesco Pico's life of Savonarola, and he had several friends familiar with that episode, including Colet who corresponded with Ficino. Take one passage from a sermon cited by Weinstein:

> Your domestic laws, Florence, make them all love, union and charity. Your external law, because not everyone is good, but for the most part bad, must be like a bridle to restrain those who wish to do you harm.[13]

12. *ibid.*, 101.
13. D. Weinstein, *Savonarola and Florence*, Princeton, 1970, p. 144.

Not so far from the Utopian position, one might say.

In the end the argument between Morus and Raphael is unresolved. Raphael will not compromise, and Morus proposes that reform must be introduced "obliquo ductu", by indirect means. It must infiltrate rather than attack. If Raphael shows the exclusive self-righteousness of the visionary, Morus suggests a less dramatic role: "What you cannot turn to good, you must at least make as little bad as you can."[14]

Scarcely the line of the revolutionary. Neither view wholly commands our sympathy, and the final words of Morus on Raphael, "though he is a man of the most undoubted learning as well as of the greatest knowledge of human affairs, I cannot agree with all that he has said", merely voices our own perplexity about the debate.

In the end, if we take *Utopia* as a specimen of utopian literature (and that question is more open than you might suppose), what does it seem to tell us about the genre? We have two elements: (i) the vision, (ii) the mediating process. In other words the central concern is epistemological rather than political. Those who scour through Raphael's account in search of Tudor reform policies have substantially missed the point. What makes More's work so perennially interesting is not just the ingenuity of its proposals but its presentation of a problem. More did become a Councillor, he disregarded Raphael's arguments, and he lost his life as an indirect result. Probably he would agree that his efforts to make the world less bad were a failure. But that does not make *Utopia* into a bad career projection. The deep ambivalence of authorial attitude which marks the book suggests how deeply More felt the issues. What he produced did not pretend to be the solution to an intractable problem, rather it was the embodiment of a dilemma, and in giving it form he drew on the deepest paradoxes of the human imagination.

Amsterdam   Dominic Baker-Smith

For a fuller discussion of this possible influence see my *Thomas More and Plato's Voyage*, Cardiff, 1978, pp. 13-16.
    14. *Utopia*, p. 101.

THE UTOPIAN IMPULSE IN SEVENTEENTH-CENTURY ENGLAND*

At the beginning of the seventeenth century the prevailing orthodoxy in England was profoundly anti-utopian. Official religious teaching was that life was necessarily imperfect. Absolute felicity had been enjoyed by Adam and Eve and would be regained by some of their descendants in Heaven. In the meantime man was fallen, nature was harsh and this life could offer only a second-best.

But the ideal of what constituted perfection was clear enough. Generations of Biblical commentators had built up an accepted picture of Eden as a place of pastoral innocence. Adam and Eve had lived among flowers, fruits and trees, naked and unashamed. They had enjoyed beauty, immortality and eternal youth. Nature had been fertile and temperate. There was work to do, for Adam had been set in the garden to dress it and keep it. But the work was "delightful" (*Paradise Lost* IV. 437). Adam and Eve had lived in an earthly paradise: a place of beauty, comfort and, in Milton's view at any rate, sexual fulfilment.

All this had been lost by the Fall. By rebelling against God, man forfeited his easy dominion over nature. The earth degenerated. Thorns and thistles grew up where there had once been only fruits and flowers. The soil became stony and less fertile, making arduous and painful labour necessary for its cultivation. Many

---

* This essay has no pretensions to be more than a general survey. It owes an obvious debt to the many recent works on the subject, notably Charles Webster, *The Great Instauration, Science, Medicine and Reform 1626-1660*, London, 1975; Melvin J. Lasky, *Utopia and Revolution*, London, 1976; Frank E. Manuel and Fritzie P. Manuel, *Utopian Thought in the Western World*, Oxford, 1979; J.C. Davis, *Utopia and the Ideal Society. A Study of English Utopian Writing 1516-1700*, Cambridge, 1981; and Miriam Eliav-Feldon, *Realistic Utopias: The Ideal Imaginary Societies of the Renaissance 1516-1630*, Oxford, 1982.

animals grew fierce and dangerous. Man himself became inherently sinful. Social and political repression was now the only way of restraining his wicked impulses. Perfection was not to be obtained in this world and the prospects of any real alleviation of the human condition were doubtful.

In Heaven, however, paradise would be regained, though only by some (the idea that all would be saved was an unacceptable heresy). Contemporary descriptions of heaven tended to be vaguer than those of hell, whose pains and torments, foul smells and hideous sounds, dark lakes and sulphurous fires were evoked with relish. But the general character of life in heaven was reasonably clear. It was not a place of sensual pleasure, as the Muslim heaven was said to be. Its delights were spiritual rather than physical. But there would be no disease and no death. Youth would not grow old and beauty would never fade. There would be "no wanton dancing, no idle sports", but there would be glorious singing of alleluias. The air would be full of delightful odours and "an unspeakable sweetness of all delectable things" would linger on the palate.[1]

This hope of heaven was the only ideal prospect in the eyes of most people. Otherwise, images of perfection were nostalgic. For the educated the myth of Eden was paralleled by the classical notion of the golden age: a time of arcadian innocence and harmony, when human needs were satisfied without strife or painful labour. The golden age had gone for ever because both men and nature had degenerated. Some explorers of the New World were ready to believe that survivors of the golden age might yet be discovered in some tropical paradise. But no one suggested that this sort of earthly paradise could be regained in Europe.

1. Christopher Hooke, *A Sermon preached in Paules Church*, London, 1603, sig. B2v; William Gearing, *A Prospect of Heaven*, London, 1673, pp. 127, 246. This entrancing prospect did not appeal to everyone. A sick woman near Lewes, Sussex, was told by a well-intentioned visitor that "if she died, she should go to heaven and be with God and Jesus Christ, and with angels and Saints"; she replied that "she had no acquaintance there, she knew nobody there, and therefore she had rather live with her and her other neighbours here, than to go thither to live amongst strangers". Thomas Brooks, *The Crown and Glory of Christianity*, London, 1662, p. 289.

Literary tradition and conventional Christian teaching thus encouraged reflection on what the ideal human condition might be. But they discouraged any hope of achieving it in this life.

During the seventeenth century this pessimistic view was seriously challenged by two associated currents of thought, each of which held out the possibility that the lost perfection might be restored in the future, and in this life rather than the next.

The first of these currents of thought came out of the Christian tradition itself. Alongside the pessimistic view of history as a story of relentless deterioration, medieval theology had bequeathed rival and more optimistic ways of thinking. The Jewish Messianic tradition held out the prospect of a future age of peace, justice and plenty; *Revelation* forecast that Satan would be bound for a thousand years; and the twelfth-century prophet Joachim of Fiore had predicted a coming age of spiritual renewal, a *renovatio mundi*.[2] Though strenuously refuted by the orthodox, these associated traditions all suggested that perfection might be achieved once more before the end of the world; and in the sixteenth century the combined effect of unprecedented geographical discovery and dramatic religious upheaval was to foster the notion that such a new age might well be imminent.

This belief in an approaching millennium became particularly strong in England during and after the Civil War, when it was encouraged by a sequence of spectacularly unprecedented events, including the War itself, the collapse of the Anglican Church, the execution of Charles I and the abolition of the monarchy. The creation of a perfect state governed by an elect minority became the objective of one sect, the Fifth Monarchy Men, and the imminence of the millennium was proclaimed by many others, who confidently awaited an era which would be characterised by universal peace and the progressive revelation of all divine mysteries.

Closely associated with this millenarian hope was the belief of many of the heterodox Protestant sects which sprang up under the favourable conditions of the mid-century that spiritual perfection could be achieved in this life: divine illumination would offset the

2. See Marjorie Reeves, *The Influence of Prophecy in the Later Middle Ages. A Study in Joachism*, Oxford, 1969.

effects of original sin and a new dispensation of the Spirit would supersede the old moral Law. The Familists, the Ranters and the Quakers all made claims of this kind; and their belief in perfectibility and universal redemption was often associated with a more practical vision of reforms in the Church, education, medicine and the law.[3]

The millenarians placed their faith in divine intervention. The restoration of Eden would be achieved by God, not man, even though man could play his part in forwarding God's objectives. For this reason, millenarianism is normally regarded as something different from the other optimistic current of thought in this period, utopianism. For a utopia envisages an ideal society created by human effort. It requires no prior transformation of man's nature, no change in the natural world, no spectacular supernatural occurrence. It is therefore usually distinguished from the millennium, which is achieved by an act of God. It is also different from nostalgic visions of Eden or arcadia, where problems disappear because men are innocent and nature obliging.[4]

The literary utopia was a genre which had been extinct since classical times. It was revived by Thomas More and developed by Patrizi, Doni, Stiblinus and other humanist writers. In the early seventeenth century its most notable European instances were Campanella's *City of the Sun* (1602; published 1623), the work of a Calabrian friar, and Johann Valentin Andreae's *Christianopolis* (1619), a vision of a Christian community composed by a Lutheran minister. Characteristically, the literary utopia describes an imaginary society which is, at least by implication, better than the one in which the author lives. This society is portrayed as actually in existence, usually in some remote location. Its workings are evoked in detail, with special attention to the political structure, the laws and religion, the system of education, the economy and the working habits and living conditions of the population. The

3. See Christopher Hill, *The World Turned Upside Down*, London, 1972.
4. For these important distinctions see M.I. Finley, "Utopianism Ancient and Modern" in his *The Use and Abuse of History*, London, 1975, and, especially, Davis, *Utopia and the Ideal Society*, whose classification of different types of ideal society deserves to be the starting-point of all future discussion.

activities of the citizens are regulated in meticulous detail; and the society exists in a timeless state of unchanging equilibrium.[5]

The sixteenth-century literary utopia, however, was not a programme for action. No route from contemporary reality to the desired state of perfection was offered; indeed the practical implications of the model were wholly unclear.[6] The vision of perfection held out by More or Doni was thus no more revolutionary in practice than were the concepts of paradise or heaven. For this reason there are modern writers like Karl Mannheim who scarcely mention More when discussing utopianism. For Mannheim "utopia" has to be revolutionary in its implications, by contrast with "ideology", which reinforces the status quo. Consolatory myths of heaven or paradise are ideology, because their effect is to reconcile people to the existing state of imperfection by proffering the hope of a better future in the next life. By contrast, a genuinely utopian vision will seek to inspire collective activity in an effort to change the world now.[7]

On this definition, it was not the sixteenth but the seventeenth century which was the decisive period in the history of utopianism because only then did there emerge the action-oriented utopia, that is to say a model of a more perfect society intended for direct human implementation. This new utopian impulse took various forms, not all of them literary. What was common to them all was that they involved both a model, explicit or implicit, of what a perfect society would be like and a desire to put the model into operation. Instead of aiming at pragmatic, piecemeal reform, the utopian was animated by a vision of the whole; and he set out to achieve goals which most of his contemporaries regarded as either impractical or undesirable or both.

There were, I suggest, at least eight different forms which the utopian impulse took during this period. The first, was the composition of literary utopias in the now traditional manner, but with an increasingly practical purpose in mind. The most notable of these works were Francis Bacon's *New Atlantis* (1624; published

5. See Eliav-Feldon, *Realistic Utopias.*

6. *Ibid.*, pp. 7, 129.

7. Karl Mannheim, "Utopia", in *Encyclopaedia of the Social Sciences*, ed. Edwin R.A. Seligman *et al.*, London, 1930-35; *id.*, *Ideology and Utopia*, London, 1936, pp. 173-4, 180-1.

1627) and its later continuations by "R.H." (1660) and Joseph
Glanvill (1676); Robert Burton's "poetical commonwealth", pre-
faced to his *Anatomy of Melancholy* (1621); Gabriel Plattes's *A
Description of the famous Kingdome of Macaria* (1641); *Nova
Solyma* (1648), a philosophical romance in Latin by the lawyer,
Samuel Gott; *Oceana* (1656), by the political theorist James
Harrington; and the anonymous *Essay concerning Adepts* (1698),
which describes a Christian community reminiscent of Andreae's
Christianopolis. There were at least a dozen other loosely comparable writings, though few of them contain the detailed social
specification characteristic of More's *Utopia* and in some of them
the element of fantasy or romance predominates. In Francis
Godwin's *The Man in the Moone* (1638), for example, the aeronaut
hero stumbles on world where all live in "such love, peace and
amity as it seemeth to be another paradise" (p.104), but the work
gives only a very brief account of this state of felicity and does not
specify how it is achieved. Many such romances or imaginary
voyages do not qualify as utopias proper because they presuppose
either an unnaturally virtuous people or a race endowed with
unusual physical properties, like the pygmies of Joshua Barnes's
Gerania (1675) or the inhabitants of Gabriel de Foigny's *Terra
Incognita Australis* (English translation, 1693), who are eight-foot
tall hermaphrodites. But some romances include descriptions of
ideal states which seem true members of the utopian genre.[8]

At least one literary utopia has not been studied because it is still
in manuscript. This is the language-reformer Francis Lodwick's
Description of a Country Not Named; it depicts a society whose
members speak a perfect language, follow a religion unchanged for
a thousand years, possess a developed system of education,
support learned philosophers who engage in experiments and
maintain a clergy who do not bother with theological disputes but

---

8. For example, Nathanael Ingelo, *Bentivolio and Urania*, 3rd edn.,
1673, I, pp. 137-148 (on the Kingdom of Theoprepia), and M. Heliogenes
de L'Epy, *A Voyage into Tartary*, London, 1698, pp. 87-183 (on the sun-
worshipping city of Heliopolis). Most of the literary utopias proper are
discussed by Davis, *Utopia and the Ideal Society*. There is a wide-ranging
list of "Utopias and Dystopias 1500-1700" in R.W. Gibson (compiler),
*St. Thomas More: A Preliminary Bibliography of his Works and of Moreana
to the Year 1750*, New Haven and London, 1961.

provide education and free medicine to the poor.[9] Other seventeenth-century utopias have been lost, like *"Jamesanna* or the pattern of a perfect city, the which, in imitation of the *Utopia* of Thomas More, representeth the good qualities, customs, perfections that both every sovereign prince and all sorts of subjects should aspire unto", a composition which the writer James Maxwell listed in 1615 among his works "not as yet published".[10]

These literary utopias served diverse purposes; Lodwick's *Description of a Country not Named*, for example, was a vehicle for the author's views on biblical criticism, the age of the world and the descent of man. But many of them were intended to offer a programme for implementation. Plattes's *Macaria*, for instance, was a scheme for a welfare state based on the increased exploitation of productive resources. The author dedicated it to the House of Commons in 1641 in the hope that the House would "lay the cornerstone of the world's happiness before the final recess". He described his model as "easy to be effected, if all men be willing" and his aim as "to make England to be like to *Macaria*".[11] Works of this programmatic kind have no real precedent in English literature.

A second form of seventeenth-century utopianism was the devising of elaborate schemes for ideal commonwealths, though without the fictional pretence that such a commonwealth already existed and without the imaginative exploration of what the texture of life in such a state might be. Both John Eliot and Richard Baxter published schemes for a theocracy or "holy commonwealth": "a divine platform of government taught by God himself", as Eliot put it.[12] In the same spirit, Gerrard Winstanley in his *The Law of Freedom in a Platform* (1652) offered

9. British Library, Sloane MS 913, fols. 1-33 (its linguistic aspects are briefly discussed in Vivian Salmon, *The Works of Francis Lodwick*, London, 1972, pp. 83-5).

10. James Maxwell, *Admirable and Notable Prophesies*, London, 1615, sig. Bl. Another lost utopia is *Eutaxia* by the Dissenter Charles Morton; F. Bastian, *Defoe's Early Life*, London, 1981, p. 56.

11. *Samuel Hartlib and the Advancement of Learning*, ed. Charles Webster, Cambridge, 1970, pp. 79, 86, 90.

12. John Eliot, *The Christian Commonwealth*, London, n.d. (?1660); Richard Baxter, *A Holy Commonwealth*, London, 1659.

a detailed code of laws for the immediate achievement of a communist state, a "Platform for the Government of the Earth without buying and selling". The most celebrated of such schemes was Thomas Hobbes's *Leviathan*. Hobbes denied that his aims were utopian: as he remarked, "the state of man can never be without some incommodity or other". Nevertheless, he presented his state as a solution to the most fundamental problems of human life and he freely admitted that it transcended anything which had ever historically existed. To many of his contemporaries his proposals seemed impossibly unrealistic.[13]

Closely associated with such ideal commonwealths was the third type of utopianism, the making of new constitutions for the government of England. The Levellers were a radical group who emerged in the aftermath of the English Civil War. They drew up the first written constitution in English history, *The Agreement of the People*, which, in its successive versions, was meant to be subscribed by all members of the population as the basis of a new state. It was but one of many such schemes for political reconstruction put forward in the Civil War period, when there was a widespread feeling that all things were now possible. In 1653 Cromwell's Protectorate was inaugurated by the Instrument of Government, a written constitution produced by the army. This was the first time that English government had been founded on a written constitution; and the adoption of the Humble Petition and Advice, which amended that constitution in 1657, was the last. Of course, such constitutions were not utopian in the full sense, for they provided a framework only for the distribution of political power and did not purport to regulate all aspects of society. But in their attempt to make the future run along ideal lines they revealed a utopian aspiration; and their invariable omission of any provision for subsequent constitutional amendment indicated that, like the literary utopians, they envisaged that future as a state of unchanging equilibrium.[14]

13. Thomas Hobbes, *Leviathan,* London, 1651, chap. xviii. Cf. Edward, Earl of Clarendon, *A Brief View and Survey of the Dangerous and Pernicious Errors to Church and State, in Mr. Hobbes's Book, entitled Leviathan,* 2nd impression, Oxford, 1676, p. 79.
14. Though the anonymous author of *Chaos,* London 1659, "a frame

Fourthly, there were idealized descriptions of other societies which did exist, or had existed, and were now perceived as perfect models of political and social organization. In the seventeenth century the most popular historical subjects for such treatment were ancient Israel, the Roman republic, the free Anglo-Saxons and the Merrie England which had existed before the Reformation.[15] In contemporary Europe, there was Venice, which was praised for its mixed constitution and political stability: "Many make [it] the very mirror of policy", wrote Thomas Gataker in 1619, "and some suppose [it] to be a model of Plato's old platform".[16] There were the United Provinces of the Netherlands, which afforded an example of hard work, political freedom, economic prosperity, care for the poor and religious toleration: in 1622 Thomas Scott thought there was no need for Plato's *Republic* or More's *Utopia*, since "the reality of their wishes and best conceptions" could be seen in action among the Dutch. Outside Europe there was China, which Sir William Temple regarded as superior to "all those imaginary schemes of the European wits, ... the *Utopias* or *Oceanas* of our modern writers".[17]

Fifthly, there was the formation of secret or semi-secret societies, pledged to the reform of the world. Particularly celebrated were the Rosicrucians, alleged authors of two manifestos published in Germany in 1614 and 1615, though it is doubtful whether any such fraternity in fact existed. The brotherhood of the Rosy Cross was represented as a mystical elite whose alchemical researches, conducted in a spirit of Christian charity, would enable

---

of government by way of a republic", admitted that "a perfect platform of government ... can only receive life and growth by time" (sig. A3v).

15. Keith Thomas, *The Perception of the Past in Early Modern England*, London, 1984; and for an earlier account of "nostalgic utopianism", Michael Walzer, *The Revolution of the Saints*, London, 1966, pp. 205-207.

16. Thomas Gataker, *Of the Nature and Use of Lots*, London, 1619, p. 57. Cf. William Bouwsma, "Venice and the Political Education of Europe", in *Renaissance Venice*, ed. J.R. Hale, London, 1973.

17. (Thomas Scott) *The Belgicke Pismire*, London, 1622, p. 90; Sir William Temple, "Of Heroick Virtue", in *Miscellanea, II*, 4th edn., London, 1696, p. 196. For a comparable passage on the supposed felicities of the Isle of Man, see *The Ferrar Papers*, ed. B. Blackstone, Cambridge, 1938, pp. 117-20.

them to eliminate hunger and painful labour and to cure all diseases. Their object was the "Universal and General Reformation of the whole wide world".[18] An English translation of the Rosicrucian manifestos was published in 1652 by Thomas Vaughan.[19] Ten years later John Heydon claimed that the Rosicrucian fraternity, "seraphically illuminated", was alive and well and living in a castle in the West of England, where they held the secret of long life, health, riches and virtue.[20] Various hermetic and alchemical groups undoubtedly existed. We can perhaps detect their influence as late as 1698 in the anonymous utopia called *An Essay concerning Adepts*, which outlines the spiritual reformation necessary before men are fit to receive the secrets of the philosopher's stone.

A more influential group was the association formed in the late 1650's by the Prussian emigré Samuel Hartlib and the Scottish minister John Dury, and later joined by the Czech educationalist Jan Comenius. Hartlib and Dury were indebted to the example of Andreae, who had urged the formation of small Christian societies, and of Bacon, who had envisaged a universal college or international association of the learned. They later adopted Comenius's Pansophism, a scheme for a unified system of learning which traced its origins to the Neoplatonic belief in the universal harmony of nature. During the 1640s Hartlib became the centre of a small but active circle pledged to the dissemination of science, the reform of schools and universities, the improvement of technology, the achievement of full employnent, the discovery of a universal language and the union of the churches. In 1649 the new Commonwealth appointed him "Agent for the Advancement of Universal Learning and the Public Good". His aim, he said later,

---

18. Frances A. Yates, *The Rosicrucian Enlightenment*, London, 1972, p. 42.

19. *The Fame and Confession of the Fraternity of R: C: commonly, of the Rosie Cross*, with a preface by "Eugenius Philalethes", London, 1652, reprinted in Yates, *The Rosicrucian Enlightenment*, appendix, See Thomas Willard, "The Rosicrucian Manifestos in Britain", *The Papers of the Bibliographical Society of America*, 77 (1983).

20. John Heydon, *The Holy Guide*, London 1662, book vi, pp. 20ff. Cf. *id.*, *The Idea of the Law*, London, 1660, sigs. B6v-7.

was "the reformation of the whole world".[21]

At various stages in his career, Hartlib hoped to found a Christian society, called Antilia and inspired by Andrea's *Christianopolis*, as a colony in Virginia or Bermuda. This dream of an ideal colonial society is our sixth form of utopianism. Obvious examples are the various efforts to create a Bible Commonwealth or New Jerusalem in Puritan New England. The covenant drawn up in 1636 by the founders of Dedham, Massachusetts, pledged its signatories to live "according to that most perfect rule, the foundation whereof is everlasting love" (significantly, it excluded "all such as are contrary-minded"). Its historian describes Dedham "a highly conscious attempt to build the most perfect possible community".[22] Pennsylvania was even more utopian in conception. Its founder William Penn regarded it as a "holy experiment", intended it as "an example ... to the nations" and named its capital Philadelphia, the city of brotherly love.[23]

Seventhly, there were smaller communities deliberately created by idealistic individuals to enable their members to live a more perfect existence. They could be a refuge from a harsh world, like Nicholas Ferrar's household at Little Gidding in Huntingdonshire, which led a semi-monastic life until broken up in 1647. Or they could offer an example which it was hoped others would follow, like Winstanley's community of Diggers, cultivating the commons at St George's Hill, or the collective settlements of Pieter Cornelisz Plockhoy in London and Bristol.[24]

Finally, there were what the seventeenth century called "projectors", ingenious people with an infinity of schemes of reform. These might range from plans to erect workhouses or introduce new crops to more ambitious programmes for a universal

21. G.H. Turnbull, *Hartlib, Dury and Comenius*, 1947, reprinted, Farnborough, 1968, esp. p. 363; *Samuel Hartlib and the Advancement of Learning*, ed. Webster; Webster, *The Great Instauration, passim; The Works of the Honourable Robert Boyle*, London, 1744, V. 293.

22. Kenneth A. Lockridge, *A New England Town. The first Hundred Years. Dedham, Massachusetts, 1636-1736*, New York, 1970, pp. 4-5, 16.

23. *The Papers of William Penn, II (1680-1684)*, ed. Richard S. Dunn and Mary Maples Dunn, Philadelphia, 1982, pp. 108, 129.

24. Jean Séguy, *Utopie Coopérative et Oecuménisme. Pieter Cornelisz Plockhoy van Zurik-Zee 1620-1700*, Paris, 1968.

language, the reunion of the Christian churches and perpetual peace. Reformers as such should not be regarded as utopian if their reforms are limited in scope and are not meant to transform the whole of sciety. But the greater their readiness to regard their particular scheme as a panacea for all the world's problems the more do they deserve the label. The later seventeenth century was what Defoe called "the projecting age" and it was the projectors who provided the object of some of Swift's most scathing satire in *A Voyage to Laputa.*

I have listed eight forms of seventeenth-century utopianism. All of them presupposed that man was fallen and nature recalcitrant. All placed their faith in human effort. I have therefore contrasted them with the millenarian impulse, which relied on divine intervention and envisaged a miraculous transformation of both man and nature.

Yet we know that this distinction is spurious. For it was precisely when the millenarian current was running most strongly that the utopian faith in human effort was most buoyant. The advancement of idealistic schemes was encouraged by the feeling that the times were special and that God had great purposes afoot. The approaching prospect of a new age of perfect knowledge explains the educational preoccupations of Comenius, while the tireless activity of Hartlib and Dury is unintelligible if we overlook their millenarian conviction that time was on their side.[25] In an atmosphere of eschatological expectation, particularly intense between 1640 and 1660, utopianism flourished most vigorously. It was because of their sense of living in a special time that, as a contemporary put it, "all sorts of people dreamed of an *Utopia*".[26] "The spirit of the whole Creation", Winstanley confidently wrote in the preface to his *Law of Freedom*, "is about the Reformation of the World".

It is therefore not easy to separate the utopian impulse from the millenarian current which accompanied it. If we examine the content of seventeenth-century millenialism and compare it with

25. Turnbull, *Hartlib, Dury and Comenius*, pp. 358-9; Katharine R. Firth, *The Apocalyptic Tradition in Reformation Britain 1530-1645*, Oxford, 1979, pp. 208-213.

26. *Persecution Undecima*, London, 1681, p. 4; *The Works of Gerrard Winstanley*, ed. George H. Sabine, Ithaca, N.Y., 1941, p. 502.

seventeenth-century utopianism we find that the two were twins.

For how was the millennium envisaged? Of course, it varied according to the millenarian concerned. For the radical sectary, George Foster, the millennium was a time when the common people would be freed from bondage and the saints would "have all things in common".[27] For the cultivated Richard Roach, the millennium would be marked by "wit and delightful conversation".[28] But the most common notion was that the millennium would see the restoration of mankind to Adam's state before the Fall. Writing at the very end of the seventeenth century, the Calvinist divine John Edwards explained just what this would mean. The earth, he said, would be renewed and become more fertile. Better air would give men "bodily strength and vigour in an unusual degree" so that everyone would be "healthful and vivacious, brisk and sprightly". There would be a vast expansion in human knowledge: even little children would know more than did the wisest centenarians at present. Natural philosophy would be "improved to the utmost". Human longevity would be enhanced by an increased understanding of the workings of the body. The nature of all vegetables and minerals would be laid open by "exquisite experiments". Wild animals would become tame and gentle. There would be more people in the world and they would live longer. But this increase in population would cause no problems. Commerce by land and sea would be "mightily increased". A common language would enable all peoples "with ease and freedom [to] confer with one another; and compare their notions together, and thereby come to an entire agreement". In this era of universal peace and concord, all religious controversies would vanish and there would be an end to warfare. Life would be "attended with all outward conveniences, comforts and refreshments of what nature soever, together with inward peace, pleasure and satisfaction". And all these earthly

27. George Foster, *The Pouring Forth of the Seventh and Last Viall*, n. pl., 1650, pp. 12-13, 29-30.

28. John Edwards, ΠΟΛΥΠΟΙΚΙΛΟΣ ΣΟΦΙΑ. *A Compleat History or Survey of all the Dispensations and Methods of Religion*, London, 1699, II, pp. 726-59.

conveniences would be as nothing to the spiritual blessings which the millennium would bring.[29]

Edwards was emphatic that this felicity would be achieved, not by human effort, but by heaven: "The Supreme Arbitrator and Manager of the World can, of a sudden, dispel all difficulties and alter the course of the universe and frame men's minds as he pleaseth". Yet his conception of ultimate happiness bears a striking similarity to the objectives of utopians who did not rely on supernatural aid. In many respects the goals were the same; only the methods were different. It would, of course, be absurd to suggest that all seventeenth-century utopians were working in the same direction. There was no single utopian impulse and the values and aspirations of the different utopian thinkers varied enormously. Even so, it is not too fanciful to detect, under the obvious differences, some abiding preoccupations; and they are ones to which the account of the millennium given by Edwards and others bears a close affinity.

For what was the aim of the utopians if not the restoration to man of what he had enjoyed in Eden: dominion over nature; comfortable living; perfect knowledge; harmony and peace? In England it was Francis Bacon who first urged that man himself could undo the worst consequences of the Fall and inaugurate a new age of knowledge. Dominion over nature, forfeited through sin, could be patiently regained by the advancement of the arts and sciences; and the state of innocence could be recaptured by the practice of piety and religion. In the "Salomon's House" of his *New Atlantis*, Bacon provided the model of a scientific institute (or "college"), staffed by a semi-priestly elite dedicated to "the finding out of the true nature of all things, (whereby God might have the more glory in the workmanship of them, and men the more fruit in the use of them)".[30]

This attempt to restore Paradise by a combination of science and Protestant piety was characteristic of an attitude which was

30. *The Works of Francis Bacon,* eds James Spedding, Robert Leslie Ellis and Douglas Denon Heath, London, 1857-74, III, p. 146.

widespread in early seventeenth-century Europe and which provided the intellectual inspiration for much later utopian activity. The Rosicrucians, for example, promised that by studying the book of nature man could return to paradise. In their case the claim took on a hermetic, mystical character, with much talk of divine illumination, universal medicine and the philosopher's stone. The Pansophists also sought to restore Eden by a combination of piety and knowledge. They aimed at a Christian synthesis of all forms of truth. Comenius believed that he was living in an era of dawning enlightenment and envisaged an international fraternity of intellectuals who would write universal textbooks in a universal language, disseminating universal knowledge for "the improvement of all human affairs, in all persons and everywhere". The *Great Didactic* was "a scheme for readily and soundly teaching everybody everything".[31]

The intellectual influence of Bacon and Comenius upon Samuel Hartlib's utopian projects in England during the Civil War period has been admirably demonstrated by Dr Charles Webster. Hartlib and his associates had schemes to achieve everything, from poor relief to the introduction of decimal currency. But their aims transcended merely material wellbeing: the accumulation and dissemination of knowledge would relieve man's estate; it would also bring him nearer to God.

In this way the utopian dreams of Bacon's *New Atlantis* bore practical fruit, though sometimes in bizarre form. In 1659, for example, the adventurer Thomas Bushell proposed to build Salomon's House in Wells, Somerset, by placing there "a select society of ... philosophers" to study the mining of underground treasures which were popularly believed to be guarded by subterranean spirits. Staffed by "six exquisite, lucre-hating philosophers" and with convicted criminals and debtors as its labour force, this "matchless academy" would ensure that "thousands of poor subjects shall eat the bread of comfort; offenders be purged and freed; trade increased and customs augmented ... new arts discovered for the universal good and honour of the nation". And when they died, the "six exquisite, lucre-hating philosophers"

would have their statues erected in the city of Wells, "and ... each...
shall hold a significant character of their peculiar invention in their
well-proportioned hands", just in the way that *New Atlantis* had
recommended.[32]

The first great utopian goal was thus the reorganisation and
advancement of knowledge by an elite of Christian scientists and
its propagation by a reformed educational system. The moral
value of learning was widely accepted. Education was the means of
undoing original sin: it aimed, said Milton, "to repair the ruins of
our first parents by regaining to know God aright".[33] The search
for lost innocence thus underlay much of the educational activity
of the period. Both Dury and Hartlib thought that the education
of the young was the quickest route to the nation's reformation;
and for Comenius the school was the solution to all problems.[34]

The second goal was the regaining of dominion over nature by
the controlled use of scientific discovery. *Macaria* set out a
programme for the state-encouraged improvement of husbandry,
fishing and trade; and many of Hartlib's projects were designed to
use new technology to enlarge the means of subsistence. Medicine
was a particularly important part of the work of regeneration.
Some form of state medical service was proposed by Plattes,
Lodwick, Hartlib and other English utopians, just as it had been
envisaged by Campanella and Andreae. The essential point was
that physical health was regarded as a necessary precondition for
spiritual well-being.[35]

This was connected with the third objective, which was the relief
of hunger, poverty and unemployment. Here, too, the primary aim
was a moral one. In their degraded state the poor were incapable
of worshipping God or leading a moral life. An adequate standard
of living should therefore be ensured for everyone. It was "to
prevent the ill breeding, wicked life and bad end that many
thousands have fallen into through idleness" that Thomas Lawson

32. J.W. Gough, *The Superlative Prodigall. A Life of Thomas Bushell*,
Bristol, 1932, pp. 116-20.

33. *The Complete Prose Works of John Milton*, II, New Haven, 1959,
pp. 366-67.

34. *Samuel Hartlib and the Advancement of Learning*, ed. Webster, pp.
141, 185; Firth, *Apocalyptic Tradition in Reformation Britain*, p. 213.

35. Webster, *The Great Instauration*, p. 263.

made his *Appeal to the parliament, concerning the Poor, that there may not be a beggar in England* (1660). In the same spirit Peter Chamberlen declared that all previous legislation for the poor had been useless. The houses of correction only degraded their inhabitants and made them desperate. Instead, the aim should be to "civilise" the poor by providing them with an honest livelihood.[36]

There were two alternative methods of guaranteeing a reasonable living for everyone. The first was to ensure that all were engaged in productive labour. Those who had no work should be provided with it in workhouses, financed by the state or by a local authority or by a private patron or group of joint-stock investors. Life within these workhouses would be so regulated as to turn them into miniature godly communities. As a result, the poor would cease to be a burden to others and become a source of strength and piety.[37] John Stratford, a Gloucestershire projector, claimed that the introduction of flax-growing would turn the idle poor into a profitable asset, living "according to God's ordinance by the sweat of their face in a more religious order".[38] The Quaker John Bellers believed that his "colleges of industry" would revive the spirit of primitive Christianity by providing a regular life, religious instruction and "easy honest labour".[39]

These proposals sound bland enough, but they were breathtaking in their ambition. No greater single transformation of seventeenth-century English society could be imagined than the conversion of the poor (whom Peter Chamberlen estimated as the majority of the population[40] into a well-fed, hard-working and religious group. It is sometimes said that one of the distinguishing features of utopianism is that it envisages an improvement in the human condition without a prior change in human nature. But what is surely notable about the full-employment utopias of this period is that their authors believed that human nature, or at least

36. (Peter Chamberlen), *The Poore Mans Advocate*, London, n.d. (1649), pp. 47, 9.
37. Davis, *Utopia and the Ideal Society*, chap. 11.
38. Joan Thirsk, *Economic Policy and Projects*, Oxford, 1978, p. 104.
39. A. Ruth Fry, *John Bellers 1654-1725, Quaker, Economist and Social Reformer*, London, 1935, p. 47.
40. Chamberlen, *Poore Mans Advocate*, p. 14.

its external symptoms, could be radically changed by social engineering.

The other method of eliminating poverty was equally ambitious. Instead of seeking to increase production, it aimed to limit consumption by forbidding luxury, enforcing greater social equality and eliminating superfluous wants. The literary utopias are particularly draconian in this respect, often prescribing uniform dress and living conditions and forbidding all forms of conspicuous display. If nothing was wasted on superfluities, declared the *Essay concerning Adepts*, there would be enough for everyone. No doubt it was hard for the rich to have to lay aside their gay attire and other luxuries, but what reason was there why they should "abound in superfluities, and others should want necessaries"? Rich garments, changes of fashion in clothes and all unnecessary expenditure should be "hinder'd by most severe penalties".[41]

The idea that happiness could be achieved by the limitation of wants was an ancient one. What is particularly striking about these seventeenth-century proposals is less their readiness to envisage equality or even communism, remarkable though that is, than their implicit assumption that the economic process could somehow be stopped, demand checked and the desire for new fashions arrested. Absurdly unrealistic though such a belief may appear to us, it was widely held, and not only by utopians narrowly defined. In 1621 a Member of Parliament called for an act to establish "a settled fashion" in clothes and a few years earlier the Church of England's canons had expressed the wistful hope that, "in time", "newfangleness of apparel" would "die of itself".[42] Not until the end of the century did economists recognize that to attempt to limit consumer demand was to fly in the face of an inexorable economic process. In the meantime the characteristic seventeenth-century utopia was based on the limitation of wants rather than the expansion of productive capacity.

Adequate living standards were only part of the utopian dream. The fourth great objective was the attainment of peace and

41. A Philadept, *An Essay concerning Adepts*, London, 1698, pp. 33, 38.

42. *Commons Debates 1621*, ed. Wallace Notestein, Frances Helen Relf and Hartley Simpson, New Haven, 1935, V, pp. 497-8; *Constitutions and Canons Ecclesiastical 1604*, ed. H.A. Wilson, Oxford, 1923, sig. N1v.

harmony between men. For religious enthusiasts like George Foster it was only in the millennium that "the root of all malice, strife, hatred and war may be digged up and ... universal love and freedom to sorts of people ... brought in".[43] But the utopians sought peace and harmony by human action. One method was by the elimination of lawyers. Like most contemporaries, the utopians were deeply hostile to the multiplication of lawyers and lawsuits which had been such a feature of the period. They romanticized the medieval past as a time when there had been few legal disputes and they regarded the growth of litigation and the rise of a legal profession as a sign of social ill-health.[44] In virtually all the literary utopias, lawyers are non-existent. They were deemed unnecessary in *Christianopolis* and deprived of civil rights in *Oceana*. There was little room for them in Francis Godwin's *Man in the Moone*, in Antoine Le Grand's *Scydromedia* or in Francis Lodwick's *Country not Named*. Winstanley declared flatly that "there shall be no need of lawyers ... for all shall walk and act righteously".[45] Even Robert Burton, whose ideals were less radical than most, prescribed that as far as possible each man should plead his own cause and that the few lawyers who were needed should earn no fees but be paid out of public funds. More realistic contemporaries protested that the growth of litigation reflected the growing complexity of economic life rather than mere professional cupidity.[46] But the utopians regarded litigation, quarrels and disputes as a symptom of imperfect human relationships; their aim was to eliminate them.

This was particularly true of the disputes caused by religion. It is a characteristic of virtually all the literary utopias that the societies they portray are free from religious debate and persecution. This happy state is achieved sometimes by toleration, as in *Oceana*, but more often by the prescription of a uniform state religion, relatively free of dogmatic content and confined to fundamentals on which all Christians could agree. In "Astreada", the ideal state

43. Foster, *Pouring Forth*, title-page.
44. Thomas, *Perception of the Past in Early Modern England*, p. 15.
45. *Works of Gerrard Winstanley*, ed. Sabine, p. 183.
46. E.g., Bulstrode Whitelocke, *Memorials of the English Affairs*, new edn, Oxford, 1853, III, p. 123.

of the anonymous *Antiquity Reviv'd* (1693), religious dogma is limited to what can be known with certainty. In Lodwick's utopia, the articles of faith are very few and the subjects must obey the rulers in all inessentials. In *Macaria* there are no religious disputes and the death penalty falls on anyone who tries to communicate new religious opinions to the common people. In the Duchess of Newcastle's *New Blazing World* (1666) the inhabitants follow a single religion and no dissent is permitted.[47]

An ever greater cause of dissension than religious disputes within the state was religious controversy between states. Ever since the Reformation there had been ecumenical attempts to close the newly-opened gaps between the Christian churches and they were kept alive by millenarian expectations of an approaching age of peace and harmony. Hartlib's associate John Dury spent over fifty years in an unceasing attempt to bring together the Lutheran and Calvinist churches of Europe. Travelling through Germany and the Netherlands, negotiating with the Danes and the Swedes, the English, the Scots and the Swiss, Dury devoted his life to a fruitless quest for ecclesiastical reconciliation on the basis of religious fundamentals declared by a Protestant General Council. There were many in England who shared his objectives, from James I onwards. "Religious division", it has been perceptively remarked, "is the great anxiety of early modern Europe, as keen a stimulus to thought and guilt as class division in modern Europe."[48] At the beginning of the eighteenth century John

---

47. Margaret Cavendish, Duchess of Newcastle, *The Description of a New Blazing World*, in *Observations upon Experimental Philosophy*, London 1666, p. 17 (separate pagination).

48. Blair Worden, "Toleration and the Cromwellian Protectorate", in *Studies in Church History*, 21, Oxford, 1984, p. 210. See J. Minton Batten, *John Dury Advocate of Christian Reunion*, Chicago, 1944; Turnbull, *Hartlib, Dury and Comenius*, part II; *A History of the Ecumenical Movement 1517-1948*, eds Ruth Rouse and Stephen Charles Neill, 2nd edn, London, 1967; W.B. Patterson, "King James I's call for an Ecumenical Council", *Studies in Church History*, 7, Cambridge, 1971; *id.*, "James I and the Huguenot Synod of Tonneins of 1614", *Harvard Theological Review*, 65 (1972); Hugh Trevor-Roper, "The Church of England and the Greek Church in the Time of Charles I", *Studies in Church History*, 15, Oxford, 1978.

Bellers, author of the scheme for "colleges of industry", was still proposing that a General Council of all Christian states should settle principles on which they could agree.[49]

The prospect of a single world religion had long been held out by millenarian and Joachimite prophets. The conversion of the Jews, for example, and their return to Jerusalem, were, on the basis of a passage in St Paul's epistle to the Romans, an accepted part of the cosmic drama, a recognized preliminary to the coming of Christ. For that reason mid seventeenth-century England was rich in prophets who offered themselves as would-be couriers, prepared to assemble the Jews together and lead them back to the Holy Land. Gott's *Nova Solyma* describes an ideal society created after the resettlement of the Jews in the Holy Land. The same millenarian concern underlay Cromwell's summoning of a conference in 1655 which pronounced that there was no legal objection to the return to England of the Jewish community which had been banished in the thirteenth century.[50] Characteristically, Samuel Hartlib wanted "to make Christianity less offensive and more known unto the Jews".[51]

Equally ecumenical in intention were the numerous schemes for a universal language which would restore to mankind the common tongue they had lost since Babel. Such a language, it was urged, would foster trade, spread true religion and achieve amity and understanding between peoples. Closely associated was the search for a "real character", that is to say a perfect language in which words corresponded exactly to things, in the way that the language of Adam had done and, it was believed, the characters of the Chinese still did. There could be no better way of eliminating all the controversies and misunderstandings which stemmed from linguistic confusion. The quest for a universal language and a real character occupied many of the best minds of the period.[52] It

49. Fry, *John Bellers 1654-1725*, p. 99.

50. David S. Katz, *Philo-Semitism and the readmission of the Jews to England 1603-1655*, Oxford, 1982.

51. *Samuel Hartlib and the Advancement of Learning*, ed. Webster, p. 95.

52. See, in general, James Knowlson, *Universal Language Schemes in England and France 1600-1800*, Toronto, 1975; M.M. Slaughter, *Universal*

would be unforgettably satirized by Swift, who in *Laputa* depicts a scheme to shorten discourse by leaving out verbs and participles and, ultimately, by abolishing words altogether; instead, the inhabitants carry about a huge load of objects to which they point when wishing to carry on a conversation.

Linguistic unity and religious pacification were means to the final objective: the prevention of war between states and the unification of the human race: "oneness" or *concordia*. Projects for universal peace and concord had less influence in England than they did on the Continent, perhaps because England was less affected by the carnage of seventeenth-century warfare. Gabriel Plattes, the author of *Macaria*, declares in one of his works that "the whole world is all of one God's making, and, no question is or should be one body politic".[53] Yet not even Hobbes put forward a plan for a world state, logical culmination of his thought though it would have been. Only the Quakers bothered with projects for international federation. William Penn propounded a scheme in 1693 for a European Parliament and John Bellers also put forward a plan for a European Senate which would settle all international disputes without bloodshed.[54]

* * * * *

It was, therefore, always the same imperfections which the seventeenth-century utopians sought to remedy; and though they differed widely in the details of their proposals, their goals display a remarkable affinity: the advancement of knowledge, the control of nature, the relief of poverty, the elimination of disputes and the atainment of universal peace and harmony. These objectives

---

Languages and Scientific Taxonomy in the Seventeenth Century, Cambridge, 1982; Vivian Salmon, *The Study of Language in 17th Century England*, Amsterdam, 1979, chap 8; Katz, *Philo-Semitism*, chap. 2.

53. Gabriel Plattes, *A Discovery of Infinite Treasure*, London, 1639, sig. A4.

54. William Penn, *The Peace of Europe: The Fruits of Solitude and Other Writings*, Everyman's Library, London, n.d., pp. 3 — 22; John Bellers, *Some Reasons for an European State*, 1710, in Fry, *John Bellers 1654-1725*, pp. 89-99.

underlay most of the literary utopias, just as they coloured the idealized accounts of other countries and inspired the activities of the projectors and colonists. The interest of these utopian goals is that they help to define the preoccupations of the age in which they originated: above all the obsession with harmony and the faith in the power of knowledge. Such preoccupations can be related to the social problems of the era, but they owe even more to the stylized preoccupations of biblical commentary. Peace and knowledge were the essential features of the New Jerusalem.

The dreams of the seventeenth century, therefore, were not those of the twentieth. There was very little concern with sexual fulfilment, for example, and no concept of utopia as a place of personal authenticity or self-realisation. On the contrary, most seventeenth-century utopias, far from encouraging human self-expression, showed an anxiety to regulate and control. "There will be rules made for every action a man can do", wrote Winstanley.[55] The literary utopians wanted a regular time-table, a clearly defined hierarchy and a firm code of rewards and punishments. Their favourite models of social organization were the monastery, the workhouse, the college and the school.

This concern with the small institution reflected another tendency — the disposition to turn away from the unregenerate mass of mankind and to withdraw into a select community of reforming spirits. Hartlib, Dury, Plockhoy, Bellers and many others were attracted by what John Beale called "the design of beginning buildings of Christian societies in small models".[56] The small, godly community, thought John Evelyn, was "the most blessed life that virtuous persons could wish or aspire to in this miserable and uncertain pilgrimage".[57] There was indeed a hermetic quality about much seventeenth-century utopianism, shown in the recurring tendency for little groups of select individuals to make private pacts in a belief that their illumination would enable them to reform the world.

After Charles II's restoration in 1660, hopes of such reform grew

55. *Works of Gerrard Winstanley*, ed. Sabine, p. 512.

56. *The Diary and Correspondence of Dr. John Worthington*, ed. James Crossley, I (Chetham Society, 1847), p. 156.

57. *Works of the Honourable Robert Boyle*, V. p. 398.

faint. England was no longer a *tabula rasa*, as she had seemed to be in the 1640s, and the prospect of radical reconstruction became remote. "The times of such a public universal happiness seem not yet to be at hand", concluded Hartlib.[58] The utopians had never been more than a tiny minority and had long been denounced as dreamers, impractical visionaries. Works like *Christianopolis* or *New Atlantis* were "witty fictions", "mere chimeras", "airy castles", "romantic whimsies". Perfection was impossible in this world, went the chorus. Human nature could never be reformed and if one evil was eliminated another would spring up in its place. "Dream not of other worlds", said Milton's Angel to Adam.[59]

This was the conservative refrain. As Mannheim says, it is the socially dominant group which determines what is or is not "unrealistic". When Parliament asked for control of Charles I's counsellors, the King denounced their demands as the "new Utopia of religion and government into which they endeavour to transform this kingdom".[60] When the Levellers put forward proposals for a more democratic regime, they were told that "the dispute is not now of what is absolutely best if all were new, but of what is perfectly just as things now stand: it is not the Parliament's work to set up an Utopian commonwealth, or to force the people to practise abstractions, but to make them as happy as the present frame will bear".[61] In 1639 Archbishop Ussher commented that John Dury would do better to come home, since England's own religious divisions made his efforts to unite the churches of Europe appear ridiculous.[62]

The ultimate refutation of utopia is dystopia, the demonstration that utopian visions are not just impractical, but potentially sinister. "I am verily of opinion", wrote one seventeenth-century

58. *Proceedings of the Massachusetts Historical Society, 1878*, Boston, 1879, p. 214.
59. Robert Burton, *The Anatomy of Melancholy*, Everyman's Library, London, 1932, I, p. 101; Gibson, *St. Thomas More: A Preliminary Bibliography*, pp. 320, 383; John Milton, *Paradise Lost*, VIII, line 175.
60. Mannheim, *Ideology and Utopia*, p. 183; John Rushworth, *Historical Collections*, London, 1721, IV, p. 727.
61. *The Leveller Tracts 1647-1653*, eds William Haller and Godfrey Davies, Gloucester, Mass., 1964, p. 120.
62. Turnbull, *Hartlib*, Dury and Comenius, p. 199.

critic, "that fantastic eutopian commonwealths (which some witty men ... have drawn unto us), introduced among men, would prove far more loathsome and be more fruitful of bad consequences than any of those of the basest alloy yet known ... because they seem all to me rather suited to the private conceptions and humours of their architects than to the accommodation and benefit of men".[63]

A Heav'n on Earth they hope to gain,
    But we do know full well,
Could they their glorious ends attain,
    This Kingdom must be Hell.[64]

Yet the only seventeenth-century work which set out to prove this was published as early as 1605 and took as its target not the millenarian utopianism of the mid-seventeenth century, but the old peasant myth of the land of cockayne. Joseph Hall's *Mundus Alter et Idem* (c. 1606) is a satirical burlesque, mocking vice of every kind, but particularly concerned to show that limitless sensual gratification generates moral and physical deterioration.It was written by a man who believed it immoral to "dream of an utopicall perfection" or to hope for paradise in this inferior world; and it is the only dystopia of the period.[65] There were some writers who expressed the modern liberal objection to utopianism, namely its implicit authoritarianism and its certainty that its exponent knows what is right for others.[66] But not until Jonathan Swift do we meet a full dystopian onslaught on the idealism of the mid seventeenth century: the reference in *Laputa* to a scheme devised forty years ago "of putting all arts, sciences, languages and mechanics upon a new foot"[67] is surely an allusion to Hartlib and his circle. Yet even in Swift it is the impracticality of the projectors

63. J. Philolaus, *A Serious Aviso to the Good People of this Nation, Concerning that Sort of Men, called Levellers*, London, 1649, p. 5.

64. Marchamont Nedham, *A Short History of the English Rebellion*, in *The True Character of a Rigid Presbyter*, 2nd edn., London, 1661, p. 64.

65. Richard A. McCabe, *Joseph Hall. A Study in Satire and Meditation*, Oxford, 1982, chap. 2.

66. E.g., Marchamont Nedham, *The Case of the Commonwealth Stated*, ed. Philip A. Knachel, Charlottesville, 1969, p. 97; Glanvill, *Essays on Several Important Subjects*, VII, p. 39.

67. Jonathan Swift, *Gulliver's Travels*, London, 1726: 1947, p. 194 (pt. III chap. iv).

which is most effectively satirized. The notion that hopes of perfection are necessarily self-defeating is less convincingly established. Swift's Struldbruggs are a dreadful warning of what immortality would mean if unaccompanied by health and energy; but since the seventeenth-century medical reformers who sought to increase the expectation of life also hoped to prolong human vigour, the criticism was unfair.

As social philosophy, the defects of seventeenth-century utopianism seem obvious enough to us. Buttressed in most cases by a millenarian belief that God was on their side, the utopians were absurdly optimistic about the possibility of attaining their objectives. With charity, faith and industry, thought John Bellers, "then mountains of difficulty will vanish away, as mists before the sun".[68] Moreover, their conception of felicity was still a largely static one. There was a dynamic element implicit in the belief that science would better the human condition by transforming man's relationship to nature, but even Bacon assumed that the achievement of science would be a finite matter. When peace, harmony and perfect knowledge had been secured, history would by implication stop. No one considered the possibility that if people were freed from pain and worry they would become bored, living a life of indifference or finding some new source of unhappiness. The practical meaning of such abstract goals as "peace" and "harmony" was never explored.

Yet we should not be too quick to condemn the utopians for a lack of realism. In the conditions of the mid-seventeenth century it really did seem possible that a gigantic reformation could take place. The old institutions had been torn down and were waiting to be replaced. Utopianism offered effective criticism because it provided an alternative model. "No wise man", thought Hartlib, "will lay his old habitation waste till he know what to erect instead thereof; hence it is that a new model is commonly first prepared before the old one be removed".[69] The aim, agreed Hartlib's friend John Pell, "is to propose to ourselves the perfectest ideas that we can imagine, then to seek the means tending thereto, as rationally

as

---

68. Fry, *John Bellers 1654-1725*, p. 153.
69. *Samuel Hartlib and the Advancement of Learning*, ed. Webster, p. 193.

46

as may be, and to prosecute it with indefatigable diligence; yet if the idea prove too high for us, to rest ourselves content with approximation".[70]

However utopian, there was nothing "unrealistic" about such an approach; and it did not prove totally unsuccessful. The foundation of overseas colonies, the return of the Jews to England and the establishment of the Royal Society were all achievements which can be credited at least in part to the utopian impulse of the age. The tireless projecting of the Hartlib circle anticipated much of what we now take for granted: a national health service, free legal aid, universal education, public libraries, decimal coinage, a university of London. The utopian faith in the power of state planning to solve problems of health, education and poverty proved genuinely prophetic. The officials who manage the economy and oversee welfare in Robert Burton's "poetical commonwealth" prefigure the modern bureaucratic state.

What above all impresses about seventeenth-century English utopian speculation is its moral and religious seriousness. Because the forces of anti-utopian sentiment rested so heavily on the theology of original sin, it was only from within a religious context that a convincing alternative current of thought could arise. It was the millenarian belief in the imminence of a new golden world which encouraged the utopian impulse; and it was the stylized, Biblically-derived assumption that harmony and knowledge were essential features of that world which shaped the objectives of utopian activity. A truly secular utopia would have to wait for another age.

Oxford   Keith Thomas

70 John Pell, *An Idea of Mathematics*, in John Durie, *The Reformed Librarie-Keeper*, London, 1650, p. 41.

RECOLLECTIONS: SIDNEY'S ISTER BANK POEM

A nineteenth-century editor of the *Arcadia* simply omitted the Ister Bank poem and the rest of the Third Eclogues because, he said, "it has nothing to do with the story, and is not remarkable for merit".[1] In this he echoed the sentiments of the Arcadian shepherds — not the noblemen in pastoral disguise, but the real shepherds — who at the end of Book III are celebrating an Arcadian wedding and who do not have the first idea what this Ister Bank song is all about. It is sung by one Philisides, a mysterious stranger dressed up as a shepherd, who has been listening to their wedding songs for a long time and in complete silence, meanwhile "revolving in his mind all the tempests of evil fortunes he had passed". Then, at length, he breaks his silence by singing the Ister Bank poem, 161 lines long; and after this sudden display of eloquence he falls silent again. The shepherds are extremely puzzled by his performance and discuss among themselves what he could possibly have meant. Then a senior shepherd, Geron, takes over. He grunts that he "never saw anything worse proportioned",[2] and so concludes the festivities with a proper wedding song of his own making.

What puzzled Philisides' audience was not only the meaning of

1. *The Countess of Pembroke"s Arcadia by Sir Philip Sidney*, London, 1893, p. 413.

2. *The Countess of Pembroke"s Arcadia (the Old Arcadia)*, ed. Jean Robertson, Oxford, 1973, p. 259. The text of the poem is reprinted from this edition (pp. 254-59) with permission. Quotations from *A Defence of Poetry* are from *Miscellaneous Prose*, eds Katherine Duncan-Jones and Jan van Dorsten, Oxford, 1973. Geron's boorish response makes an amusing contrast to the civility of Sannazaro's Italian shepherds who, in his *Arcadia*, commented on one occasion: "If by reason of the covert language it was little understood by us, nevertheless it did not follow that it was not heard by each man with the closest attention". Jacopo Sannazaro, *Arcadia and Piscatorial Eclogues*, tr. Ralph Nash, Detroit, 1966, p. 118.

the song but also its quaintness. They, the real rustics, sing
epithalamia like true Elizabethan gentlemen, but the pseudo-
shepherd Philisides ineffectively completed his disguise by singing
a "rustic" poem — and about animals, too. The Ister Bank song is
Sidney's only "archaic" poem (somewhat in the manner of
Spenser's 1579 *Shepheardes Calender*, dedicated to Sidney, which
also contains a beast-fable),[3] and a very rare instance of his using
the Chaucerian stanza — which, incidentally, should remind his
readers of Chaucer's *Parliament of Fowles*. If his Arcadian
audience was baffled, we too may wonder why he wrote the song in
the way he did, particularly because in these same months (in *A
Defence of Poetry*, speaking *à propos* Spenser's *Shepheardes Calender*) he remarked that Spenser's "framing his style to an old rustic
language I dare not allow". Here is his own text:

As I my little flock on Ister bank
(A little flock, but well my pipe they couthe)
Did piping lead, the sun already sank
Beyond our world, and ere I gat my booth
Each thing with mantle black the night did soothe,
   Saving the glow-worm, which would courteous be
   Of that small light oft watching shepherds see.

The welkin had full niggardly enclosed
In coffer of dim clouds his silver groats,
Ycleped stars; each thing to rest disposed: 10
The caves were full, the mountains void of goats;
The birds' eyes closed, closed their chirping notes.
   As for the nightingale, wood-music's king;
   It August was, he deigned not then to sing.

Amid my sheep, though I saw naught to fear,
Yet (for I nothing saw) I feared sore;
Then found I which thing is a charge to bear,

---

3. In the May eclogue; however, several analogies with Spenser's
February eclogue are even more striking. The fable (though not a beast
fable) told by Thenot in "February" is "a tale of truth", also on religio-
political issues, which the speaker has learned from one "Tityrus in his
youth". Contrary to what E.K. suggests in his notes, the tale is not
Chaucerian or based on Phaedrus, but largely the poet's own invention,
as is the beast fable in "May".

For for my sheep I dreaded mickle more
Than ever for myself since I was bore.
  I sat me down, for see to go ne could,   20
  And sang unto my sheep lest stray they should.

The song I sang old Languet had me taught;
Languet, the shepherd best swift Ister knew, ·
For clerkly rede, and hating what is naught,
For faithful heart, clean hands, and mouth as true.
With his sweet skill my skill-less youth he drew
  To have a feeling taste of him that sits
  Beyond the heav'n, far more beyond our wits.

He said the music best thilke powers pleased
Was jump concord between our wit and will,   30
Where highest notes to godliness are raised,
And lowest sink not down to jot of ill.
With old true tales he wont mine ears to fill:
  How shepherds did of yore, how now, they thrive,
  Spoiling their flock, or while twixt them they strive.

He liked me, but pitied lustful youth.
His good strong staff my slipp'ry years upbore.
He still hoped well, because I loved truth;
Till forced to part, with heart and eyes e'en sore,
To worthy Coredens he gave me o'er.   40
  But thus in oak's true shade recounted he
  Which now in night's deep shade sheep heard of me.

Such manner time there was (what time I not)
When all this earth, this dam or mould of ours,
Was only woned with such as beasts begot;
Unknown as then were they that builden towers.
The cattle, wild or tame, in nature's bowers
  Might freely roam or rest, as seemed them;
  Man was not man their dwellings in to hem.

The beasts had sure some beastly policy;   50
For nothing can endure where order nis.
For once the lion by the lamb did lie;
The fearful hind the leopard did kiss;
Hurtless was tiger's paw and serpent's hiss.
  This think I well: the beasts with courage clad
  Like senators a harmless empire had.

At which, whether the others did repine
(For envy harb'reth most in feeblest hearts),
Or that they all to changing did incline
(As e'en in beasts their dams leave changing parts),   60
The multitude to Jove a suit imparts,
    With neighing, bleaing, braying, and barking.
    Roaring, and howling, for to have a king.

A king in language theirs they said they would
(For then their language was a perfect speech).
The birds likewise with chirps and pewing could,
Cackling and chatt'ring, that of Jove beseech.
Only the owl still warned them not to seech
    So hastily that which they would repent;
    But saw they would, and he to deserts went.   70

Jove wisely said (for wisdom wisely says):
'O beasts, take heed what you of me desire.
Rulers will think all things made them to please,
And soon forget the swink due to their hire.
But since you will, part of my heav'nly fire
    I will you lend; the rest yourselves must give,
    That it both seen and felt may with you live.'

Full glad they were, and took the naked sprite,
Which straight the earth yclothed in his clay.
The lion, heart; the ounce gave active might;   80
The horse, good shape; the sparrow, lust to play;
Nightingale, voice, enticing songs to say.
    Elephant gave a perfect memory;
    And parrot, ready tongue, that to apply.

The fox gave craft; the dog gave flattery;
Ass, patience; the mole, a working thought;
Eagle, high look; wolf, secret cruelty;
Monkey, sweet breath; the cow, her fair eyes brought;
The ermine, whitest skin spotted with naught;
    The sheep, mild-seeming face; climbing, the bear;   90
    The stag did give the harm-eschewing fear.

The hare her sleights; the cat his melancholy;
Ant, industry; and cony, skill to build;
Cranes, order; storks, to be appearing holy;

Chameleon, ease to change; duck, ease to yield;
Crocodile, tears which might be falsely spilled.   '
   Ape great thing gave, though he did mowing stand:
   The instrument of instruments, the hand.

Each other beast likewise his present brings;
And (but they drad their prince they oft should want)   100
They all consented were to give him wings.
And ay more awe towards him for to plant,
To their own work this privilege they grant:
   That from thenceforth to all eternity
   No beast should freely speak, but only he.

Thus man was made; thus man their lord became;
Who at the first, wanting or hiding pride,
He did to beasts' best use his cunning frame,
With water drink, herbs meat, and naked hide,
And fellow-like let his dominion slide,   110
   Not in his sayings saying 'I', but 'we';
   As if he meant his lordship common be.

But when his seat so rooted he had found
That they now skilled not how from him to wend,
Then gan in guiltless earth full many a wound,
Iron to seek, which gainst itself should bend
To tear the bowels that good corn should send.
   But yet the common dam none did bemoan,
   Because (though hurt) they never heard her groan.

Then gan he factions in the beasts to breed;   120
Where helping weaker sort, the nobler beasts
(As tigers, leopards, bears, and lions' seed)
Disdained with this, in deserts sought their rests;
Where famine ravin taught their hungry chests,
   That craftily he forced them to do ill;
   Which being done, he afterwards would kill

For murder done, which never erst was seen,
By those great beasts. As for the weakers' good,
He chose themselves his guarders for to been
Gainst those of might of whom in fear they stood,   130
As horse and dog; not great, but gentle blood.
   Blithe were the commons, cattle of the field,
   Tho when they saw their foen of greatness killed.

But they, or spent or made of slender might,
Then quickly did the meaner cattle find,
The great beams gone, the house on shoulders light;
For by and by the horse fair bits did bind;
The dog was in a collar taught his kind.
  As for the gentle birds, like case might rue
  When falcon they, and goshawk, saw in mew.   140

Worst fell to smallest birds, and meanest herd,
Who now his own, full like his own he used.
Yet first but wool, or feathers, off he teared;
And when they were well used to be abused,
For hungry throat their flesh with teeth he bruised;
  At length for glutton taste he did them kill;
  At last for sport their silly lives did spill.

But yet, O man, rage not beyond thy need;
Deem it no gloire to swell in tyranny.
Thou art of blood; joy not to make things bleed.   150
Thou fearest death; think they are loath to die.
A plaint of guiltless hurt doth pierce the sky.
  And you, poor beasts, in patience bide your hell,
  Or know your strengths, and then you shall do well.

Thus did I sing and pipe eight sullen hours
To sheep whom love, not knowledge, made to hear;
Now fancy's fits, now fortune's baleful stours.
But then I homeward called my lambkins dear;
For to my dimmed eyes began t'appear
  The night grown old, her black head waxen grey,   160
  Sure shepherd's sign that morn would soon fetch day.

The first point that needs to be made is that the Ister Bank poem
is very much a 1579/80 composition. All the eclogues were
presumably written before the spring of 1580, and several details
(apart from the Spenserian link mentioned before) connect this
particular piece with the preceding months. Lines 150-51 are a
paraphrase of Seneca's *Oedipus*, 705-6, which he also quoted in
Latin in the *Defence of Poetry*, the *Letter to Queen Elizabeth* and
Certain Sonnets 14 (with a translation); clearly this succinct
definition of a tyrant was very much in his thoughts in the winter
of 1579/80. Next, the Ister Bank poem, though seemingly unre-
lated, is placed in the middle of a pastoral wedding scene and

thereby invites association with Alençon's wooing during these months. Finally, Queen Elizabeth always enjoyed giving animal names to politicians, but 1579, with Alençon ("my frog") around, was a peak-year for animal nick-naming. This is Sidney's only beast fable, and its chief source — apart from Ovid, the Bible (1 Sam. 8; Isaiah 11), and the Prometheus myth — is the famous Phaedrus fable on tyranny, the fable of the *frogs* who wanted to have a king.

We know that 1579/80 was Sidney's most prolific time as a writer. Writing was his only outlet because, as we know from his own correspondence, 1579/80 was also his most frustrating year as a budding politician. The international situation had developed in such a way that he should now have been playing the active part for which Languet and others had cast him for so long. Instead he was doomed to be an onlooker, watching his neighbour's house go up in flames as he liked to call it (borrowing a phrase from Horace). It often drove him to despair. "My only service is speech", he wrote to his uncle the Earl of Leicester; adding sarcastically that he now had such a bad cold that he had lost even that.[4] And it is not surprising that during these months he often reflected upon the previous years, recalling his travels from princes' courts to centres of learning, as he prepared himself for great tasks to come. This, too, is what the Ister Bank poem is about.

The Ister Bank peom is a poem of retrospection. (As I have explained elsewhere, this also accounts for its literary quaintness, for like Spenser's *Ruines of Time*, Philisides' song recaptures some of the earlier literary experiments).[5] It is Sidney's most autobiographical poem, the only instance where his mentor Languet is introduced in a literary context, and it offers one very precise circumstantial detail: the Ister Bank setting. This location, the bank of the river Danube, clearly refers to the trip which Sidney and some of his companions made to Hungary in the late summer of 1573 (11. 13-14). Languet had not joined them. In fact he had

4. *Prose Works*, ed. A. Feuillerat, Cambridge, 1963, III, 129.

5. "Literary patronage in Elizabethan England", in *Patronage in the Renaissance,* eds Guy Fitch Lytle and Stephen Orgel, Princeton, 1981, p. 205.

discouraged Sidney from undertaking the journey. But Sidney went, in spite of his tutor's advice, because he wanted to see with his own eyes — though from a safe distance — the common enemy of Western Europe: the Turks. However, this kind of simplistic analysis appears to have been revealed in its true nature to him as he found himself surrounded by the complexities of Europe in 1579, when the enemies to "the religion", "the people", or "the state" seemed legion, and the light of truth and wisdom that should guide Europe's leaders shone so very dimly. Whether real or imaginary, the Ister Bank setting of the early 1570s served as a revealing analogue to his predicament in the late 1570s. For he may once have thought that he knew "the enemy", but did he — or, does he now?

The beast-fable, the poem's story-within-a-story (within the tale of *Arcadia*), is a political allegory and should therefore be able to tell us more. The allegory itself is straightforward enough: from a golden age of harmony, peace, and tolerance, to war, bloodshed, tyranny. It is fair to expect a moral, some sort of conclusion, in the last stanza of the fable (11. 148-54). The tone certainly changes. This is Sidney, not some disguised "Philisides". There is no trace of the neo-rustic idiom, or even fable language. The Chaucerian stanza — or should we say Rhyme Royal? — begins:

But yet, O man, rage not beyond thy need;
Deem it no gloire to swell in tyranny.

Here at last the theme is named: tyranny. Then Sidney paraphrases those two obsessive lines from *Oedipus* "Qui sceptra saevus duro imperio regit/Timet timentes, metus in auctorem redit".

Thou art of blood; joy not to make things bleed.
Thou fearest death; think they are loath to die.

It is followed by the line which because of its rhyme sticks out so much in a rhyme royal stanza:

A plaint of guiltless hurt doth pierce the sky.

(I can think of no other line in a Sidney poem that is quite so direct and emotional as this.) We now reach the beginning of the conclusion,

And you, poor beasts, in patience bide your hell,

which is very close to the conclusion of Phaedrus' fable, "submit to the present evil" ("malum perferte"). But to one's surprise, the final line only says

Or know your strengths, and then you shall do well.

What does it mean? It cannot be explained from the context. The Arcadian shepherds were at a loss "what he should mean by it"; and even today's commentators have been unable to solve the "moral" convincingly. The fable, I think deliberately, ends in an enigma.

It is time to consider the rest of the poem, the framework around the fable: the six opening stanzas (or perhaps, more accurately, the first three because the next three are transitional) and the concluding stanza which, in the poem's own terms, are Sidney's lines, not Languet's. What needs to be realized is that this is a poem of day-break, a "dawn poem". The genre is familiar.[6] There appear to be very few countries in the world where dawn poetry does not exist in one form or another. In many cases, as in England, it is associated with lovers' parting, or with the bridal night. By choosing this genre Sidney adopted a formula that could have been in tune with the Arcadian wedding. But he decided to be different, as usual, and ignored this opportunity to contribute a song in the *alba* tradition (as in Shakespeare's *Romeo and Juliet*), or to adopt the Ovidian model from the *Amores* (which Dr Faustus remembered even in his final hour) upon which Renaissance poets liked to play variations (such as Donne's "The Sunne Rising"). Instead he wrote a very personal variation on the dawn theme and focused almost exclusively on its most basic motif: light and darkness.

In this, he did something of which no other instance in English Renaissance literature is extant but which comes very close to certain continental traditions. In the Low Countries, most notably, a special kind of dawn poetry had become popular in which the "watchman" plays a prominent role. Posted on duty on the watch tower, he is the first to perceive and to announce the break of day. (In Dutch literature dawn poems are in fact referred to as *wachterliederen*, watchman's songs). In such poems a note of moral seriousness may be introduced which the Ovidian model tends to lack. The singer invites association with the Old Testament watchman and often adopts a symbolic, indeed prophetic,

6. See *Eos*, ed. A.T. Hatto, The Hague, 1965.

role. He can see the light before anyone else. He announces the new day, the light to come. He watches over us all, and his role often blends with that of the Good Shepherd who protects his flock at night and guides it towards the light of the new day.

Sidney's dawn poem fits the tradition of "watching shepherds" (1. 7):

> As I my little flock on Ister Bank
> (A little flock, but well my pipe they couthe)
> Did piping lead, the sun already sank
> Beyond our world, ...

Yet the poem does not quite fit the tradition. Again, Sidney chooses to differ from the literary conventions, in a truly "Mannerist" way. It happens in the third stanza, our crucial key to the poem's meaning:

> Amid my sheep, though I saw naught to fear,
> Yet (for I nothing saw) I feared sore.

The watchman-shepherd must play his part. But for once the shepherd, rather than the sheep, is afraid during the dark hours before dawn. He is not afraid because of what he sees — for he sees nothing — but *because* he cannot "see" anything. And it is this which makes him realize for the first time what it is to be the leader of others when you yourself do not "see":

> Then found I which thing is a charge to bear,
> For for my sheep I dreaded mickle more
> Than ever for myself since I was bore.

This realization, then, is located in Hungary in August 1573, but it seems fair to argue that it reflects Sidney's thoughts in late 1579. He was feeling frustrated in the political ambitions which he and Languet and others had cultivated; but, the Ister Bank poem seems to say, what if he were to be given leadership at last? Expectations were high, yet how much wiser, better equipped to be a leader of others, was he now compared with the days when an apprehensive inexperienced eighteen-year-old English gentleman travelled with his companions along the Danube to take a look at the enemy of Christendom? How much more does he "see" in 1579 than he did six years earlier? Once again he calls upon his teacher, "old Languet"; but even his fable on tyranny ends without a clear conclusion.

Sidney died a few years later, in the Netherlands in 1586 — the only year in which he was allowed to be actively involved in the Protestant cause, unlike in 1579.[7] At his funeral, in 1587, a banner with the motto "Per Tenebras" was displayed, which he himself had designed some years earlier.[8] It was embroidered with silver stars against a blue background, the stars of Astrophil or Philisides, that should lead the way *per tenebras* to the invisible light:

To have a feeling taste of him that sits
Beyond the heav'n, far more beyond our wits.

This "the shepherd best swift Ister knew" had taught him more than anything else. The same *per tenebras* appears to be the central motif of the autobiographical framework of the Ister Bank poem of 1579/80.

In *A Defence of Poetry* written in these same months Sidney stressed the responsibilities of a poet; for did not the Romans call him a *vates*, "which is as much as a diviner, foreseer, or prophet", and have poets not been "the first light-givers to ignorance"? Shepherds, too, must sing unto their sheep "lest stray they should" (1. 21); but how can all these seers — poets or politicians — claim to be reliable guides when they themselves see with "dimmed eyes" (1. 159)? The Ister Bank poem is rather more than a political allegory containing powerful warnings against giving up one's freedom and about the evils of tyranny. It is a crucially autobiographical poem, and a much more private, intimate statement of faith and inadequacy than it might seem to be.

This, I think, is where the poem becomes particularly intriguing. The poet tells us a story which he claims to have heard from his own tutor — a councillor of princes, and a man therefore for whom clarity of vision is no problem. But having narrated Languet's lesson, the poet cannot now remember, or will not remember, Languet's solution to the problem of tyranny (about which there was so much talk in 1579). And so his fable fades out on the enigmatic note "know your strengths ...". Perhaps, if he had

7. On Sidney's mixed feelings about leadership in 1586, see my forthcoming essay "The Final Year" in *Sir Philip Sidney: 1586 and the Creation of a Legend*, Leiden, 1986.
8. See Katherine Duncan-Jones, "Sidney's personal *imprese*", *JWCI* XXXIII (1970), pp. 321-4.

written a philosophical treatise, not a poem, he would have remembered Languet's answer to tyranny: kill the tyrant.[9] (In the Ister Bank fable, incidentally, that solution might have been too drastic, since killing the tyrant would involve killing mankind.) But instead we have a poem — which, says the *Defence*, is just as well because poetry is a better instrument for presenting true wisdom than even philosophy or history, because poetry does not affirm but teaches idealistically, allegorically, delightfully, This, obviously, is what the Ister Bank poem sets out to do: with "an old true tale" (1. 33) of the kind that can hold "children from play, and old men from the chimney corner", a "perfect picture" is drawn of one of the most pressing political themes of the 1570s. Rhetorically, this is the simplest kind of poetry: pastoral and the "pretty allegories" of a beast fable, the two humblest of the genres. And yet this very poem, the most emphatically didactic one Sidney ever wrote, lacks a firm, useful conclusion. The Arcadian listeners were puzzled, quite rightly, and one of them ("old Geron") commented: "this is the right conceit of young men who think then they speak wiseliest when they cannot understand themselves." What Geron was made to say, was of course very near the truth. The young man had attempted to speak wisely, but lacked full understanding. His conclusion, therefore, remained "dimmed".

The phrase "... or know your strengths, and than you shall do well" is not self-explanatory. Sidney certainly never advocated a revolution of the masses, or even what we now call democracy, and it would be fatal to read such an interpretation into his poem. Some have argued[10] that "strengths" refers to the (lower) aristocracy — the horses and the dogs of the fable — but the poem itself, which is so clear in every other respect, does not actually make this point. Therefore such a reading, too, must be rejected. But are we to believe, then, that Sidney was just being honest, saying that tyranny is a terrible thing but that even as a poet he has

9. See Martin N. Raitiere, *Faire Bitts: Sir Philip Sidney and Renaissance Political Theory*, Pittsburgh, 1984. Because my approach is different I have not changed the shape of this essay since the publication of Raitiere's excellent study. In some important respects, however, our conclusions are the same.

10. Cf. *The Poems of Sir Philip Sidney*, ed. William A. Ringler, Jr., Oxford, 1962, pp. 414-5.

no firm solution to offer? It would certainly fit this highly idiosyncratic poem, and really turn it into a "self-consuming artifact".

There is, however, one other way to make sense of what appears to be a non-conclusion. In the final paragraph of Henricus Cornelius Agrippa's *De Incertitudine et Vanitate Scientiarum et Artium* (1530) there is one crucial sentence that seems to apply to Sidney's predicament. "You, therefore, o ye asses", Agrippa writes, "if you desire to attain to this divine and true wisdom, not of the tree of knowledge of good and evil, but of the tree of life, reject all human learning ... and, once you have entered into your very selves, you will have full knowledge of all things."[11] If this is at all applicable to what Sidney was thinking as he completed his Ister Bank poem in 1579, "know your strengths" may be read as the Delphic "know thyself". Sidney was deeply influenced by Agrippa's treatise which (as *A Defence of Poetry* shows) he had studied that same winter.[12] And it seems particularly revealing that one of the most famous paragraphs of the *Defence* is built on examples from Agrippa, proceeds to the same "know thyself", and culminates in Sidney's personal doctrine of "well-doing":

But when by the balance of experience it was found that the astronomer, looking to the stars, might fall in a ditch, that the inquiring philosopher might be blind in himself, and the mathematician might draw forth a straight line with a crooked heart, then lo, did proof the overruler of opinions, make manifest that all these are but serving sciences, which, as they have each a private end in themselves, so yet are they all directed to the highest end of mistress-knowledge, by the Greeks called αρχιτεκτονικη, which stands (as I think) in the knowledge of a man's self, in the ethic and politic consideration, with the end of well-doing and not of well-knowing only ... (pp. 82-83).

Interestingly, the paragraph ends:

So that, the ending end of all earthly learning being virtuous

11. "Vos igitur nunc o asini ... si divinam hanc et veram, non ligni scientiae boni et mali, sed ligni vitae sapientiam assequi cupitis, proiectis humanis scientiis ... ingressi in vosmetipsos, cognoscetis omnia ..." *De Incertitudine*, Cologne, T. Baumius, 1584, sigg. Cc5v - Cc6r.
12. *Miscellaneous Prose*, p. 193.

action, those skills that most serve to bring forth that have a most just title to be princes over all the rest.

One final comment needs to be made. Whether or not Hubert Languet was the author of the influential "monarchomach" treatise *Vindiciae contra Tyrannos* of 1579, this essay reaches almost the same conclusion as a recent, totally different, book-length study of the Ister Bank poem.[13] Although Sidney was deeply committed to pan-European protestantism and its political aims, he did not share the radical, revolutionary ideas of some of its intellectual leaders. (Perhaps this why William the Silent and other moderate protestant politicians put so much trust in him.) This reading of the Ister Bank poem indicates some of his most private doubts about authority and leadership, which were to surface more clearly in his final year when leadership had become fact, not fiction.[14]

Jan van Dorsten

13. Above. n. 9. Raitiere argues that Languet did write *Vindiciae*. See also David Norbrook, *Poetry and Politics in the English Renaissance*, London, 1984.

14. Above. n. 7. The present article is based on my inaugural lecture (*Terug naar de toekomst*, Leiden University Press, 1971) and various versions of a paper read at Berkeley (16 January, 1978), U.C.L.A. (18 February 1982), and Amsterdam (13 September 1984).

PLOCKHOY'S *A WAY PRONOUNDED*: MENNONITE UTOPIA OR MILLENNIUM?

J.C. Davis, in his book *Utopia and the Ideal Society, A Study of English Utopian Writing 1516-1700*, distinguishes two major types of ideal society, one of which he labels Utopia and another the Millennium. The distinction he makes between the two is based upon the way in which they deal with the major source of conflict and misery in any society, the problem of relating the existing and changing supply of satisfactions and goods to the wants of a heterogeneous group. Davis argues that the millenarian ideal society tends to shelve the problem of the reconciliation of limited satisfactions and unlimited human desires by invoking a force or agency that will miraculously and from outside the system change and perfect the old order. He then goes on to claim that the utopian ideal society is more "realistic" or tough-minded, in that it seeks to devise a set of strategies to create and maintain social order and perfection in the face of the deficiencies of nature and the wilfulness of man.

In this paper I shall try to answer the question whether Pieter Plockhoy's *A Way Propounded to Make the Poor in These and Other Nations Happy* falls within the category of utopian ideal societies or of millenarian ideal societies. An examination of the degree of "realism" or tough-mindedness in Plockhoy's blueprint may serve to confirm our first impression of a reformer both inspired and practical and tolerant almost to a fault in an intolerant age.

By the middle of the seventeenth century the Dutch anabaptists or Mennonites had lived down the disastrous and bloody events of the years 1534 and 1535, when in the city of Münster, in a radical attempt to realize their chiliastic expectations, their ancestors after a mass-emigration from Holland had helped to establish the New Jerusalem or the Kingdom of God in this world. After a long siege the final assault by the Prince Bishop and his troops upon the

Münster experiment in theocracy took place in June 1535, when most of the defenders were butchered by the victors. Fierce persecution of the radical anabaptist minority in particular spread rapidly and the fall of Münster indirectly led to the victory of the more pacific wing of the anabaptists over those who were prepared to use force in order to achieve their aims. The leader of the more moderate and sensible of the Dutch anabaptists was an ex-priest from Witmarsum in Friesland called Menno Simons, after whom his followers were called Mennonites.

In the hundred years after the traumatic failure of the Münster utopia the Dutch Mennonites earned themselves the nickname "stillen in den lande", that is, "the quiet in the land", which may be seen as proof of their renunciation of violence and their dwindling hopes of establishing a millenarian society on earth. The Mennonites emphasized adult baptism, inner religion and the separation of church and state. They rejected child baptism, military service and the swearing of oaths and adopted a role of passive obedience to government. They strove to achieve a primitive Christianity based upon scriptural authority, particularly the Sermon on the Mount, and simplicity in life and dress.

It would seem then that most members of the Mennonite congregations in seventeenth-century Holland were satisfied to avert their eyes from the world outside, which was seen as an overgrown, untidy garden in which sin and corruption were raging, and cultivate their own enclaves of salvation whose boundaries formed a colony of heaven. However, not all Mennonites were as inward-looking as this character sketch would seem to indicate. In 1658 near the close of Cromwell's protectorate, there appeared in London a Dutch Mennonite who in his pamphlets signed himself Peter Cornelius Van Zurick-Zee. Like many contemporary English reformers, notably Gerrard Winstanley and John Bellers, he was a radical preacher on religious liberty and the ideal society. Apparently the toleration granted by the Cromwellian government inspired him and he believed that the time had arrived for the practical realization of his democratic and cooperative concepts. To him Cromwell was not just a reformer in England, but a type of the "universal Magistrate" who would "break forth as a light to all other Countreys and Nations".

Two American historians, Leland and Marvin Harder, in their book *Plockhoy from Zurick-Zee: The Study of a Dutch Reformer in Puritan England and Colonial America*, have carefully traced Plockhoy's mission to England, which can be documented by two publications. The earlier, entitled *The Way to the Peace and Settlement of These Nations*, is dated January 24, 1659 (new style) and consists of three letters which together had been addressed to the Parliament convened on January 27, 1659. The second and third letters are printed copies of ones originally delivered to Oliver Cromwell. The letter addressed directly to Parliament reveals that Plockhoy obtained an interview with Cromwell and "was severall times heard by him with patience".

The Way to the Peace and Settlement of These Nations is an appeal to the Commonwealth government to establish freedom of speech for all religious sects and inaugurate universal toleration. One of the more remarkable recommendations made by Plockhoy in this pamphlet is for the State to nurture and protect a kind of ecumenical Christian society. To provide common religious meeting-places for all Christians, he proposes that the government

> Institute ... in every City and in every County throughout England, Scotland, and Ireland, one general Christian assembling or meeting-place in such a form that all people may see one another round about by the help of seats, rising by steps, having before them convenient leaning-places to read and write upon; also one desk aloft on one side or end to hear the holy Scriptures read at a set time, giving freedom after that reading to all people, orderly to confer together concerning the Doctrine and Instruction of their Lord and Master Christ....

We shall see that this manner of meeting in common assemblies in which the Scriptures are read receives a central emphasis in Plockhoy's second pamphlet too. It is entitled *A Way Propounded to Make the Poor in These and Other Nations Happy*. The year of publication is 1659. The title page also bears the following note: "Printed for G.C. at the sign of the *Black-spreadeagle* at the West-end of Paul's Church-yard". We know that G.C. represents the initials of Giles Calvert, bookseller and agent for the Levellers. This suggests that Plockhoy had connections with some of the English radical social reformers.

A Way Propounded contains Plockhoy's proposals for an ideal, cooperative society. His motives for "bringing together a fit, sutable and well-qualified people into one Houshold-government, or little Commonwealth" appear to be twofold. In the first place he seeks to reduce unemployment amongst the poor through a policy of full-employment and an improvement of their work discipline ("Being the way ... to rid these and other Nations from idle, evil, and disorderly persons"), and secondly, his "little Common-wealth" will put an end to the exploitation of the poor by "all such as have sought and found out many inventions, to live upon the labour of others".

It would be a mistake to think of Plockhoy's original inspiration for this ideal society blueprint as primarily socio-economic and secular. From the opening paragraphs it is evident that his desire to reform the world in which "Temporal and Spiritual Pharaohs ... have long enough domineered over our bodies and souls", by setting up again "Righteousness, love and Brotherly Sociableness", must be qualified as moral and religious. It is the pattern and "doctrine of the Lord Jesus, who came not to be served, but to serve" that underlies and shapes his reforming zeal. That Plockhoy and his supporters took concrete steps to practice what they preached, may be inferred from the following note appended to the pamphlet:

> One Society being setled in order (as a nursery) about London, to imploy the Poor, we may have a Second about Bristol, and another in Ireland, where we can have a great deal of Land for little money, and plenty of Wood for building of Houses, Ships, and many other things.

For the society to get started it is necessary that a few able men put in sums of money to raise a starting-capital with which they can buy a piece of land. The next step is the recruitment of "Husbandmen, handy Craftsmen, Tradesmen, Marriners, and others (coming in with their moveables as Cattel, Money, or any other Commodities)". It is stipulated that only "honest, rational, and impartial persons" will be received as full members of the society, but it is possible for others who are not (yet) of such disposition to be employed by the little Commonwealth, working

12 hours in a day, against a working day of 6 hours for the members.

On a reassuring note Plockhoy adds that the people who join the society are not expected to make their goods common, for "according to the tenth Commandment none ought to covet another man's goods".

Two centres are to be established, a city "Warehouse" (i.e. a kind of department store) and, close to a river, a large house in the country. The country house for farmers, craftsmen and sailors, will produce corn, flax, hemp and other raw materials for manufacture, to be transported by water to the city "Warehouse" and, it is hoped, in due time exported to Flanders, Holland and France in their own ships. The plans for the house in the country strike a sensible balance between communal and private demands. Besides a common dining-room, kitchen and lecture-hall, there are "for freedom and conveniency a chamber and a closet for every man and his wife". The house in the city has to be big enough for 20 to 30 families to sell from shops a great variety of goods such as cloth, linen, stockings, men's and women's apparel, shoes and hats. In keeping with the Mennonite insistence on simplicity in dress the members of the society would in principle "make all things for sale without unnecessary trimmings". Yet, almost in the same breath we are given an instance of the flexibility of Plockhoy's Mennonite (commercial) conscience: "Unless ... any buying of us, would have any trimming upon them, those we shall endeavor to give content, if they bring to us those unnecessary trimmings, which we our selves have not, doing our endeavor to keep their custom, that so in time they may be convinced of their folly, being better with us, who give them reasons for alteration, than with others who bolster them up in pride and excess".

If for a moment we recall J.C. Davis' criterion for distinguishing between a utopian and a millenarian ideal society, the extent to which "realistic" strategies are devised to achieve and maintain a social order without undue neglect of natural deficiencies or human weaknesses, then surely our last example reveals a "realistic" appraisal of both the customers' and the members' weaknesses. As an earlier example of such a "tactical withdrawal" I would cite Plockhoy's rejection of the sharing of goods through an appeal to the tenth commandment. Further, more substantial proof of a certain tough-mindedness can be found in the procedure adopted for the selection of prospective members: he carefully excluded dishonest and irrational people. It would perhaps be no exaggeration to claim that in the earlier millenarian anabaptist experiment in Münster irrationality in a brother or sister was considered a distinct advantage!

The society's centre in the city would not only house tradesmen and craftsmen, there would also be skilled book-keepers, navigators, astronomers, physicians and teachers of Latin, Greek and Hebrew, offering their services to "the Rich, without the society, for money and the Poor gratis". Plockhoy quite confidently predicts that the commercial centre will be competitive for three reasons: there will be no "overasking in price, contrary to the common custom of the world", the overhead expenses are lower (lower rent, plain life-style) and the morale of the workers will be higher, because the profit is used for the common good.

For the government and the administration of the little Commonwealth the pamphlet contains a number of detailed and sensible suggestions, most of which testify to the "realistic" insight and shrewd business acumen of its author. There is, for instance, this cautious provision with regard to the control of the society's funds: "One man alone ... shall not be Master of the Cash or Treasury; but three of the uppermost in the Government shall always have the keys, so that one, or two, unless the third were with them, would not be able to open the Chest; A threefold Cord doth not easily break, saith Solomon." This practice, which has been preserved in some Dutch Mennonite congregations to this very day, evinces the same combination of a pious appeal to biblical wisdom and a full recognition of human weakness that we saw earlier.

In the same spirit Plockhoy specifies the chief regulations concerning the society's form of government, which is essentially democratic, with terms of office limited to one year. No "Governour is to rule according to his own pleasure; but according to such Orders as the whole People shall make." Perhaps there is an underestimation here of the passion for power when he writes apropos of the office of Governour "but who would not rather ... work quietly six hours in a day (the working day of an ordinary member), than to bee in a perpetual disturbance of his thoughts, being imployed in multiplicity of businesses?"

Given the equality of all men and women in the sight of God, it is not surprising that every member is allowed to vote. But the principle of equality has one or two less predictable consequences: in waiting at the table the younger members take turns, "that so one may not be respected above the others" and the "ceremony of putting off the Hat" is abolished, because there is no need of those demonstrative gestures of respect, assured as they are of one another's love.

A remarkably enlightened attitude to the position and role of women is reflected in regulations concerning the education of girls: "The maids shall not onely be be fitted to do the housewifery, and order children, but also in case hereafter they be minded to leave the Society they shall learn a good Handy craft-Trade, that ... so they may be able to get a livelihood." This advanced approach is further supported by the conviction that "many women will rather work together with men for the common good than to be a whole day troubled with diversities of cares".

As a final example of Plockhoy's liberal, non-sectarian idealism one may adduce the fact that in his Commonwealth outside marriages are permitted: "If any desires to marry, he shall not be tyed to marry one of our Society; if he will have a vertuous person abroad, out of the Society, and dwell with her, or have her come into the society, every one is left to his liberty."

Towards the end of the first part of *A Way Propounded* Plockhoy considers the advantages and benefits to those who join his ideal community. He claims that his Commonwealth would, in particular, appeal to all those worried about making provisions for their old age, for their children, or for the time they should find themselves out of work, warning those who are successful in business and in good health against the day that they may lose their health and good fortune. In his cooperative society people would be freed from all wordly cares, surrounded as they are by many good people willing to take care of their neighbours, contrary to the way of the world in which men are exclusively concerned with their own affairs. Therefore he concludes that it would only be natural and reasonable for people to be desirous of serving the common good and, in so doing, their own interests.

In the second part of the pamphlet, with the subtitle *Shewing the Excellency of True Christian Love*, Plockhoy develops, in the manner of a sermon, the Christian foundation of his ideal society. It is Christ, he says, who by his example has taught a partnership or society of mutual love: "abolishing amongst his disciples, all preheminency, or domineering of one over another, requiring that the gifts and means of subsistence in the world ... should be common; ... so that all Christendome ought to meerly be a certain great fraternity consisting of such as (having denied the world and their own lustes) conspire together in Christ, the sole head and spring of love; doing well to one another, and for his sake distribute their goods to those that stand in need."

Despite the unmistakably Mennonite tone of his apology — just for once he sheds his guise of the urbane and tolerant social innovator in a fierce denunciation of the "many Orders of lazie and wanton beasts, (I mean Monks and the like)" — he is as determined as in *The Way to the Peace and Settlement of These Nations* in his advocacy of the elimination of denominational differences in religious faith and practice. Only Christ and the gospels are to be accepted by all members, otherwise dogma would be kept to a minimum. Again he urges that a meeting-place, with seats in an amphitheatre form, and an emphasis on the reading of the holy scriptures be provided in the community. He states expressly that children are not to be taught merely "Humane forms of religion", clearly trusting them to be able to read and understand the Bible by the light of their own reason, and he concludes: "So doing there will be no foundation for sects, fractions, and schismes layd in their heartes."

In this reaction against prescribed dogma and the traditional liturgy of the churches, Irvin Horst, who has called Plockhoy "an apostle of the Collegiants", sees the influence of the Collegiant movement, which had its origin among the Dutch Remonstrants (Arminians). It was vigorous at the time of Plockhoy and growing by the absorption of Mennonite and Socinian elements. The Collegiants sought a fellowship across the lines of religious sects, and they rejected the strict dogmatism and control of the Reformed Church. It is true that Plockhoy's nonconformist and undogmatic ideas owed much to Collegiant thinking, yet his unique brand of pragmatism — pious and shrewd — remains the distinctive feature of his blueprint for a utopian ideal society. His anxiety to avoid a repetition of the grievous disappointment caused by the dashing of the millenarian hopes in Münster in 1535 must have been the product of a mind, careful and empirical, placing a great trust in man's reason. It is such a "realistic" temperament that we see reflected in *A Way Propounded*. Plockhoy never lost sight of his objective, "to leave the world to my posterity in a better condition than I found it". The modest phrase is characteristic of a man who never cherished the illusions of his Mennonite forefathers.

Cromwell's death and the Restoration of the monarchy were fatal blows to any hopes Plockhoy and his supporters may have had of establishing a network of ideal communities in England. In 1662 he is back in Amsterdam persuading the authorities to help him set up a similar experiment in the New Netherlands. But that's another story.

Amsterdam   Bouwe Postmus

LUNA MENDAX:
SOME REFLECTIONS ON MOON-VOYAGES IN EARLY SEVENTEENTH-CENTURY ENGLAND

On July 16, 1969, the spacecraft Apollo 11 was launched: destination Moon. Four days later, at 02.55 hrs. Greenwich Mean Time, the American airman Neil Armstrong became the first human to set foot on its surface. "A small step for a man", he was recorded as saying when he had got down from his spacecraft-ladder, "and a giant stride for mankind".

Whether the statement was truly improvised or a ghost-writer's carefully memorized text is neither here nor there, the point was perfectly valid. And it was so in more respects than one. For after Armstrong's historic words, we would nevermore be in a position to lend credibility to tales like the one which will furnish us with our present point of departure: a tale printed in London in 1638 and entitled *The Man in the Moone: a Discourse of a Voyage thither by Domingo Gonsales, the Speedy Messenger.* This was the first full-length moon-voyage in the English language. It was read and re-read, reprinted and translated, copied and imitated for well-nigh two centuries. And it was followed in that same year of our Lord 1638 by another, entitled *The Discovery of a New World: or, a Discourse tending to prove, that it is probable there may be another habitable World in that Planet.*

The interest, in other words, of their themes lies in the sequence, at close quarters, of these two publications; it lies in the *pas de deux* through the entire civilized world of these slender twins-in-12°, the one (posthumously and under a Spanish pseudonym) by the Bishop of Hereford, Francis Godwin, the other (under his own name) by the vicar of Fawsley, later Bishop of Chester and First Secretary of the Royal Society, John Wilkins. For thus was born the ever-swelling stream of modern books of air-based "popular science" which, time and again, would be merging with "science fiction" and prove inconceivable without its admixture of utopian bias.

1

The idea of human flight has, of course, engaged the waking and sleeping hours of men from the time when they first developed their imagination and began to regard birds with awe and envy. Together with the envy came the ambition to emulate. Remarkably enough, flying has never appeared to its devotees as a mere method of transportation, faster and more convenient than travel by land or water. Nor was it finally achieved by any pressure of economic need. From its earliest beginnings aviation has drawn its strength from an appeal to the emotions, an appeal, that is, to the longing for escape, or to the desire for exhilaration and power. Some, in fact, have seen it as the very symbol of aspiration.

But there is more. Until recently, i.e. until the end of the days when Scripture was still read for its own sake, no treatise on the history of flying could afford to miss quoting verse 6 of Psalm 55. This verse reads: "O that I had wings like a dove". But even in that distant past, the sequel, more often than not, was omitted. And yet, it is *there*, it would seem, that we may find the real point, since it is in this sequel that the Psalmist exclaims: "for then would I fly away and be at rest".

Even nowadays aircraft-pilots are known to feel, as they close their hands over the controls at take-off, that little by little in their bare palms they receive this gift. But then, have we not here precisely one of the prime movers of the writers of utopias? Is not the utopian dream the dream of a world where the inhabitants are essentially "at rest"?

Of course, focussing on the moon as the site of such an "other world" is as old as the hills. In a utopian context, though, such moon-focussing is a special thing. For, in this case there is no question of a "NO-place". The moon is there for all to see in its various phases, and has always been there, has always been reached for, and has always been cried for: an almost tangible *topos*, particularly since the invention of an effective telescope.

Prior to this invention — a very Dutch invention, incidentally, at once reported to his masters by the Venetian Ambassador — "Luna" had been a beloved poetical or fantastic theme. The moon was the unattainable abode of the moon-goddess, to be peered at with love and awe. From the moon the goddess might descend to enchant or to madden mortals at will. But, throughout, the moon was a power-house of fancies for artist and layman alike. Usually such fancies had erotic overtones, and long after the "realistically" conceived moon-voyage became popular in fiction, vestiges of the older attitudes persisted, even among scientists. In poetry and painting, the poignant lot of Endymion continued to inspire, the chastity of Diana to tantalize, the cool beauty of Cynthia to fascinate.

But Galileo the Florentine had not lived in vain. In 1638, on the title-page of Godwin's booklet, one Domingo Gonsales could only be apostrophized as "the speedy messenger" because in 1610 the *Sidereus Nuntius*, "The Starry Messenger", had been published. This was the slender treatise in which the Italian scientist-philosopher had revealed details of the new heaven and new earth which he had been the first to observe through his "optick tube". Not least because of its illustrations the repercussions had been enormous. In 1604, the ironic introduction in the German writer Johannes Kepler's *Astronomia Nova* of a "new star" had already shocked orthodoxy when described in none too classical Latin. After all, so far, the Church Fathers believed, as the Greek philosophers had taught, that the heavens were as immutable as they were incorruptible. "Change and decay" had been limited to the earth, to "sublunary" nature. The heavens were eternal, the firmament declared the glory of God, the stars had been counted. A new star, therefore, was either a miracle, as at the birth of Christ, or a dire warning of God's anger.

Whether miracle, however, or sign of divine anger, a "stella nova" *had* appeared. It had actually been discovered as early as 11 November 1572 by the Danish astronomer Tycho Brahe in his unique observatory at Oranieborg on the island of Hven. A generation later, as Professor of Mathematics at Padua, Galileo had been in a position to declare that the "strange visitants", first seen by his late lamented master in Denmark and recently by his friend Kepler in Prague, were indeed entirely new stars. Through his own telescope he subsequently observed millions of other stars never before seen by mortal eyes: the Milky Way. He also thought he discovered four new planets, though in fact these were the satellites of Jupiter. And, finally, he was able to offer the world what he described as "the body of the moon", the first scientifically based lunar topography.

The moon-passage in Galileo's *Starry Messenger* of 1610 represented a milestone in the history of Western thought. For, the telescope had proved, and the printing-press had broadcast, what reason had only been able to offer as a supposition. Instead of a smooth surface with an intriguingly anthropomorphic design, Galileo concluded that, like the earth, the surface of the moon was everywhere varied by lofty mountains and valleys and that some of its dark spots were seas and lakes. The moon, in fact, could be described as another earth; and so after earthly and celestial globes, map-makers now went on to manufacture beautifully decorated lunar globes and thereby to further concretize the idea of the moon as a "new world".

Is it surprising that, as time went on and the excitement, and horror, caused by Galileo's discoveries wore off, this "zooming in" on our ancient satellite first made for romance, then for comedy and eventually for satire? In her pioneering *Voyages to the Moon* of 1948, to which much in this article is indebted, Marjorie Nicolson indicated how only a few months after the appearance of the *Sidereus Nuntius* (which King James's Ambassador to Venice, Sir Henry Wotton, had at once sent to the Earl of Salisbury), Ben Jonson offered his Court-masque *Love freed from Folly and Ignorance*. In it, the character personifying Love is wisely counseled to seek a world outside our own by a Sphinx. To this, Love replies:

I say, that is already done,
And is the new world in the Moone.

His was not, of course, a startling reference to the new astronomy. Ten years later, however, he presented *News from the New World Discovered in the Moon* and another five years after, *The Staple of News*, the first full-length play Jonson had written in a decade. From the former we learn that the telescope had really ceased to be a novelty in England to the extent of even inspiring that wonderfully apt pun on "perspective glasses" (the customary name for the instrument), viz. "perplexive glasses". And in the latter we find for the first time the term "engine" for flying-machine. This is when, in the context of ridiculing the general avidity for news, the supplier of an utterly impossible novelty provokes the comment:

Witness the engine they have presented him
To wind himself up into the Moon,
And thence make all his discoveries....

No English poet showed a more direct response to the new astronomy than John Donne. In the analyses of his many references to the sun, the moon and the stars — no matter how we choose to interpret these references — the effect of the writings of Galileo and Kepler can hardly be overestimated. The role of Sir Henry Wotton in introducing Galileo to Britain has been mentioned above; in Kepler's case it was King James himself who had been told of the great German by Tycho Brahe in 1598, when this peace-loving monarch sailed to Denmark to collect the wife he had been married to by proxy. It is fascinating to follow the trail of those references and realize the links that must have existed between both Galileo's *Sidereus Nuntius* and Donne's *Conclave Ignatii* as well as the absolutely surprising connections of the latter with Kepler's *Somnium* (printed 23 years after and therefore only known to Donne in manuscript). For the surprise lies in the fact that, after the first scientifically-based moon-topography, the first scientifically-based cosmic dream-voyage should have come so late in the day. But this is another story; after all, it concerns an "actual" dream.

What constitutes the importance of Jonson and Donne for our purpose is the openly confessed or ingeniously disguised obsession with the notion of a plurality of worlds. It is less the disruption of ours that seems to trouble their minds, than the realization that this little world of ours plays so incredibly slight a part in an expanding and continuously expanding universe. It is true that after a few years, Donne's interest in astronomy seems to have declined. But in the 1635 edition of his *Poems* the printer included a verse-letter entitled "To Mr. Tilman after he had taken Orders". This intriguing valuation of the Ministry contains the lines:

If then th'Astronomers, whereas they spie
A new-found Starre, their Opticks magnifie,
How brave are those, who with their Engine can
Bring man to heaven and heaven againe to man!

Both Donne's and Jonson's use of the term "engine" takes us back to Bishop Godwin and the astonishing achievements with the "engine" of his hero-in-Spanish-disguise — a disguise that seems perfectly feasible in the light of the immense popularity still enjoyed by Columbus at the time. But then, the Spanish-sponsored Italian arch-discoverer is referred to in Godwin's "Epistle to the Reader" in so many words, when this reader is significantly informed:

> In substance thou hast here a new discovery or a new *world*, which perchance may finde little better entertainment in thy opinion, than that of *Columbus* at first, in the esteeme of all men. Yet his than [*sic*] but poor espiall of *America* betray'd unto knowledge soe much as hath since encreast into a vast plantation.

The passage is no less revealing — even to the use of such a term as "plantation" — than the epistle's final paragraph where we are told that

> the knowledge of this may seeme more properly reserv'd for this our discovering age: In which our *Galilaeusses* can by advantage of their spectacles gaze the Sunne into spots, and descry mountaines in the *Moon*.

Now, John Wilkins, the second of our authors of 1638, felt that neither hero nor engine were required to beguile his readers. His is a cogently argued presentation, as indeed was his subsequent *Discourse concerning Flying* in which he declared that there were "four several ways whereby flying in the air hath been or may be attempted". In our context, the list is remarkably helpful in that the first way is defined as "by the strength of spirits or angels", the second "by the help of fowls", the third "by wings fastened immediately to the body", and the fourth "by a flying chariot".

Of course, even in Wilkins' days it would never do to ignore the supernatural with which flight had been associated from time immemorial. But enlisting either devils or angels was as obviously beyond the grasp of ordinary humans (who were not prepared to follow in Faustus' footsteps) as weaving a magic carpet or mounting a witch's broomstick. So much for the oldest method.

The next method, while being as ancient in conception, was a second-best proposition which hailed from the Middle East and classical Greece. In Greek romances, for instance, we read about

Alexander the Great who fastened eagles to his throne and enticed them to take wing by suspending raw meat over their beaks. But this method, too, was fated to remain legendary.

The third method was epitomized, it need not be recalled, in the story of Daedalus and Icarus, a story doubly pathetic since the father of the unfortunate youth was also credited with having invented the square sail for ships.

As for the chariot or engine, this fourth method has its beginnings in far-off China with kites big enough to carry a man attached to their tail and used, like present-day satellites, primarily for military observation. The kite or dragon had been introduced to Europe as a toy — like the horizontal propellor derived from the horizontal windmill and recognized by Leonardo da Vinci as the potential helicopter. From Daedalus' square sail, and in combination with the kite, were developed ingenious prototypes of the parachute and glider. These first lured man into jumping from towers (and so mostly to their deaths) but ultimately, after the problem of adequate propulsion had been solved, they led to the primitive aeroplane. And this, as we all know, proved the real "upstart crow" that defeated the "cloud in a bag" represented by the balloon, the aeroplane which in turn was to be overtaken by the (once more Chinese-born) rocket that led to Neil Armstrong's "small step for a man to take".

To this history-of-aviation-in-a-nutshell there is a dual purpose. For, metaphorically, that nutshell is the same nutshell, in the kernel of which our first modern anatomist, the Dutchman Andries van Wezel (alias Andreas Vesalius) had shown the resemblance to the human cranium. His *De Humani Corporis Fabrica* of 1543, impressively illustrated by J.S. van Calcar, had also been written at Padua and proved no less a "messenger" throughout the Western world than the *Sidereus Nuntius*. In fact, it seems more than plausible that Van Calcar's drawing of a man's brain must sometime somewhere have been seen by Shakespeare and surfaced in his mind when writing Hamlet's "O, I could be bound in a nutshell/ And call myself King of infinite space". It seems equally plausible that it subsequently inspired Rembrandt to paint the indeed uniquely moving *Anatomy-lesson of Dr Deijman*, a picture which (some ten years after those imaginative Anglican Bishops and some forty years after Donne's "Anatomy of the

World") clearly symbolizes even more than the earlier *Anatomy-lesson of Dr Tulp*, the discovery of no less a mysterious new world than those sensational little publications. Together, in fact, the new Astronomy and the new Anatomy ushered in a new Awareness.

And so, the point of cultural-historical glosses of the kind is primarily to emphasize once again the extraordinarily close intertwining of science and art in our present context, and their joint connection with the utopian impulse. Needless to say, this intertwining revealed both optimism and pessimism. It is not by chance that "A Digression of Air" should occur in the second book of Burton's *Anatomy of Melancholy* of 1621, that Bacon's *New Atlantis* should be published with the *Sylva Sylvarum* in 1627, that Kepler's *Somnium* should have appeared in 1634, and that this drug-inspired dream of a voyage to the moon should date from the same year as the English translation of Lucian's *True History*. The latter, moreover, is the tale of a ship that sailed beyond the Pillars of Hercules, was hurled into the air by a waterspout, and was then carried to the moon by the wind. The original story, greatly admired by Erasmus and Thomas More, goes back to the second century A.D. and the ship, as may have been guessed, was wearing a square sail — the Daedalus-invented type of sail that was to engender the parachute.

2.

Let us, then, examine more closely what our two authors actually have to offer. If we start with Godwin's *Man in the Moon*, what we find is that, as in countless other tales of adventure, the story opens with a sea-voyage and a forced exile in an uninhabited island. Conventional as this promises to be, the framework, however, is frankly picaresque. Thus the hero, writing in the first person, is of noble Spanish parentage, but reduced to poverty. After more or less shady vicissitudes as a mercenary with the Duke of Alba in the "expedition against the Prince of Orange", he finds himself grievously sick on board a Spanish East-Indiaman from which he is eventually put ashore, together with, *mirabile dictu*, a faithful negro-servant, called Diego. The island on which they have been landed turns out to be a minor paradise, called St Helens. It is in this exotic scene, in which they will stay for the space of a year, that the climax begins.

Among the richly varied fauna of the island there appears to live "a certain kinde of wild Swans" who in a particular season "vanish away". Gonsales calls them "ganzas", a name which in spite of its Spanish ending is strikingly reminiscent of the Dutch for "geese", that is, "ganzen". He trains a number of these birds to carry small burdens to his black servant who, in embryonic *apartheid*, had been ordered to camp in another part of the forest, recognizable by a white sheet in a clearing. What follows was to be expected. By a clever application of pulleys with weights, and linking his ganzas to a small raft which resembled the customary travelling-litter or sedan-chair, Gonsales succeeds in teaching his birds to form a team and in the end to transport a lamb. This lamb (comparable to the cock, sheep and duck sent up by the brothers Montgolfier in their hot-air balloon in 1783, and to the monkey in the original Sputnik) became the first living creature to fly and come back to earth all in one piece. Gonsales is at once overcome by the perennial longing for the wings of a dove. His Moor is likewise affected, but finds himself peremptorily dismissed by a master who "simply" wanted to be the first human to fly.

It is thus that the great experiment starts with, as runway, a flat rock on a river's edge. After he has got safely across managing to avoid a ducking, Gonsales has only one more wish to be safely home so that he might, as he says, "fill the world with the fame of my glory and renown". And this wish is almost at once fulfilled. The Spanish East-Indiaman, on its return-trip, comes to pick him up. Gonsales embarks with both ganzas and "engine", overjoyed at his luck. His only worry is that the Captain might do him in and subsequently present the invention as his own. But fate intervenes in the shape of the Royal Navy. Some ten miles from the Canary Islands a British squadron appears on the horizon. The Spaniard, outnumbered and outgunned, decides to run his ship aground. Gonsales at once climbs into his engine that has been parked on the quarter-deck and finds that, as the vessel strikes, birds and raft are hurled aloft with the shock and that he is carried ashore. Alas, the natives prove unfriendly. And so, once again, he gives the reins to his faithful dozen, expecting to be put down on the island's snow-covered mountain. To his immense surprise, however, the ganzas this time climb higher and higher in the

THE
MAN IN THE
MOONE:
OR
A DISCOVRSE OF A
Voyage thither
BY

DOMINGO GONSALES

The speedy Messenger.

LONDON, *1711*
Printed by JOHN NORTON, for
Ioshua Kirton, and Thomas Warren. 1638.

direction of the moon. It was in this very moon that the wild swans, as everyone knew, were accustomed to hibernate and for which Gonsales' team had been overdue — a small detail he had clean forgotten, but which causes his space-trip to begin in earnest.

It is clear that the greatest technical problem facing the writer of a scientific fiction, whether he belongs to antiquity, to the seventeenth or to the twentieth century, is from the outset that of securing credibility. Any fiction with its central experience outside the normal range of everyday life can no longer rely on the universality of associations of thought; it has to ensure that the reader is prepared to suspend his disbelief in order to enter imaginatively into the story proper. The oldest and soundest method for securing this willing suspension of disbelief is that of embedding any and every strange event in realistic detail about everyday occurrences. That, obviously, is what lies behind the opening chapters of Godwin's *Man in the Moon*. The next thing, needless to say, is rational plausibility on the basis of generally known scientific fact and technological skills. Only thereafter is there room for clever speculation, witty, ironic, or emotionally overpowering.

Bishop Godwin's performance, when viewed from the narratological angle, is truly astonishing. Having made his début as an author with *A Catalogue of the Bishops of England* (with their lives) and with *Annales* of the reigns of Henry VIII and Mary Tudor, and ending his writing-career with a proposal for a universal language for scientists, he presents us, half a century before Newton's apple and the announcement to the world of the laws of motion and gravitation, with something completely unexpected: Domingo Gonsales' experience with diminishing gravitational attraction in space. In fact, Godwin's intrepid aeronaut meditates that things "do not sinke towards the Center of the Earth as their naturall place..., but are drawen by a secret property of the Globe...in like sort as the Loadstone draweth iron". We are further informed that between the earth and the moon Gonsales rests in gravitational equilibrium. Also, it appears that without any effort on the part of his ganzas, he is held at a constant speed on a direct course, that is, he follows the moon as it circles the earth which turns under him like "a huge mathematicall Globe". Gradually, as he approaches the moon, the earth is seen more like the moon and the moon "more like a World" — a sensation which today has become so

THE DISCOVERY OF A WORLD IN THE MOONE.

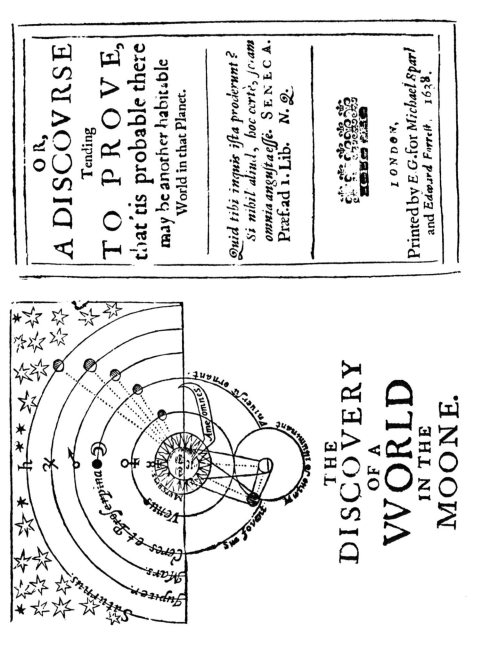

OR,

A DISCOVRSE

Tending

TO PROVE,

that 'tis probable there may be another habitable World in that Planet.

Quid tibi inquis ista proderunt? Si nihil aliud, hoc certè, sciam omnia angusta esse. SENECA. Praefad 1. Lib. N. Q.

LONDON,

Printed by E.G. for *Michael Sparke* and *Edward Forrest*. 1638.

familiar to us that it is even regularly used by advertisers. And all the time the birds flow on, "as easily and quietly as a fish in the middle of the Water", carrying their weightless passenger higher and higher; if "higher" it was, since (as Gonsales conscientiously records) "whether it were upward, downward, or sidelong, all was one". Like Hamlet, he had taken out his tablets, feeling that meet it was he set it down while, systematically, he asked himself all the questions of the great philosophers and there and then noted his answers in light of his unique experience. They make fascinating reading.

They confirm that for Gonsales Ptolemy was wrong and Copernicus, Brahe, Galilei and Kepler were right; indeed, it was the earth that moved, as Godwin's colleague John Wilkins actually illustrated in his frontispiece. But as his flight continued, atavistic (as well as Freudian) notions presented themselves to him in the form of hallucinations. Thus, characteristically reminiscent of Kepler's dream-vision, he traverses regions in which flying demons appear to dwell, both male and female, demons that tempt the traveller with promises of safety, sexual gratification, and unsuspected powers. Gonsales, finding that they understand several languages, proves a true diplomat. Without saying yea or nay, he obtains foodstuffs from them for future eventualities and in the end is able to continue unhindered. Thereafter he has to pass through an enormous cloud of locusts. But at long last he does reach the moon and his ganzas gently put him down. It has taken him eleven days in all and the date is Tuesday, 11th September ("at what time the Moone being two days old was in the Twentieth degree of Libra").

What he finds upon landing is that, like the earth, our satellite planet is largely covered by water. But it is also inhabited. Apart from migratory birds, the lunar animals and vegetation are strange and extraordinarily abundant. There is a particular shrub among the latter that produces leaves of highly nutritive value, for instance. As for the moon's inhabitants, while tasting leaves of this wonder-shrub, Gonsales is suddenly surrounded with "a kind of people" twice the size of his own, beautiful and pleasing in demeanour beyond words, their "habit" of a colour never seen before. These lunarians appear to be governed by twenty-four princes, ruled in turn by one Supreme Monarch. As a result of the reduced gravity on the moon, they all move about, like any twentieth-century astronaut, at gigantic strides through the air in slow-motion, while using small fans by way of rudder as we would small rockets. Gonsales goes to wait upon the Supreme Monarch and in exchange for some earthly trinkets receives three precious stones with remarkable properties and a mineral which, as a magnet in reverse, can neutralize the moon's gravitational pull and so, he feels, will enable him eventually to return to the earth. But that is still some way off and not, as yet, our concern. For, the question that imposes itself first is that of the quality of Godwin's work and whether it justifies our going into greater detail.

Its value is not in its profundity or in its wisdom. The book openly reflects some of the psychology and many of the generally available notions of its time in astronomy and science. But it is larded with realistic *minutiae* which bespeak an extremely rich and rationally nimble imagination on the part of its author. Of course, what Godwin writes does not all come as a surprise, nor is everything he offers the reader quite new. Lucian's *True History* also begins with an Odyssey and his vessel also lands on an inhabited and cultivated moon where the travellers are also presented to a king. Only, with Lucian, the rest is un-scientific fiction. Again, the first moon-voyage to be really based on science is Kepler's *Somnium*, circulated in manuscript from 1610 onwards. It is true, the device that Kepler used for his flight is a drug and still looks back to the supernatural, not forward to the flying-machine, and the flora and fauna on his moon are still grotesque. But the geology — if we may use so earthly a term — was in accord with what could be seen through a telescope. Moreover, he suggested that given a suitable means of conveyance, the moon could be colonized — an idea to which we shall return.

To what extent was Godwin's fantasy visionary, one wonders. It is certainly amazing that quite early in his story he should write:

> You shall see men flying in the air from one place to another; you shall be able to send messages many hundreds of miles in an instant and receive answers immediately without the help of any creature on earth.

On the other hand, as his hero's opening adventures are Robinsonian, so is Godwin's moon decidedly Brobdingnagian.

Diego is his Man Friday, but one type of lunarian is completely Swiftian. For instance, all proportions on the moon were answerable to the surprising height of its inhabitants. Lunar days and nights are each a fortnight long. Gonsales found that on the moon, too, there were social classes, that is stratified differences depending, interestingly enough, on the individual lunarian's capacity to bear the various kinds of light to which they were exposed. It was this capacity that determined their ability to stay awake during the entire lunar day. Only the third class was comparable to terrestrians in this respect: that group served the others like slaves, since they were esteemed to be no more than bastard-men, that is, counterfeits. As for communication, like all travellers to any utopia, Gonsales set himself to learn the language. This, like the lunarian colours, was for him literally unheard-of, since it consisted not of words but of "tunes and musical sounds". Need we point out that in Bishop Godwin's days call-signs and signature tunes had as little been dreamt of as aeroplanes and telephones? Yet, this is what Gonsales recorded even down to the musical notation of the lunarians' forms of salutation. And again like all visitors to utopias in the past, he proved at once to be an apt pupil and a keen linguist.

But then, in addition to all this, Godwin's moon-state was really Arcadian. Men and women were chaste and by nature mono-gamous, notwithstanding the extremely alluring physical appear-ance of male and female. There were no prisons either, nor judges and lawyers, since there were no crimes. Murder was unknown and actually impossible to commit, because there was no way to inflict injuries that might not be cured by a particular herb. Besides, lunarians were able to detect signs of innate depravity at birth and were accustomed to exile potential sinners to earth. There they exchanged these so-called "green children" for better products — a practical notion that evidently enabled Gonsales to account for the obsessive idea of the "changeling" in his own seventeenth-century world. The same radical attitude was applied to death. When his time had come, the moon-dweller would welcome it and organize a banquet as a festive farewell to all his friends. His body would not putrify and, in obvious anticipation of the modern American's mortician's usage, would be exhibited in all its glory.

For Gonsales, however, time had not come to a stop. Godwin's ingenuity as a writer charmingly solved the problem of devising a plausible return. His hero, in fact, discovered that of the original number of his ganzas he had already lost three as a result of pining away for want of their customary spring-migration. The others in their cage had also begun to droop, and even the Supreme Monarch could perceive "by the oft baying of my birds", as Gonsales writes, "a great longing in them to take their flight". And so preparations were made accordingly, his engine "trimmed up", fond farewells taken, and the reins let go. "With greediness the birds took wing", we read. Quickly they carried him out of sight of the huge lunarian crowd that had gathered to see him off. Once more, he was alone in space.

His return-trip was short and lasted only nine days. He was set down in China — a detail not devoid of poetic justice, when we consider the part played by that country in the pre-history of aviation. And from there he was able to send word to, and eventually reach, the Jesuit fathers in Portuguese Macao. With their help he could "lay a foundation" for the return to his wife and children, the "dear pledges" who had been as much the cause of his wishing to leave the moon as his desire "to enrich my Country with the knowledge of hidden mysteries whereby I may once reape the glory of my fortunate misfortunes". Thus the famous last words of *The Man in the Moone*.

3.

As has been emphasized from the outset, the significance of 1638 in the present context is its being the year in which two publications saw the light of day, which together could be considered to represent the *fontes et origines* of the science-fiction space voyage in English. Indeed, we may well state that, if Bishop Godwin was its Founding Father, Bishop Wilkins was its Founding Uncle. For, Dr John Wilkins, sometime member of the Philosophical Society of Oxford and subsequently founder-member of the Royal Society, whose first Secretary he became, was basically a man of science. His discourse on the *Discovery of a New World in the Moon* is made up of four pages "To the Reader" (which also serve as a Table of Contents) and two hundred and nine pages of propositions and their closely argued proofs. John

Donne, in his "Second Anniversary", while going back to the technique of medieval celestial voyages, may have demonstrated the disengagement of a deceased girl's soul (in the description of how "dispatching in a minute all the way twixt heaven and earth", she "carried no desire to know" about meteors or the nature of the middle and upper air). It is significant that he went on to declare:

She baits not at the Moon, nor cares to trie
Whether in that new world men would live or die.

Dr Wilkins did care.

In his *Discourse* he offers no solution to the problem of propulsion in flight; that of the force of gravity, however, is expertly settled by him. The same applies to the problem of the speed of the traveller, once he is above the "sphere of magneticall virtue" proceeding from the earth. Typically, the passages about a man's diet and sleep in space are the most fanciful. The flyer, he tells us, will need neither, since beyond the influence of gravity there will be no labour and no wearing down of the physical system. Accordingly, in a free mixture of science and legend, Wilkins declares that it was quite conceivable that once a year a human being might be carried to the moon on what to all intents and purposes must be a shuttle-flight. And in an almost lyrical finale, he defines "the great benefit and pleasure to be had by such a journey, (as enabling man to gage) the strangeness of the persons, language, arts, policy, religion..., together with the new traffic that might be brought thence". And this was not the end of the author's realistic appraisal. What is particularly striking is that one of the great attractions of an ability to reach the moon appears to have been that it offered the British a place to dump disturbers of the realm. The first time such a suggestion was made goes back twenty-seven years when Ben Jonson in his *News from the New World* stated in so many words:

It is the opinion of Keplar that, as soon as the art of flying is found out, some of their nation will make one of the first colonies that shall transplant into that other world. I suppose his appropriating this preheminence to his own countrymen may arise from an over-partial affection to them.

Of course, the extent to which "over-partial affection" to one's countrymen may be dangerous, particularly in nations avid for "new traffic", is too well-known to require elaboration. But it seems beyond doubt that one type of stimulus for the seventeenth-century development of cosmic flight-fantasies was this firm, and prophetic, belief that the first nation to discover the practicality of aviation would also be the first to plant its flag on the moon. Even in that stage of the history of human endeavour, one nation watched jealously the aeronautical progress of another. Oliver Cromwell, who was John Wilkins' brother-in-law, could as Lord Protector have used a technical feat of the kind. And satirists such as Samuel Butler in his "Elephant in the Moon" were not slow to spot ulterior motives.

Was it "to spot" or "to impute"? For an example of the latter in our lunar context, we only have to go back to the nation of which a member first efficiently ground lenses at Alkmaar to fit into an optic tube powerful enough to form a telescope (at once offered, incidentally, to Prince Maurice of Orange to aid in his military operations against the Spanish super-power). In the generation after the inventor — Lippershey by name and a fellow-townsman of Drebbel who produced the first submarine — the Dutch started draining the English fens. Their workmen, as could be expected, were attacked by the local population, picket-lines organized, dykes ruined. And the streets of Wisbech and Ely rang with ballads linking the proverbial Dutch thirst to their proven skill at draining lakes and reclaiming swamps and marshes. In one such ballad the singer denounced the Dutch as threatening "to drain the Kingdom dry", roaring:

Why should we stay here and perish with thirst?
To the new world in the Moon away let us goe;
For if the Dutch colony get thither first,
'Tis a thousand to one but they'll drain that too!

So far, the Dutch have not done so. But the ideas of Godwin and Wilkins had also reached France. There Cyrano de Bergerac followed suit and wrote two fantastic voyages, *L'autre monde, ou les états et empires de la Lune* and *Les états et empires du Soleil* (both posthumously published, in 1657 and 1662, and both also in the first person). For his moon-trip, however, he did not employ "ganzas" but glass vials filled with dew and strapped to his body. The sun, he reasoned, sucks up dew. If a man were to fasten about himself vials filled with dew, would not he too be sucked up through the air? And indeed, the contraption worked. Nay, so strong was this "solar attraction" which hurried him up with dizzying rapidity that, fearing to by-pass the moon, he had to break some of his vials and in this way adjust the forces of attraction and gravity in order to achieve a safe landing. *Selenarchia, or the Government of the World in the Moon*, as the English title reads when this "Histoire Comique" was translated in 1657, is only one example of the world-wide effect of our 1638 publications.

Of all their off-spring the most charming as well as the most learned, however, was Christiaen Huygens's *Cosmotheouros, sive de Terris Coelibus*, a booklet translated as *The Celestial Worlds Discovered: or Conjectures Concerning the Inhabitants* of 1698, the year of the author's death. To Christiaen Huygens, the first foreign member of the Royal Society, the planets were the heavenly cities of the idealistic philosopher who believed that possessing a rational mind and being well-versed in the essential disciplines of the mathematics, astronomy and music was the basis of human happiness. Huygens was not interested in playing about with imaginary devices for travelling through space in order to reach planets with which he had long been familiar through his marvellous self-made telescope. He simply printed "Suppose ourselves there" and went on to pour out a veritable flood of breath-taking scientific conjecture cast into a truly Utopian mould. And this leads us to our conclusion.

If, in the course of the seventeenth century, the supernatural voyage died out as a literary form expressive of the utopian impulse, this is because the New Science, no matter how elementary in its revolutionary line of thinking, had come to stay. If, moreover, writing a utopian tale had so far largely been a playful game, it was now becoming a serious exercise — an exercise in which the laws of nature were more and more consistently incorporated. Only, where the moon is concerned, the process is not as simple as that.

The title of this paper was phrased as *"Luna Mendax"*, the Deceptive Moon. One reason for doing so was that the earliest moon-trips in English literature, while in effect inaugurating the novel genre of science-fiction, were — and could not but be — deceptive as utopias. They stood for a classical ideal of reasonable societies with individual wisdom deepened by Christian piety and presented as larger, indeed inconceivably larger, than life. In fact, they represented the Senior Service, as it were, in the pre-Copernican, long drawn-out war against the man-centred conception of the universe, even if they did not as yet win any decisive victory.

Our opening quotation was Neil Armstrong's "small step". Our next was the Psalmist's full text where he sighs "O that I had wings like a dove...for then would I fly away and be at rest". In the seventeenth-century tales of moon-trips it is implied that if only, like a pre-historic aeronaut, one could land "out there", the "rest" would follow (*pace* George Herbert). So after the various parallels — spoken and left unspoken — between certain details imagined by our two astute Anglican Bishops in 1638 and the actual experience of our own successfully accomplished moon-voyages, the lesson, surely, is this: if one *does* set foot on the moon, what one brings back is no more than a handful of dust and neither gold, nor precious minerals, nor even the remotest signs of life. What does this mean?

A few months after 19 July 1969, the date when the first human stepped down from a moon-lander and became world-news, an elegant little book appeared in France, entitled *Adieu à la Lune*. It contained a remarkable collection of prose and verse on the Moon from all ages and many countries, including Godwin's *Man in the Moon*. This now unobtainable little volume by Alain Bosquet is introduced by a short piece directly addressed to the Moon by the anthologist:

Dorénavant [he laments] il nous est plus possible de fabuler sur votre nature .... Vous nous privez du rêve et du mystère.

Soon, he goes on, you, Luna, will be no more than a junction, a station on our sidereal cruises to Mars and Saturn, where we shall seek other moons:

Mais [he concludes] à cause de vous c'est avec une infinie tristesse.

At first glance, this curtain-line may seem touchingly apt. Yet, once again, we are deceived. Whether young and in love, or old and fond, we may be sure that the actual, unaided sight of the moon in the night-sky will continue to cast a spell which neither the most gigantic mirror-telescope nor the most sophisticated space-lab will ever prove able to destroy. But then, what could be more genuinely utopian?

Leiden   A.G.H. Bachrach

BIBLIOGRAPHY

H.J.M. Bos, M.J.S. Rudwick, H.A.M. Snelders and R.P.W. Visser, *Studies on Christiaen Huygens*, Lisse, 1980.
A. Bosquet, *Adieu à la Lune*, Paris, 1969.
H. Butterfield, *The Origins of Modern Science*, London, 1949.
R. Calder, *Leonardo and the Age of the Eye*, London, 1970.
Ch. Gibbs-Smith, *Aviation: An Historical Survey from its Origins to the End of World War II*, London, 1970.
A. Rupert Hall, *From Galileo to Newton*, New York, 1963.
A. Koestler, *The Sleepwalkers*, London, 1959.
A. Koyré, *From the Closed World to the Infinite Universe*, Baltimore, 1957.
L. Mumford, *Story of Utopias* (1922), new edn with a new introd., New York, 1972.
M. Nicolson, *Voyages to the Moon*, New York, 1948.
M. Nicolson, *Science and Imagination*, Oxford, 1956.
R. Ruyter, *L'Utopie et les Utopies*, Paris, 1950.

SWIFT AND ORWELL: UTOPIA AS NIGHTMARE

It seems appropriate that, at a Utopian conference in 1984, one should think of Swift in relation to this significant date and with substantial reference to Orwell's view of *Gulliver's Travels* as well as to his own dystopian fictions. Utopian fictions (to give definitional priority to the positive side of the genre), being essentially timeless and placeless, cannot be considered only in terms of the time at which they were written, or of particular local circumstances in the real world. They have a habit of breaking down tidy period divisions and neat chronological ordering. The year 1984 will pass; indeed it was pointed out several years ago by some expert on our calendar that we are some six years adrift in our calculations, so that here we all are in 1990.[1] With the suspense gone, and also the pressure to pass or fail Orwell's novel according to how accurately it predicted the way we now live, we may set about the serious task of placing it in the broader utopian literary tradition.

Gulliver's Travels is a long-established utopian text in its own right, but it is also one of direct importance to Orwell. Eric Blair, as he then was, read *Gulliver's Travels* at the impressionable age of eight — or, rather, just before: I first warmed to him as a human being on reading that he had stolen the hidden birthday present from his mother to read surreptitiously in advance. If he then felt guilty at the difficulty of pretending sufficient surprise on the day, the occasion perhaps provided an appropriate foundation for the guilt he so regularly expressed in his own writings. In 1946, between publishing *Animal Farm* and writing *Nineteen Eighty-Four*, Orwell wrote his essay "Politics vs. Literature: An Examination of *Gulliver's Travels*", and there he lists Swift's book among the six which he would preserve if all others were to be destroyed (*CEJL*,

---

1. *The Guardian*, 6 December 1978, p. 2.

IV, 257).[2] The conditions themselves sound suitably Swiftian, and the selectivity is reminiscent of Gulliver's (or Swift's) reduction, to the same number, of those "heroes" who deserve the name throughout history: "*Brutus* ... his Ancestor *Junius, Socrates, Epaminondas, Cato* the Younger, Sir *Thomas More* ... A *Sextumvirate* to which all the Ages of the World cannot add a Seventh" (p. 196).[3]

My comparisons between Swift and Orwell, however, must go beyond the obvious relationships between the best-known fictions of each. For both, the creation of a utopia or dystopia was a climactic achievement in a lifetime of political writing, and the form chosen may be seen as one way of putting into literary perspective the urgent concerns of each with the conditions of his own time. Rival prognosticators can no longer limit our attention to the merits or demerits of Orwell's last book as any kind of specific prophecy,[4] and while our fears for the future are more about whether there is to be one than about what form it may take, we are likely to think of our own time as not post-utopian but post-*dy*stopian.[5] Among all the other posts we are passing is this year: 1984, like 1948, will be lost to us as a period of particular impact, but using a date for his title was a clever choice on Orwell's part, and showed that he knew the rules of the utopian/dystopian game. Just as distance in space was once essential to the positive utopia, so the date of a dystopia had to press hard and close on

2. References in the text are, unless otherwise stated, to the Penguin edition of *The Collected Essays, Journalism and Letters of George Orwell* (*CEJL*), eds Sonia Orwell and Ian Angus, 4 vols, Harmondsworth, 1970, rpt. 1984.

3. *Gulliver's Travels* is quoted from *The Prose Works of Jonathan Swift*, ed. Herbert Davis and others, 16 vols, Oxford 1939-74, XI, rev. 1959.

4. See Raymond Williams, "Nineteen Eighty-Four in 1984", in *Orwell*, Flamingo edition, London, 1984, pp. 95-126, and compare his Chapter 6, "Projections", pp. 69-82.

5. Marijke Rudnik's account of "Women and Utopia: Some Reflections" (see p. 172 ff. below) mentions a number of recent feminist utopias. Their authors would probably not subscribe either to the view that utopias are not meant to be realized, or to the classical definitions of the genre as I am using them.

readers urged to avoid its seeming inevitability. Hence the useful-
ness of such teasing ambiguities as Thomas More's punning on the
good place being noplace, of Butler's Erewhon being Nowhere
spelt backwards: the fact that Nowhere, without any reordering
tricks, is also Now Here, might almost serve as a mnemonic for
definitions of the genre.

But since time passes, and we must look at the relationships
between ephemeral and permanent features, we can, as "post-
realists", stand back from the *form* of *Nineteen Eighty-Four* as a
novel, to adjust the perspective in which it stands alongside the
slighter but equally powerful text of *Animal Farm*, which uses the
ancient form of the fable and gives an interesting twist to a
theriophilic tradition reaching back through Swift's Houyhnhnms
to Erasmus, and further back to Plutarch and to Cynic and even
Stoic philosophies.[6] The animal fable, as both Orwell and Swift
used it, simplifies and universalizes at the same time, to make a
statement that cannot be confined to one series of events or set of
particular circumstances. *Animal Farm* is a warning, if you like,
just as *Nineteen Eighty-Four* is, as well as a fictionalized account of
actual happenings, but it is also, like *Gulliver's Travels*, a description in narrative form of natural and social forces perennially
interacting in an imperfect human world, its central concern being
not only with Party but with the old civic morality and its
expression in government.

While we rescue *Nineteen Eighty-Four* from temporal limitations, *Gulliver's Travels*, too, is enjoying the insistence of critics on
its wider scope. A recent book by F.P. Lock, *The Politics of
Gulliver's Travels* (Oxford: Clarendon Press, 1980), is one that
urges universality of application for the seemingly most local of
satiric attacks. He cites, for example, that passage in the "Voyage
to Lilliput" (p. 39) where "the Emperor lays on a Table three fine
silken Threads of six Inches long. One is Blue, the other Red, and
the third Green. These Threads are proposed as Prizes, for those
Persons whom the Emperor hath a mind to distinguish". Obliga-

---

6. The term may originate with George Boas. For a detailed treatment
see James E. Gill, "Beast over Man: Theriophilic Paradox in Gulliver's
'Voyage to the Country of the Houyhnhnms'", *SP*, 67, 1970, 532-49, and
"Theriophily in Antiquity: A Supplementary Account", *JHI*, 30, 1969,
401-12.

94

tory footnote references usually gloss this allusion to the Orders of the Garter, the Bath, and the Thistle, and, as Lock puts it, "most readers ... would ... be surprised to learn that [in the first edition of 1726 these were coloured] purple, yellow, and white". He then offers the suggestion that, far from being motivated by fear of censure, the purple, yellow, and white were chosen for the universally symbolic values of silver, gold, and imperial purple, and that blue, red, and green were introduced in later editions to sharpen and update the satire with topical allusions to Walpole's exercise of patronage (pp. 79-80).

Lock is speculating, but in doing so he is looking for a broader relevance of the kind not only Swift but also Orwell may claim in the utopian tradition. The impulse seems ahistorical, which lifts concepts out of the temporal confines to which a choice of words (or even literary forms) may confine them, when the "real" values of those words have been corrupted by the world's usage. There is significance in the number of worldly things for which Swift's Houyhnhnms have no words (their language has an innocent perfection which Orwell's Newspeak aims to pervert), but the model for this particular utopian concern with language is, I think, in Thomas More's ironic dismissal of Hythloday's Utopia, of a communism that "utterly overthrows all the nobility, magnificence, splendor, and majesty which are, in the estimation of the common people, the true glories and ornaments of the commonwealth" (p. 245).[7] With "nobility, magnificence, splendor, and majesty", More puts emphasis on concepts which have in European life, never mind "the estimation of the common people", been sullied by local practice but *could* be restored and purified and given the original and timeless meanings of *nobilitas, magnificentia, splendor, maiestas*: *Utopia* was not written in the vernacular.

The same sense of perspective can be applied to literary forms.

7. *Utopia* is quoted from the Yale *Complete Works*, Volume IV, eds Edward Surtz, S.J., and J.H. Hexter, New Haven and London, 1965. I have discussed this point in "Utopia and 'the Thing which is not': More, Swift, and Other Lying Idealists", *University of Toronto Quarterly*, 52, 1982, 40-62 (pp. 55-56). On ideas about language in Swift and Orwell, see Charles Scruggs "George Orwell and Jonathan Swift: A Literary Relationship", *South Atlantic Quarterly*, 76, 1977, 177-89.

Animal Farm and *Nineteen Eighty-Four*, it is suggested, were intended as two parts of a trilogy, which would show life before, during, and after a particular kind of revolution.[8] The fable sandwiched in the centre breaks up the consistency of form we might expect from a series of novels, but not the expectations we have of works in the utopian tradition, where the useful term Menippean satire enables us to bridge gaps not only between Orwell's separate late fantasies but between Books I and II of *Utopia*, and as one way of accounting for disunities between the four books of *Gulliver's Travels*. It then does not matter that Orwell's *Nineteen Eighty-Four* has what may already be seen as the outmoded "novel" form, with its limiting representation of ordered reality. That form may eventually be looked at as a concession to, and comment on, the time for which it was written, just as *Gulliver's Travels* exploited a prevailing fashion for traveller's tales, or Rabelais's *Gargantua* and *Pantagruel* make use of a popular vernacular tradition of anonymous "Chronicles". The juxtaposition of ancient with modern forms forces us to become conscious of the relationships of literature to life, learned to popular culture, written to oral modes of transmission, and is, I believe, indicative of an author's claim on tradition for the permanence and universality of his values.

I have already mentioned the centrality of *moral* philosophy in the politics of the great utopists. For Swift this is a crucial element in the battle between Ancients and Moderns, Homer versus the Royal Society. I want to highlight the part played by the animal fable in the fictions of Orwell and Swift because both seem uneasy with man's dependence on that reasoning faculty which should make Utopia so easy to realize and which instead appears to bring about dystopia. The theriophilic fable undermines the basic distinction men like to make between themselves and the beasts, either by suggesting identifications, and thus equality (as in Aesop's fables) or by making animals superior to men.[9] A

8. See Bernard Crick, *George Orwell: A Life,* Penguin edn, 1982, pp. 387-89. On *Animal Farm* and its Swiftian fable form, see Scruggs, p. 178.
9. J.A. van Dorsten, in "Recollections: Sidney's Ister Bank Poem" (see pp. 47-8 above) argues for an interesting variation. For complexi-

Renaissance *locus classicus* is the adage which Erasmus might almost have written expressly to place alongside Pico's "De dignitate hominis", reminding us as he does that "dog does not eat dog, fierce lions do not fight each other, there is peace between snake and snake, venomous creatures agree together", but men "use instruments invented against nature by the art of demons, to arm men for the destruction of men".[10] In one of his most striking essays, "Shooting an Elephant", Orwell works hard to discover in his human self the fellow-*feeling* (not reason) that enables him to register the nobility of the falling elephant, and it is a *dog* that shows him the humanity of a prisoner about to be executed in "A Hanging". No one should be surprised that the discomfort we feel on getting to know certain domestic details of Houyhnhnm life in *Gulliver's Travels* (their threading needles, or riding on sledges for long journeys) is due to the fact that these creatures are neither men nor horses, as we recognize each with our Lockean faculties. Orwell brings us back to Aesop's humbling simplifications, when men and pigs become indistinguishable at the end of *Animal Farm*. The rat that is Winston Smith's undoing in *Nineteen Eighty-Four* is a creature I shall return to: the creature of the sewer that, with Swiftian recognition of heights meeting depths, Orwell chose as the ultimate inhuman weapon of the Party's political science, when words had failed to persuade and convert.

When I offered the title "Utopia as Nightmare" I meant to suggest a paradox, for it is of course the *dys*topia that is the nightmare in Orwell, presented, as is generally the rule, as a positive utopia by those in the fiction who take pride in its realization. It is easy enough to discover dystopia behind the initial attractions of Swift's Lilliput, less easy to appreciate that the grossness of life in Brobdingnag, a mirror which distorts only the superficies of human life, may offer some sober recommendations after humbling our vanity. But the Houyhnhnms, whether or not

---

ties in Stoic and Cynic views which filtered into the Renaissance and beyond, see again James E. Gill, "Theriophily in Antiquity".

10. "Dulce bellum inexpertis", quoted from Margaret Mann Phillips, *Erasmus on his Times: A Shortened Version of the Adages of Erasmus*, Cambridge, 1967, pp. 111-12. Erasmus's "demons" perhaps partly absolve "natural" man.

one believes as I do that Swift offers their principles seriously as a model for humanity, are both utopian and nightmarish. They are classically utopian in the strict forms of Spartan conduct that Swift took from Plato, with Stoic embellishments.[11] Their lifestyle denies most of the human values we treasure. They are nightmarish (to us) in their deviation from the natural, from a nature that we know has room for both the innocent brutish strength of the horse and the perverse passions of feeble man: above all in their usurpation of our precious capacity for reason.

Swift, calling man *rationis capax* instead of rational, aimed to vex rather than divert the world, but he, like Orwell, has been variously misunderstood. Partly he meant to mislead of course — to have his fiction taken for real, to shock all the more for being amusing, to anger those in power by making accusations which were not quite actionable. Both Swift and Orwell have been seen as traitors to their own parties, advocates for the wrong side. But this is *because* they may be read too narrowly, with application to local and specific temporal allegiances: Orwell was certainly a Socialist; Swift was variously a Whig and a Tory. But then, Thomas More was some kind of Communist. The labels are too small, and therefore open to contradiction. Raymond Williams aptly describes Orwell's attachment to England, for example, as a "conscious affiliation" rather than "membership" of a society (*Orwell*, pp. 16-17). Swift and Orwell experienced colonial rule in opposite situations, but some of Swift's local espousals might similarly be called "conscious affiliations", principled but pragmatic, necessary but lacking the freedom of the Erasmian spirit he might have preferred to imitate. Texts *about* propaganda are easily adopted and misunderstood *as* propaganda, in a narrower and thus misleading interpretation of what the author may have thought he intended, let alone what he believed.

Some sympathies and similarities between Orwell and Swift have all along been generally recognized, and my concern here is to investigate differences in spirit, which interestingly are most striking where the two writers seem superficially most close. Bernard Crick, in his introduction to the new Oxford edition of

11. The fullest recent discussion is Ian Higgins's "Swift and Sparta: The Nostalgia of *Gulliver's Travels*", *MLR*, 78, 1983, 513-31.

Nineteen Eighty-Four, refreshingly absolves Orwell from blame for inaccuracies in his picture of the world we have experienced in 1984. The reorientation Crick presents concentrates on Orwell's intentions, and emphasizes the connection with Swift. *Nineteen-Eighty Four*, Crick says, is "specifically 'Swiftian satire'". "Many of the features of Oceania", he goes on, are "wickedly comic". Even the scenes in Room 101 are "not uncomic" (the litotes suggests some awareness that his reading may be a provocative one), and when "smell and oppression, as well as dirt, are once more linked", "all this is farce". The end of *Nineteen Eighty-Four* Professor Crick sees as "comic, grotesque", centring on the phrase "two gin-scented tears trickled down the sides of his nose" to describe the emotional force of Winston's final submission to Big Brother, and pointing to the textual significance of the words "The End" as echoing the winding-up of a Hollywood B-movie at the close of the narrative.[12] A new bit of significance perhaps creeps in at this stage in Crick's edition, for there the words "The End" are accompanied prominently by the superscript number "102", which, though presumably merely a footnote reference, accidentally opens up a whole new dimension for speculating that Winston's struggle with the Party may not, after all, be over.

The reader who comes to Orwell from Swift is unlikely to find the smells and squalor and oppression funny in either writer; and Orwell lacked the "savage indignation" which makes a certain *kind* of comedy possible in Swift. Orwell, for that matter, did not seem to find *Gulliver's Travels* funny when he wrote about it in 1946. He calls it "a rancorous as well as a pessimistic book" and describes "the inter-connexion between Swift's political loyalties and his ultimate despair" as "one of [its] most interesting

---

12. *Nineteen Eighty-Four*, ed. Peter Davison, with a Critical Commentary and Annotations by Bernard Crick, Oxford, 1984, pp. 7, 50, 55. Quotations from the novel give page references to this edition hereafter. On "Swiftian satire" Crick is quoting Czeslan Milosz, *The Captive Mind*, New York, 1953. For farce *without* comedy, Crick might aptly have included among his "bodysnatchers" Richard I. Smyer, *Primal Dream and Primal Crime: Orwell's Development as a Psychological Novelist*, Columbia and London, 1979. Smyer quotes C.M. Kornbluth, who in 1959 saw Room 101 as "the uterus ... these numerals [being a] sketch of the female genitalia" (p. 159).

features". He then goes on to puzzle over what it is that makes the book enjoyable (*CEJL*, IV, 243, 257-58). He is right about the pessimism, and my argument is, first, that though the pessimism of Orwell's own dystopia is apparent, there is a world of difference between presenting a dystopia on the assumption that it can be avoided, and offering a *u*topia (that of the Houyhnhms) from which man is by nature excluded; secondly, that if Orwell is like Swift, then the affinity is to be found more at an unconscious than at a conscious level.

Orwell allows that "Swift was an admirable writer of comic verse"; he also recognizes that Gulliver is "ridiculous" and "silly" at times, and that (presumably like Winston Smith, given that both protagonists are provided with names to express their social status and values), he represents the average Englishman of his time: "bold, practical and unromantic, his homely outlook skilfully impressed on the reader" (*CEJL*, IV, 256, 242, 241). It is important to the effect of both narratives that the reader should be obliged to identify with the "hero", not just initially but to the end of each work, but if Gulliver is eventually ridiculous (particularly in neighing and trotting like a horse on his return home), an element of humour is available only through the reader's determination to separate himself from Gulliver (not entirely what Swift intended). Winston Smith's "two gin-scented tears" may also be ridiculous, but he remains a steadily sympathetic character, a victim of social circumstances, not culpably perverse by nature, and I doubt whether laughing at him would serve Orwell's purpose. As for Swift, we have it on good authority that he *could* "laugh and shake in Rab'lais' easy chair", but Pope's words (*Dunciad*, I. 22) do not necessarily refer to *Gulliver's Travels*. Moreover, Pope admitted that he did not understand Rabelais at all, and Swift told him that he did not always understand Swift.[13]

Rather than reiterate accounts of those features which make Swift's clean, rational, passionless Houyhnhnm utopia so unattractive to most readers, its lifestyle reminiscent not only of ancient

13. See, for example, the tone of slight rebuke in the letter of 29 Sept. 1725, answering one from Pope of 14 September (*Correspondence*, ed. Harold Williams, 5 vols, Oxford, 1963-65, III, 102-03, 96). For Pope on Swift and Rabelais, see Spence's *Anecdotes*, ed. James M. Osborn, 2 vols, Oxford, 1966, I, items 133, 511, 512.

Sparta but of the rigours of English public-school life (so often rendered as a nightmare experience), I will summarize very briefly a few salient points. What is most fully realized in Houyhnhnmland is glimpsed earlier on, in the three previous Voyages, as something lost, forgotten, or disregarded by most men. The faint "otherworldliness" of the good life is made more striking by the fact that it tends to be presented not so much as Gulliver's own experience but at second hand: in discussions reminiscent of Socratic debate (for example in audience with the King of Brobdingnag) or in surveying the history of the land he visits. This usually happens somewhere near the centre of each Voyage, or, more accurately, at the deepest point of Gulliver's discoveries before leaving a country (in Book III there is an actual visit to the underworld), all of which may remind us of classical and even epic procedures.

It is, Gulliver reminds us, only in their "original Institutions", not their current corrupt application, that the Lilliputians "have more Regard to good Morals than to great Abilities" in government, and "suppose Truth, Justice, Temperance, and the Like, to be in every Man's Power" (pp. 60,59). Crimes against the State are (were) severely punished, but good men are honoured. The Lilliputians believe in divine Providence. Their children are removed from their families to be educated by the State, and parents may occasionally visit but not fondle their offspring. Training is modified according to class and gender, but breeding, as distinct from nurture, is not strictly controlled as in Houyhnhnmland, or More's Utopia, or in Plato's Republic. From the King of Brobdingnag we learn more about ourselves, as Gulliver takes his turn at giving an account of our own customs, our degenerate aristocracy, our warring religious and political factions, our invention of gunpowder as a triumph of civilization. The King's values are those of "common Sense and Reason", "Justice and Lenity", and he believes that "whoever could make two Ears of Corn, or two Blades of Grass to grow upon a Spot of Ground where only one grew before; would deserve better of Mankind ... than the whole Race of Politicians put together". The Brobdingnagians have no standing army, no colonizing ambitions, their learning is limited (in that they have need of few books), and they write simply and economically in a "clear, masculine, and smooth" style (pp. 135-37). (The Houyhnhnms have of course no written literature, though they excel in poetry on "exalted Notions of Friendship and Benevolence, or the Praises of those who were Victors in Races, and other bodily Exercises" (p. 274).

Book III is the most thoroughly dystopian, in that it presents a fragmented society (morally, physically, geographically, and institutionally disorientated) which is seen by its privileged classes, and by Gulliver at salient points, as utopian. Only one character, Lord Munodi, in his would-be Horatian retreat to a country estate, is admirable: out of favour at court, perhaps suggestive both of Sir William Temple and the Earl of Oxford, he cultivates his land and cares for his tenants in the old way, but is vulnerable to the imposition of disastrous new methods in estate management. The Houyhnhnms, whose Spartan and Stoic features are too well known to need description here, are of course most striking in their relationships with their subject race of Yahoos: troublesome creatures mainly because Gulliver identifies himself (and therefore the reader) as one of them. One way in which Houyhnhnmland is nightmarishly utopian is in its presentation of the passions, which, like the imagination that includes Swift's own fantasy, are governed by reason: not human reason but Houyhnhnm reason. Gulliver is allowed by Swift to come home, but only to confirm that passionate unreason can indeed not be eradicated in humanity. His return to the cave, or the stable, shows him devoid of the qualities Socrates, and Thomas More, envisaged in the hypothetical figure of the philosopher. The Houyhnhnms would leniently have castrated him, their reason allowing something mercifully short of extermination, hinting even at scope for improvement.

I am on the side of those who believe Swift seriously admired Houyhnhnm values, to their last degree of severity. The other nightmare quality, at the climax of Gulliver's (or the reader's) educative adventures, is the way he must be expelled from his utopia, however creditably he has performed to show himself superior to other Yahoos. I believe we are not meant to laugh at his wish to be a Houyhnhnm and if we find him ridiculous when he tries to be a horse, back home, we risk a lot by dissociating ourselves not only from his practices but from his desires as well. We make distinctions too easily, while Gulliver does not make them easily enough.

Orwell and Swift plainly hated and feared extremism, but Orwell saw that Swift's utopia was itself extremist: a totalitarian state in which the Yahoos, he notes, are treated like Jews in Nazi Germany. Swift might argue that the whole point of *Gulliver's Travels* is that the extremism of Houyhnhnmland is not for man; that man cannot handle the absolutism of a virtue which is pure reason since human reason is perverted by passion. Orwell proves the point with his invention of Newspeak: the society of Oceania, like that of Houyhnhnmland, has simplified language to a level at which there *can* be no ambiguity of meaning, and *should* be no variety of experience. "Neither is *Reason* among them a Point problematical as with us, when Men can argue with Plausibility on both sides of a Question; but strikes you with immediate Conviction", as Gulliver says of the Houyhnhnms (p. 267). For Swift the enemy is not unity of opinion but open disagreement.

There are awkwardnesses in Orwell's illustrations of non-reason disguised as reason, however. "2 + 2 = 5" does not strike Winston Smith with immediate conviction. The sum is an innocent abstraction abused for the sake of power which is craved and exercised with passion, but the "common sense" opinion that $2 + 2 = 4$ is also an abstraction. Winston's real appeal is to the individual reader's experience, and it might be more interesting if some men thought that $2 + 2 = 3$. It is not reason but lack of imagination that disables the innocent Houyhnhnms from believing that Gulliver travelled across the sea in a boat. Swift's reader, laughing at their naivety, draws on a fund of human knowledge, which is not always the same as wisdom, and there are circumstances in which Swift *would* ask us to accept that $2 + 2 = 5$. Orwell described him as a "Tory anarchist" (*CEJL*, IV, 253), and probably recognized that the term allows some breadth and variety of reference.

The real difference between the two, and between the effects of their powerful fictions, is that Orwell had faith in human nature, which he achieved by dint of taking on himself certain kinds of expiatory guilt; whereas Swift had no such faith and projected guilt on to his fellow men as punishment for the fact that he was one of them. This is why Orwell's dystopia is in fact optimistic, if not comic, and Swift's utopia is pessimistic. One of Swift's more notorious statements, in a letter to Pope, was "principally I hate and detest that animal called man", as he prepared to launch *Gulliver's Travels* in a mood of defeatist irony that it would "wonderfully mend the World" (*Correspondence*, III, 103, 87). Orwell, believing in progress, and in revolution if unavoidable, recognized the basic dilemmas which separate the methods of the Romantic utopist from the Classical utopist: "The one, how can you improve human nature until you have changed the system? The other, what is the use of changing the system before you have improved human nature?" (*CEJL*, I, 469). His outlook is clear in the application of "change" to "system" and "improve" to "human nature", and his use of "until and "before" instead of "unless".

Swift's orthodox Christian pessimism *was* extreme: man is wilfully depraved, using his reason only to perverse ends (Gulliver's excuses for travelling are vain, worldly, scientifically curious, and socially irresponsible, and the outcome is total disorientation). Man is seen as corrupt when in power, ignorant, lazy, and dirty when poor, full of proud self-delusions that guarantee an interdependence between fool and knave, the gullible and the dishonest. Swift's realistic aim might be that men could be protected from their worst excesses by being forced to live with an appearance of tolerable civility within a decent orthodox institutional framework. This is not to say that Swift had no ideals, only that his ideals were too radical for human application, and his conservatism was *all* application, shallower than any creed — so Orwell's phrase "Tory anarchist" may be about right.

Orwell, forgiving *us*, is able eventually to forgive himself. He thought Swift sick and diseased in mind. "The most essential thing in Swift", he says, "is his inability to believe that life — ordinary life on the solid earth, and not some rationalized, deodorised version of it — could be made worth living" (*CEJL*, IV, 253). The protest, like some of Orwell's comforting (and nowadays embarrassing) beliefs about the English (for example in "England your England"), suggests a degree of romantic self-delusion which Swift would have dealt with savagely. "Part of our minds", says Orwell, " — In any normal person it is the dominant part — believes that man is a noble animal". He talks of Swift's "endless harping on disease, dirt and deformity", expanding repeatedly, and with gratuitous inventions of his own, on the kind of thing he means. "Something in us", he claims, though with a comforting generality, "responds to [Swift's pessimism] as it responds to the gloomy words of the burial service or the sweetish smell of corpses in a country Church" (*CEJL,* IV, 259, 260).

Orwell's own poking about in the hovels of the poor, his

obsessively detailed recording of stinks and other human un-
pleasantnesses (but especially stinks) is mostly justified in *The
Road to Wigan Pier* by its propagandist aim against social inequality and in his evident assumption that a general decency of
spirit will come to light if given material decency of circumstance.
The insanitary rooms and smelly drains around which Orwell
seems to linger are, I think, never satirically presented, in the
manner of Swift's poem (which Orwell cites) "The Lady's Dressing
Room", where Strephon has his illusions shattered about art and
nature in woman:

> But oh! it turn'd poor *Strephon's* Bowels,
> When he beheld and smelt the Towels,
> Begumm'd, bematter'd, and beslim'd
> With Dirt, and Sweat, and Ear-Wax grim'd ...
> Nor be the Handkerchiefs forgot
> All varnish'd o'er with Snuff and Snot.
>
> (11. 43, 48)[14]

Swift puts the fascination and the shock equally far from himself
through the mediations of both a character (Strephon) and a
moralizing narrator, but Orwell's habit is to grasp these emotions
to himself. His sense of guilt is at being clean, not at the rest of
humanity being dirty. He evidently never recovered from the
trauma of being told as a boy that the poor smelt, and privilege
seemed to be a cross he continued to bear, with self-inflicted
punishments reminiscent of Thomas More's famous hairshirt: "It
is a kind of duty to see and smell such places now and again,
especially smell them, lest you should forget that they exist", he
remarks of slum dwellings in *The Road to Wigan Pier*, but it is
rather as though he undertakes this duty on our behalf, protecting
us where Swift would expose us.[15]

If we grant that both men, in their writings, were in some sense
idealists (as one might expect a utopist or dystopist to be), we may
suspect that the idealism at its deepest was a private affair. In

14. *The Poems of Jonathan Swift*, ed. Harold Williams, second edition,
3 vols, Oxford, 1958, II, 527.
15. *The Road to Wigan Pier*, Penguin edition, 1962, rpt. 1984,
p. 16.

Swift's case it is not just that, as a satirist, he conventionally leaves positive views to be taken for granted, but that he deals with the world in manageable fragments through a range of personae each of which can contain one particular issue at a time. He is rarely the authority speaking for all men, but by turns the mad, wordy prose hack of *A Tale of a Tub*; the hoaxer gossip Isaac Bickerstaff; the commonsense materialist who argued for all the wrong reasons "Against Abolishing Christianity"; the solid Dublin Drapier defending the rights of a nation he disliked being a member of; the Modest Proposer whose cold logic reveals the distress Swift felt for that same nation's inhabitants. The partiality is usually eccentric and provocative, so that it is we, the rest of society, that must unite in common sense to resist. Gulliver is the obvious exception in so far as he is Everyman — but then that is even more of a shock, requiring efforts of dissociation which leave the reader asking "what must I do to be human?".

Orwell, on the other hand, makes himself a kind of universal social conscience, putting aside, as Swift does, his own private identity, though in favour not of a multiplicity of occasional voices but of the one figure, George Orwell, whose name of course has the stability of a refuge — if not pastoral then certainly bucolic; of the land, specifically of England. Orwell, running away from the stigmas of Eton and imperialist officialdom in Burma, tried hard to be a tramp, one of the faceless proles that in *Nineteen Eighty-Four* may eventually rise in revolt but have meanwhile the saving grace of being irresponsible. In a totalitarian dystopia they are city slum dwellers, though the woman hanging out washing, and even the unattractive and corrupted Parsons, have a physique suggestive of rural peasant origins in a happier world, the Golden Country.

Orwell's attempts at anonymity, or at belonging unobtrusively to the mass in order to speak or even fight for it, are not entirely successful, though the regular expression of a sense of superiority, when not unconscious, shows that he is aiming at those who need converting, hardly the proles themselves. There are, however, moments when he sounds comfortingly snobbish, as when Winston Smith observes Parsons making up his notebook in "the neat handwriting of the illiterate" (p. 205). More deliberate, in its self-mocking honesty, is the class-directed moralizing of "Down the Mine": "In a way it is even humiliating to watch coal-miners working. It raises in you a momentary doubt about your own status as an intellectual and a superior person generally. For it is brought home to you, at least while you are watching, that it is only because miners sweat their guts out that superior persons can remain superior" (*The Road to Wigan Pier*, p. 31).[16] There is even a hint of that theriophilic strain I mentioned earlier, in Orwell's description of the miners' "most noble bodies": they have "wide shoulders tapering to slender supple waists, and small pronounced buttocks and sinewy thighs" (p. 21), sounding not unlike Blake's "Tiger, tiger, burning bright/ In the forests of the night", an awesome conjunction of the divine and the infernal.[17]

But Orwell, taking us on a conducted tour, doing the thinking and, more importantly, the feeling, for us may no more be Eric Blair (though I am not suggesting deception or dishonesty) than Swift is the Modest Proposer, whose description of the Irish poor moves along at so brisk a rate as to leave no space for the feelings we must find for ourselves, in order to protest at the inadequacy of his emotions: "It is a melancholy Object to those, who walk through this great Town" is his opening response to "*the present deplorable State of the Kingdom*", in which the "prodigious Number of Children" is a "very great additional Grievance", though the old are no problem, who "are every Day *dying*, and *rotting*, by *Cold* and *Famine*, and *Filth*, and *Vermin*, as fast as can be reasonably expected" (*Works*, XII, 109, 114).

It was as the Drapier, stirring up resistance to the imposition on the Irish of one of Walpole's shadier fiscal schemes (or so it seemed to them), that Swift became a public hero. Orwell, a less provocative, and less isolated, fighter for less local causes, seems to have indulged in heroic acts of a more private kind. At an Orwell conference in Birmingham early in 1984, a surprise guest was Douglas Moyle, a retired (and retiring) veteran of the Spanish Civil War whom Orwell mentions several times as a comrade alongside him during incidents he records in *Homage to Catalonia*. Mr Moyle's own anecdotes (which had not been available to

16. The sentiments expressed here have, for a British reader in 1984, a rather different poignancy from anything engendered by *Nineteen Eighty-Four*.

17. Interestingly, he contrasts Swift's treatment of the body with Blake's, in his Swift essay (*CEJL*, IV, 259).

Orwell's biographers) included lively memories of Orwell's personal courage and highly individualistic leadership. He instigated night patrols to reconnoitre enemy positions, and on one occasion asked Mr Moyle to accompany him so far, then to wait (as an observer, or witness, perhaps) as he went on alone. Mr Moyle recalled being terrified on his own account, let alone Blair's, since it was a night of brilliant moonlight which made every detail of the landscape clearly visible — though Blair would not have it that they, too, could be seen. In the book, Orwell underplays his personal leadership, mentioning merely that "at night small patrols *used to be sent* into no man's land to lie in ditches near the Fascist lines", etc. (my italics).[18]

Swift had no occasion to flirt with death is such a manner. Instead he is often censured, as Orwell is not, for seeking out dirt, disease, and depravity and rubbing the reader's nose in all three. It may be natural enough that his Houyhnhnm utopia is a cleaner place than Orwell's dystopian London (except for the messes made by the Yahoos), but Swift's real world of Dublin was almost certainly more depressing, and without the same prospects for renovation, than Orwell's London in 1948. In a recent study Carole Fabricant supplies documentary evidence of conditions in Dublin at the time that make Swift's responses to life about him seem not especially perverse.[19] To be Dean of St Patrick's was not a privileged situation to a man who had once had hopes of preferment in England, on Orwell's side of the colonial fence. London's streets might flow copiously, in 1710, as

> Sweepings from Butchers Stalls, Dung, Guts, and Blood, ⎫
> Drown'd Puppies, stinking Sprats, all drench'd in Mud, ⎬
> Dead Cats and Turnip-Tops come tumbling down the Flood,⎭
> ("A Description of a City Shower", *Poems*, I, 139)

18. *Homage to Catalonia*, Penguin edition, 1962, rpt. 1983, p. 72. The occasion referred to was an Extra-Mural Dayschool on "George Orwell: The View from 1984", University of Birmingham, 11 February 1984, at which an earlier version of this paper was read, and at which Bernard Crick was introduced to Douglas Moyle. I have since confirmed details of the anecdote with Mr Moyle, and am grateful for his permission to relate it.

19. *Swift's Landscape*, Baltimore & London, 1982.

but Dublin struck people used to ordinary eighteenth-century city filth elsewhere as particularly appalling. St Patrick's was in the oldest and poorest part of the city, among the Liberties, an area exempt from the city jurisdiction.[20] A survey later in the century reported that, as Carole Fabricant quotes (pp. 27-28):

> The streets ... are generally narrow, the houses crowded together; the rears or back-yards of very small extent, and some without any accommodation of any kind .... I have frequently surprised from ten to sixteen persons, of all ages and sexes, in a room not 15 feet square, stretched on a wad of filthy straw, swarming with vermin and without any covering, save the wretched rags that constituted their wearing apparel .... This crowded population wherever it obtains is almost universally accompanied by a very serious evil — a degree of filth and stench inconceivable except by such as have visited these scenes of wretchedness.

This could easily be a passage from *The Road to Wigan Pier*; the scandal for the twentieth century is that the reports should be so similar. But Orwell had to go and look for squalor, sometimes offending his northern hosts by finding it, as Crick reports in his biography (pp. 281-82), whereas for Swift it was all on his own doorstep: closer, in fact, for his cathedral, built on very low ground, was periodically flooded to a depth of some seven feet. Such floods were not, of course, made up of clean water, in a district where, as Carole Fabricant reminds us (pp. 29-30), ordure was simply thrown out of the windows, or deposited directly in the street by its human donors, in the manner, but more offensive in matter, of Gulliver's admired Houyhnhnms.

With his eye firmly on the world as it is, since its improvements seem largely cosmetic, Swift's ideal of civilization might have been relatively available in London, were it not for other kinds of corruption in spheres less physical. To leave the court for a cultivated Horatian retreat, in the style of Sir William Temple (of course in *England*), and locate a pastoral or even a Tory land-owner's utopia in some country estate, was a model sharply in contrast to the reality of Swift's own exile in an unhospitable Irish environment where (again according to Carole Fabricant's des-

20. *Swift's Landscape*, p. 25.

cription of the typical Irish "cabin") his own house was a poor thing he had largely to build for himself, and his church or churches were in ruins. W.B. Yeats, who admired Swift's spirit and elitist values, and who was himself an "Ancient" (with a nostalgia for Swift's own time, at that), regretted the "high horse riderless,/ Though mounted in that saddle Homer rode". Sharing Swift's ambivalent feelings about his fellow Irishmen, he was nevertheless, as he claimed, one of "the last Romantics" as Swift was not (even in poetry), and could make much, in verse, of custom and ceremony while a protégé of the Gregorys. Swift's familiarity with great houses showed him only an aristocracy hardly worthy of the name, for he saw them as absentee landlords or as frivolous incumbents, with none of the traditional virtues of the outcast Lord Munodi in Gulliver's third voyage — their lands resembling more closely the Balnibarbian norm: "I never knew a Soil so unhappily cultivated, Houses so ill contrived and so ruinous, or a People whose Countenances and Habit expressed so much Misery and Want" (p. 175). Swift's "Market-Hill" poems best express his unillusioned irreverence towards his social superiors the Achesons, whose hospitality is described in thoroughly unYeatsian fashion, and to whom the guest could best pay tribute by building a privy in their grounds, as though to teach them better manners.[21]

Orwell did find sources of trust and hope in nature, human and other. His adopted name asserts it, as does his choice of "Animal Farm" for the location of a utopian experiment; his period as contented rural shopkeeper and allotment-gardener confirms it; his final retreat to Jura stretches it to the limit. Even there, though making much of the complicated journey in a letter of travel itineraries to Sonia, he characteristically refers to daffodils planted, hoping for "quite a nice garden" next year — and Bernard Crick reminds us that the climate in those parts is quite mild.[22] It is as though Orwell chose for himself, however, the utopian Spartan existence that Gulliver recommends, but pri-

21. See "A Panegyrick on the D[ea]n, in the Person of a Lady in the *North*", *Poems*, III, 886. Swift cultivated a certain boorishness when among friends, which contained an element of mock-insult, so it is never easy to know how seriously to take the apparent rudeness, even when the relationship is known to have been quarrelsome.
22. *CEJL*, IV, 375; *Orwell: A Life*, p. 511.

vately, not with any zeal to impose it on society at large. His was self-consciously a working man's idyll, though one cannot imagine many real "working men" sharing his ideal. By contrast, Winston Smith's "Golden Country" seems classically pastoral, a recurring dream, a nostalgia for something he cannot be sure was ever real, until it materializes in the woodland scene with Julia at the novel's centre to sharpen our sense of treachery before and after. But the strength (more than hope) which Winston finds immanent in the proles could give rise to Gulliver's dream of Houyhnhnm aggression. "They needed only to rise and shake themselves like a horse shaking off flies", says Winston (p. 216), and Gulliver asks us to "imagine twenty Thousand [Houyhnhnms] breaking into the Midst of an *European* Army, confounding the Ranks, overturning the Carriages, battering the Warriors Faces into Mummy, by terrible Yerks from their hinder Hoofs" (p. 293).

The animal association brings fear, as well as hope, most strikingly in the rat (which was not only Winston's undoing but Orwell's own pet phobia: "If there is one thing I hate more than another", he confessed in *Homage to Catalonia*, "it is a rat running over me in the darkness" (p. 81), as "the filthy brutes came swarming out of the ground on every side"). Orwell's socialism obliges him to envisage a classless utopia in *Animal Farm*, but there are barriers to overcome. The animals are presented in a natural hierarchy, and their attempts to change it are not entirely convincing. "'Comrades, [asks Major] .... the wild creatures, such as rats and rabbits — are they our friends or our enemies? Let us put it to the vote .... Are rats comrades?' The vote was taken at once, and it was agreed by an overwhelming majority that rats were comrades".[23] This has about it an element of $2 + 2 = 5$, and is also reminiscent of the unashamed squeamishness with which the creatures of the Wild Wood are treated in Kenneth Grahame's *The Wind in the Willows*. Raymond Williams notices "the speed of [Orwell's] figurative transition from animals to the proletariat ... showing as it does a residue of thinking of the poor as animals: powerful but stupid" (*Orwell*, pp. 71-72). In *Nineteen Eighty-Four* the proles are in fact reassuring in their passivity, lacking the noble violence inherent in the horse, and the treachery of the rat: "Left to

23. Quoted from Secker & Warburg "Cheap Edition", London, 1949, rpt. 1955, pp. 13-14.

themselves, like cattle turned loose upon the plains of Argentina, they had reverted to a style of life that appeared to be natural to them, a sort of ancestral pattern" (p. 217).

Hope, on the other hand, seems captured in the washerwoman's singing, her words ironically those of a mechanically-composed song, on the theme of "it was only an 'opeless fancy" — but life-renewing (she has "powerful mare-like buttocks") regardless of the words: "though it might be a thousand years, they would stay alive against all the odds, like birds, passing on from body to body the vitality which the Party did not share and could not kill", Winston thinks, a moment before Charrington's treachery is revealed (p. 348). He is remembering the thrush in the wood:

> A thrush had alighted on a bough not five metres away.... It ... began to pour forth a torrent of song. In the afternoon hush the volume of sound was startling .... The music went on and on, minute after minute, with astonishing variations, never once repeating itself, almost as though the bird were deliberately showing off its virtuosity. Sometimes it stopped for a few seconds, spread out and resettled its wings, then swelled its speckled breast and again burst into song. Winston watched it with a sort of vague reverence. For whom, for what, was that bird singing? No mate, no rival was watching it. What made it sit at the edge of the lonely wood and pour its music into nothingness? (p. 263)

Orwell's source for this epiphanic passage (and if it is imitative the literary allusion brings extra support for its power) is surely in the work of a different kind of pessimist — and pastoralist — Thomas Hardy, in a post-millenial New Year poem (31 December 1900):

> I leant upon a coppice gate
>   When Frost was spectre-gray,
> And Winter's dregs made desolate
>   The weakening eye of day.
> The tangled bine-stems scored the sky
>   Like strings of broken lyres,
> And all mankind that haunted nigh
>   Had sought their household fires.
>
> The land's sharp features seemed to be
>   The Century's corpse outleant,

His crypt the cloudy canopy,
   The wind his death-lament.
The ancient pulse of germ and birth
   Was shrunken hard and dry,
And every spirit upon earth
   Seemed fervourless as I.

At once a voice arose among
   The bleak twigs overhead
In a full-hearted evensong
   Of joy illimited;
An aged thrush, frail, gaunt, and small,
   In blast-beruffled plume,
Had chosen thus to fling his soul
   Upon the growing gloom.

So little cause for carolings
   Of such ecstatic sound
Was written on terrestrial things
   Afar or nigh around,
That I could think there trembled through
   His happy good-night air
Some blessed Hope, whereof he knew
   And I was unaware.

("The Darkling Thrush")[24]

The optimism in Orwell's thrush, as in Hardy's, passes humanity by, enabling Orwell both to render acceptable the class distinctions which continually associate the proles with animals, and to avoid Swift's dismissal of all humanity (in the King of Brobdingnag's terms) as "the most pernicious Race of little odious Vermin that Nature ever suffered to crawl upon the Surface of the Earth" (p. 132). The pessimism of Swift, savage rather than gloomy in its excesses, is not, as Orwell thought, life-denying, however. It offers not hope but energy, an energy Orwell recognized as anarchic: a radical energy of intolerant and intolerable ideals, and of the utopian nightmare.

Warwick   Jenny Mezciems

24. *The Complete Poetical Works of Thomas Hardy*, ed. Samuel Hynes, Oxford, 1982, Volume I, pp. 187-88.

GARDENS IN UTOPIA: UTOPIA IN THE GARDEN

Singe die Gärten, mein Herz, die du nicht kennst...

Speakers' Corner is aptly located in Hyde Park, which is historically the extended garden of Kensington Palace [Fig.1]. This privileged place of utopian discourse, where proposals to right the wrongs of this world are formulated and entertained, would be unthinkable outside the green world of the landscaped park. For utopias have frequently invoked the special and resonant spaces of gardens, just as gardens have often been utopian in impulse, design and meaning. It is this exchange of symbolic meanings that I want to explore: I shall be concerned somewhat less with the place of gardens in utopian literature, though that will be my starting point, than with the strongly utopian dimension of some Renaissance and post-Renaissance gardens. I have tried to invoke English materials where possible,* but in gardenist matters as in utopian traditions it is of course impossible to ignore Europe.

Indeed, the first garden we come across in More's *Utopia* is the one in Antwerp where the discussions that form the book take place. We are told little about it, except for one feature to which I shall return. But in the actual description of the Utopian cities in Part Two gardens are more prominent: behind the houses are "broad gardens", of which the inhabitants are proud and in which they take great pleasure:

> In them they have vines, fruits, herbs, flowers, so well kept and flourishing that I never saw anything more fruitful and more tasteful anywhere. Their zest in keeping them is increased not

---

* The text is substantially that delivered as a lecture to a conference of Dutch university teachers of English, with a few changes made to make more feasible a reading of it without the slides that originally accompanied it. A few references have been added within the text to clarify some of my sources and debts.

merely by the pleasure afforded them but by the keen competition between [city] blocks as to which will have the best kept garden.

So not only do gardens feature centrally in the utopian cityscape, but they are the occasion for some good citizenly rivalry. And just as More and his companions retire to a garden for their discussions, so the inhabitants of the utopian cities resort to their gardens in summertime for "recreation".

More had perhaps personal and certainly literary reasons for this emphasis upon gardens. His own at Chelsea was famous and cherished in its owner's lifetime and mythologized after his death. The oil painting in the Victoria and Albert Museum attributed to Rowland Lockey depicts More, his family and descendants sixty-five years after his execution in a domestic space which conspicuously includes a garden [Fig.2]. This is a simple area, walled but with a gateway that either gives access to less carefully plotted grounds beyond or permits direct access to the garden without passing through the house; the beds are laid out in a simple geometric pattern (a maze shape that is readily traced); at one corner of the garden is a pavilion, a summer house or study. By 1600 when this picture was painted More's garden had passed into the possession of Sir Robert Cecil, but he was so busy completing Hatfield that it is doubtful whether he had much time for this garden in Chelsea. Therefore we may see here something very like the garden of More's time, though the corner pavilion looks to me of later construction. But the point is that the artist felt it was part of the Morean myth to invoke a garden. More had himself been proud of his garden's natural and emblematic richness: "As for Rosemarine I lett it run alle over my garden walls, not onlie because my bees love it, but because 'tis a herb sacred to remembrance, and therefore to friendship...." And one of his friends, Thomas Heywood, has left us an equally resonant description of a place "Wonderfully charming, both from the advantage of the site...and also for its own beauty; it was crowned with almost perpetual verdure; it had flowering shrubs, and the branches of fruit trees interwoven in so beautiful a manner that it appeared like a tapestry woven by Nature herself".

Unfortunately we know little else about More's garden. It has

Figure 2. Attrib. Rowland Lockey, *Sir Thomas More and his Family,* 1600, Victoria and Albert Museum.

been suggested by Craig R. Thompson that Eusebius's garden in Erasmus' colloquy *The Godly Feast* may have as one of its models that of More at Chelsea. Dates, however, suggest the reverse: *The Godly Feast* appeared in 1522 and it was only in the following year that More purchased the land at Chelsea; Erasmus might well have been thinking of More's other gardens at Bucklersbury. But over and above the matter of models and who influenced whom is the kind of vision of gardens that More and his friends like Erasmus would have shared. We can already detect in his own remarks, just quoted, and especially in Heywood's description, that gardens were not simply, God wot, lovesome things. Herbs like rosemary were emblematic, and they served the bees which Virgil's *Georgics* had celebrated; nature was so contrived by the gardener as to imitate the craft of tapestry, yet "Nature herself" was the artist; the garden's verdure was "almost perpetual", the closest that Chelsea could come (even then) to an eternal spring. Such rhetoric recalls the traditions of garden imagery from which no garden description of the sixteenth and seventeenth centuries, nor probably any contemporary garden either, could manage to free itself. The one Erasmus describes is no exception.

It is divided into five sections: a flower garden to the front, a herb garden in the courtyard, and beyond a combined kitchen and medicinal garden, then a grassy meadow enclosed by a quickset hedge for strolling, and an orchard. The dining room has a triple view of these various gardens through sliding windows and is adjoined by a library with a balcony overlooking the garden, by a small study and a chapel. More, too, at Chelsea interestingly developed both spatial and intellectual relationships between the garden and the library, gallery and chapel. Erasmus also pays especial attention to the decorations and iconology: the open gate of the flower garden is guarded by a painted image of St Peter. A small chapel to the right contains a figure of Christ (but not, apparently, Christ as Gardener). Biblical inscriptions in Latin, Greek, and Hebrew accompany each of these figures. The fountain of the flower garden — a traditional feature of mediaeval gardens — is said by Eusebius to signify the heavenly stream for which the human soul pants.

The symbolism of all flower gardens is discussed extensively in Chapter III. But it is the herb garden which is fashioned most elaborately — as a kind of multi-dimensional lesson in divine and human artistry. This herb garden is enclosed on three sides by galleries with painted marble pillars: on the wall of one gallery is painted a fresco of trees, in whose branches are shown representatives of rare or renowned species of bird, while on the ground beneath are depicted such animals as a piping monkey, a dancing camel, and a chamelion. The fresco of the second gallery is dedicated to famous plants, especially poisonous ones, every kind of serpent, the scorpion, basilisk, and armies of ants. The third gallery shows lakes, rivers and seas, with their fishes, amphibians and wildlife of their shores. Eusebius frequently draws his visitors' attention to the accuracy of the frescoes: every variety of hellebore is distinguished; the poisonous plants are so realistic one fears to touch them; an attempt, however crude, is made to place every species in its natural environment.

This garden which Erasmus describes is, as Marilene Allen suggested in *Literary and Historical Gardens in Selected Renaissance Poetry* (University of Edinburgh Ph.D., 1980), contemporary with the rise of botanical studies in Europe and its inclusiveness of reference recalls some of the early cabinets of curiosity, especially those in the Holy Roman Empire. But the main impulse behind the garden is not scientific: it is an exercise in art, nature and illusion for devotional ends. The herbs in their separate beds are reflected in the channels of water that flow from the central fountain. The paving stones of the galleries are painted green with representations of small flowers, while the green hedges of the garden are also painted. The "marble" of the pillars, fountains and channels is imitated in paintwork. One of his guests is deceived, then delighted, by the deception, and Eusebius comments:

> We are twice pleased when we see a painted flower competing with a real one. In one we admire the cleverness of Nature, in the other the inventiveness of the painter; in each the goodness of God, who gives all these things for our use and is equally wonderful and kind in everything.

Nature and art cooperate to celebrate God's universe; it is the metaphysical as much as the physical world which Eusebius tends.

The herb beds have scientific labels giving name and special virtue, but also banners with mottoes on them. That of the marjoram says, "Keep off, sow; I don't smell for you", and Eusebius points up the old and popular proverb by explaining that swine hate what for men is a pleasant scent.

I have spent so much time rehearsing details of this fascinating description because it epitomizes much of what I would call the utopian dimension of gardens. It draws upon literary and rhetorical traditions of garden description, with all their emphasis upon ideal and perfect places. Yet it is also in touch with — or imaginatively anticipates — actual Renaissance gardens where those ideals were realized in some shape and form: whether or not we can include More's as one of his models, Erasmus certainly knew Johann Froben's at Basel and from his correspondence it is clear that Erasmus studied, exercised and conversed in Froben's garden as he makes Eusebius do in *The Godly Feast*. But not only is Eusebius's garden a mingling of traditional and actual possibilities, it is instinct with some of the tensions which are endemic to all postlapsarian garden art. The fiction of the colloquy expects us to believe the garden is real, that it has realized in its architectural space and botanical fullness the ideals which classical and Christian literary traditions have identified with gardens. But Erasmus was perfectly aware that any garden is always and essentially a compromise between ideals located in the past and the practical exigencies and possibilities of the present. More's garden, according to Heywood, achieved only "almost perpetual verdure". Eusebius depicts the serpent and poisonous plants to remind us of the evils and inconveniences of a fallen world. Even the play between illusion and reality must recall us to a world where human art ($T\epsilon\chi\nu\acute{\eta}$) must intervene to create the fulness of the natural creation dispersed since our banishment from Eden. (This is a theme taken up prominently by botanical gardenists of the seventeenth century, and I shall be returning to it later.)

Erasmus, not surprisingly, presses his description close to irony or satire when we arrive at such an item as the labelled marjoram: for the swine and the marjoram, which also (as Marilene Allen, *op.cit.*, has noted) appear on the frontispiece of Sidney's *Arcadia* and of two editions (1611 and 1617) of *The Faerie Queene*, signal the animosities in nature that never existed in Eden, Arcadia, the

Io.Clemens. Hythlodæus. Tho.Morus. Pet.Ægid.

Figure 3. Ambrosius Holbein, illustration of a garden scene placed at the start of Book One of the 1518 edition More's *Utopia*. A turf seat held by wooden boards can be glimpsed beneath the figure of Hythlodaeus especially.

Golden Age or any such mythical *locus amoenus*. Gardens in our world, lovesome things maybe, are always a sharp reminder of the needs that have urged man to create and cultivate them, needs that are not necessarily satisfied even then. And finally Erasmus's garden is substantially architectural: walled, with galleries and pillars, it may be seen as much as a city as a garden ; indeed it takes its place (as I shall explain) at some strategic point along the human route from the Garden of Eden to the City of God.

It is here perhaps that it is worth taking up the one item of garden description which More allows himself of that Antwerp garden in the *Utopia* [Fig.3]. We are told that the discussants take their place "on a bench covered with turfs of grass" and More repeats this feature — the only one, as I say, singled out — at the beginning of the second part. Should we assume any particular significance in this isolated feature? Some recent and extensive researches by Martine Paul at the University of Paris (see *Journal of Garden History* V/1, 1985) suggest that More may have wished to emphasize two features of this garden seat: first, it appears to be associated with patrician establishments and to be used by the most courtly figures therein; but at the same time (and this is the second feature) it is the most natural of a garden's artificial creation, for the seat, which we associate with indoors, is constructed of grass sods laid upon earth which is retained inside a woven wattle fencing (sometimes, brick walling was used). Does More perhaps wish to underline unobtrusively the simple, non-architectural elements of the garden where the utopian talks take place? Certainly the gardens in the cityscapes of the second part are firmly vegetal — no mention, for instance, of pergola or arbour. He may also have wished to suggest that those who seek to recover, if only in discourse, the ideal perfections of the world must remain (literally) close to nature. The paradox of courtly or patrician behaviour in firm alliance with true simplicity (what Spenser urges too in the sixth book of *The Faerie Queene*) is not without point for gardens and for gardens in utopias. Both gardens and utopias combine what man recall imaginatively of perfect worlds now lost with an essential element of the impossible (a point Erasmus also seems to be making). Paradoxical, too, in both gardens and utopias is their timelessness within time, as well as their naturalness that is the work of human art & craft. More's coinage of "utopia" significantly derives its etymology from a combination of the Greek for "good place" ($\epsilon\dot{v}\tau\acute{o}\pi o\varsigma$) and for "no place" ($\dot{o}\nu\tau\acute{o}\pi o\varsigma$). The man who sits on that turf seat in Antwerp and discourses of utopias is called both Raphael (which signifies, "God has healed") and Hythlodaeus (dispenser of nonsense). Ideal gardens — with their illusion at least of perpetual spring — and perfect societies can only be located nowhere, in no place; to linger in both is to partake of refreshment, even perhaps some healing quality; but about both is also the tincture of nonsense. It is as much for the absurdity of his claim as for his verbal bathos that we smile at the poet's "A garden is a lovesome thing, God wot".

If we discount Erasmus's explicitly Christian lessons, his garden in *The Godly Feast* anticipates the physical disposition of many Renaissance gardens in the next hundred years. These princely gardens, like More's and Eusebius's, were realized from a combination of received garden forms and ideas in both literary and rhetorical traditions, classical largely but subsuming the Christian. To start with, the ideal Renaissance villa (a term used to include house and garden) was likely to recall the younger Pliny's description of his villas in Tuscany and at Laurentinum (the most extensive of such descriptions from antiquity) and attempted to recreate Pliny's account of a series of spaces for different purposes and times of day; this clearly had links also with the Pindarian (*Fragments*, 129 & 130) and Virgilian (*Aeneid*, VI, 637 ff.) visions of the Elysian Fields, where were incorporated grounds for a whole range of activities, athletic, musical, amorous and contemplative: "green pleasaunces and happy seats" is a version of Virgil's phrase, suggestive of a succession of garden spaces. Christian emphases could well translate such enclosures, either individually or as an *ensemble*, especially when they were associated with a religious house, into the closed garden of the Canticles.

One Renaissance garden above all others in Italy determined the shape and spirit of the art: that was the complex begun by Bramante when he was asked to turn the Belvedere into a garden for the Papal collection of antique sculpture and at the same time to link it with the Vatican Palace by a series of ramps copied from a pagan temple-theatre and by a courtyard to be used for ceremonial and entertainment purposes [Fig.4]. Equally Utopian, too, is the determination to bring hortulan space into creative relationship

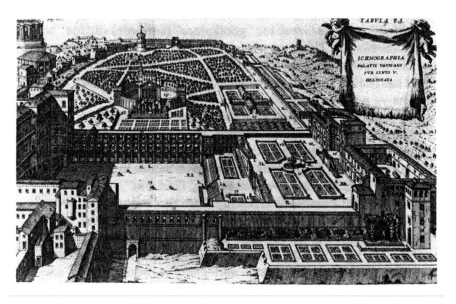

Figure 4. Engraved view of the Vatican gardens, Rome. The Belvedere Villa is to the right, and Ligorio's casino in the rear centre.

with the church of St Peter, with political ceremony and with the Vatican libraries. In the more private gardens beyond the courtyard Pirro Ligorio later designed the casino for Pius IV, finding the prototypes for it in a whole range of antique buildings and decorating it with elaborate stucco work on the outside and frescoes (by Zuccaro) inside. The decorations unite pagan and Christian worlds; classical mythology and church fathers are drawn upon to make this elaborately wrought garden house what Burckhardt (quite rightly) called "the most beautiful resting place for the afternoon hours which modern architecture has created".

Since most sixteenth and seventeenth-century guide books to the Eternal City began their modern sections with these Vatican Gardens, their richness and emblematic fullness and their union of pagan and Christian worlds encouraged visitors to look elsewhere for such an ideal garden. Since the Belvedere courtyard provided physical, architectural models for later Italian gardens, it was in fact easy enough to find examples of its metaphysics elsewhere.

The conceit that earlier and legendary places of perfection could be realized in modern gardens was a dominant theme of designers and users alike. The Medici villa at Pratolino had its Parnassus, with a small arena for visitors to use while they listened to its concert. The D'Este gardens at Tivoli were elaborately designed to reconstitute the Gardens of the Hesperides, for Hercules (the patron alike of the Estes and the town of Tivoli) had simply brought the dragon to guard an even more perfect spot. The sight of oranges everywhere in Italy encouraged northern visitors to read into their garden settings a whole series of Hesperidean relocations. Just as Eusebius's garden had offered moral and religious lessons, so Renaissance gardens were provided with the iconography to promote virtue: Roman emperors and imitation bas-reliefs that form the perfect circle of the little garden at Villa Brenzone on Garda were installed to induce recollections of imperial values, while the gardens of the Villa D'Este with their series of forking paths realized the Choice of Hercules (one series of routes leading the visitor to representations of vice, another to ones of civic and moral probity).

Sometimes it is true the iconography was both less precise and less uplifting. But its appeal to visions of legendary worlds, realized in modern villa complexes, was still potent. At Genoa, often the first opportunity visitors from the north had to encounter modern

Italian architecture, its villas and palaces recalled the hanging gardens of Babylon, its garden enclaves such fabled places as the paradise of the Old Man of the Mountain, the Hesperides or the Elysian Fields. Garden statuary in the Doria gardens (still surviving amid the incursions of modern urbanism) took a traveller like John Evelyn into a familiar but hitherto largely literary world of ancient heroes which now seem realized before his very eyes. These Genoese palaces cast such a spell that it was perfectly apt for an earlier visitor, Jan Massys, to use the Doria gardens as background for his *Venus Cytherea* [Fig.5].

Gardens were thus constituted as places of hitherto lost perfections. Not perhaps surprisingly, most Renaissance iconographical programmes were classicizing; but the pagan virtues had been absorbed into a Christian ethic (as is shown by a few surviving programmes). And some gardens did, like Eusebius's, focus unequivocally upon Christian matters. Near Siena the Villa Cetinale garden is still decorated with classical figures; but its striking feature is a complete circle of stations of the cross encircling the garden. Yet if one leaves this earthly though Christian paradise and climbs the

Figure 5. Jan Massys, *Venus Cytherea*, 1561, Nationalmuseum, Stockholm.

hill behind to the hermitage (palatial enough, it must be admitted, in terms of living accomodation) and from *that* vantage point (nearer Heaven, perhaps) looks down towards the garden, it appears diminished and minute in the Tuscan landscape. At Bomarzo, the so-called monster garden near Viterbo, a dystopia of classical legend is explicitly established in opposition to the utopian vision of God's temple at the end of the garden journey: wrestling colossi, mythical beasts, leaning houses, marine monsters, a hell-mouth and siren-like illusions of easy virtue have all to be safely negotiated (i.e. passed in the full consciousness of their negative values) before the visitor ascends a staircase guarded by the three-headed Cerberus to take sanctuary in Vignola's magnificient and austere temple, dedicated to the true and only God and erected in memory of the deceased wife of the garden's creator, Vicino Orsini.

But as Eusebius shrewdly noted these hortulan lessons and realizations of lost perfection depend upon the specific garden skills of bringing art and nature into creative association. This has, of course, always been a garden's particular distinction: one essential point underlying the end of Marvell's "The Garden" is that what appeared ineluctably natural ("green thoughts in a green shade") has by the end to be recognized as the gardener's art. Notions of art and of art's involvement or interference in a garden's nature have fluctuated through the ages. Eusebius's naturalistic frescoes might well strike us as naive: after all, piping monkeys and dancing camels sound as quaint as Milton meant his prelapsarian animals to appear in the Garden of Eden or as Roelandt Savery makes his in analogous visual exercises. But the theme of art and nature — whether cooperating or vying in *paragone* — is certainly crucial to gardens and, arguably, to utopias.

At least one garden, that of the Villa Lante at Bagnaia near Viterbo, established its whole iconographical programme around the necessarily different roles of art and nature in the Golden Age and its dystopic successors. But sixteenth and seventeenth-century gardens everywhere elicited from visitors an appreciation of exactly this same theme; the literary traditions which sustained garden design endorsed it. In Achilles Tatius's romance of *Clitophon and Leucippe* the actual garden that adjoins a character's house is described in exactly the same detail as he had used to describe the painting of a meadow at the start of the story — crystal fountains, cloistered walls, foliage that filters sunlight to the grass beneath. Similar confusions occur in Renaissance gardens and indeed it is sometimes as hard to distinguish in verbal accounts between what is actual and what is imagined or painted, as it was difficult to make such discriminations on the ground.

English visitors reported their delighted confusions: when trellis work with vines and birds turns out to be painted; when what should be a sculptured stone group of animals turns out so realistically coloured and equipped with real horns and tusks that one expects them to move. Grottoes make stones into flower shapes that deceive the eye in the gloom of the cavern, which is itself artificial, resonant with many literary, especially Ovidian, references to *natural* springs in the rock. Indeed, the metaphorical world of Renaissance gardens is arguably their distinguishing feature, and Ovid's poem is drawn upon more frequently than any other source for iconographical detail and for decorative subject matter (see my *Garden and Grove*, J.M. Dent, 1986). It is precisely this Ovidian colouring of garden design — water forced into a tunnel of arches, balustrades of running water which you cannot grasp, artificial birds singing, and so on — that made the Renaissance garden a fabulous place. Even giants seemed to be represented realistically — either bending down to pick up a rock to hurl at one or in the very process of metamorphosis (from rock to living being or from living being into rock is the ambiguity that makes the colossus at Pratolino so intriguing).

But the point at which the rivalries or cooperations of art and nature become most intense was in the flower garden, and this will therefore serve me conveniently as the stepping stone into that most utopian of Renaissance garden worlds: the botanical garden. The art/nature dialogue was focused in the very layout of botanical (and by inference of all) gardens. At Mantua, for example, the beds of the Duke's botanical garden were clearly the work of ingenious man, forming what Agostino del Riccio called "beautiful patterns in the forms, variously, of pyramids, maps, dragons, stars, and other *fantasie*". But other botanists attacked this artful complexity of presentation: Giovan Battista Ferrari argued that elaborately shaped beds were scientifically inappropriate — "quite unsuitable both for sowing seeds and for growing them". Such pragmatic considerations obviously obtained at Leiden, where the rectangular

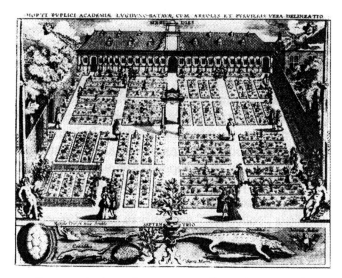

Figure 6. Engraved view of the Hortus Botanicus at Leiden, with the repositary of some of the non-botanical specimens across the end of the gardens.

beds were as readily accessible to the mind's categorizing and understanding as to the gardener's hands and care [Fig.6].

There are of course more aspects of this topic than I have time for: Keith Thomas has shown in *Man and the Natural World* that the energies which went into botanical gardens were an escape from older anthropomorphic perspectives (assessments of a plant's moral status, for example) and part of a search for the intrinsic qualities of each item in the natural world; yet this search and its physical embodiment in the precise beds of a botanical garden also declared man's pride in his control over the world of fallen nature. A botanical garden was a possible, a feasible utopia rather than one of those that Milton derided in his *Areopagitica*: "To sequester out of the world into Atlantick and Eutopian polities, which never can be drawn into use, will not mend our condition."

There was much that seemed useful to man's condition in the scientific study of the natural world. Nor did that study confine itself within botanical limits. Most botanical gardens of the sixteenth and early seventeenth centuries were linked (often physically) to cabinets of curiosity. The engraving of the Leiden Hortus displays examples from its natural history museum which was housed after 1599 in the specially built *Ambulacrum*. At Pisa, where the botanical garden was founded thirty-four years before Leiden's, adjoining the plants beds was a gallery which in 1641 Evelyn found "furnish'd with natural rarities, stones, minerals, shells, dryed Animals, etc". The inventories of the gallery and garden (which survive) show that by the time of his visit the collection included not only natural objects — what the famous Bolognese botanist, Aldrovani, called "le cose sotterranee e le altre sopraterranee" — but landscape, portraits of European botanists including Clusius, beautiful albums of flower paintings, birds and animals, and even religious pictures. Its gallery recalls those of Eusebius's garden, though all of his "collection" was only in painted representations.

The combination of botanical gardens and their associated cabinets of natural and artificial rarities seemed to present a utopian opportunity to reconstitute the whole natural world in its Edenic perfection. No longer did it seem necessary to speculate upon the exact situation of Eden when the fullness of Eden was beginning to be made available in many botanical gardens in Europe. The discovery of the New World as well as extensive travels into the near and far east brought a huge influx of new plants and other specimens (shells, native art and dress) into Europe. It seemed suddenly possible that man was in a position to design a garden which would (in John Evelyn's words) "comprehend the principall and most useful plants, and...be as rich and noble [a] compendium of what the whole Globe of Earth has flourishing upon her bosome". The new world, with its variety of plants and trees, struck many of its first European visitors with the appearance of a garden. Thus Hakluyt reports in "A briefe relation of Newfound-land" of about 1582 (Everyman edn, VI, 17):

> The next morning being Sunday and the 4 of August, the Generall and his company were brought on land by English marchants, who shewed unto us their accustomed walks unto a place they call the Garden. But nothing appeared more then Nature it selfe without art: who confusedly hath brought foorth roses abundantly, wilde but odoriferous, and to sense very comfortable.

When the profusion of the Americas was put together with the

Figure 7. Engraved view of the Musei Wormiani, Copenhagen, 1655.

riches of Asia, Africa and Europe, the potential for man's new gardens was utopian. The titlepage of John Parkinson's *Theatrum Botanicum* of 1640 shows the four continents contributing to this plenitude, while the first gardener, Adam, faces Solomon, representing the modern man who has the intelligence to recover Adam's knowledge, in a garden that was indeed a theatre — a complete collection *and* a stage for its display.

This determination to collect together in many single places the variety of the world's natural and artistic creation is widely attested in visual evidence — luckily, since the *Kunstundwunderkammern* have been almost all completely dispersed and can only be theoretically reconstructed. (See *The Origins of Museums: the Cabinet of Curiosities in Sixteenth and Seventeenth-Century Europe*, eds O.R. Impey and A.G. MacGregor, Clarendon Press, 1985, for further details.) There is the famous engraving issued in Leiden of the Worms cabinet [Fig.7]; a later anonymous Dutch painting at Norwich displays part of the Yarmouth collection. Or there are those paintings by Rubens and Breughel in Madrid which bring together all of the material subject to each of man's senses. The suggestion of

130

the profusion of the cabinet, its extension into neighbouring rooms and even out into a garden beyond, is ample visual evidence of the utopian enterprise which I have been sketching. Jan van Kessel's *Europe* (Munich) repeats this popular motif; no doubt popular, too, for its demands upon painterly skills — but of course painterly virtuosity exactly answers the efforts of the virtuoso who makes such collections in the first place. We have evidence that these virtuosos' collections were recognized at once for their utopian ambitions: Christopher Arnold, afterwards Professor of History at Nuremberg, noted in 1651 his impressions of what remained of Lord Arundel's gardens and gallery beside the Thames: "certain gardens on the Thames where there are rare Greek and Roman inscriptions, stones, marbles: the reading of which is actually like viewing Greece and Italy at once within the bounds of Great Britain."

These gardens and cabinets attest to the scientific dimension of the Utopian impulse in seventeenth-century Europe (though inevitably in widely different dimensions). Many of these garden-cum-cabinets also included some form of laboratory [Fig.8]. At the

Figure 8. Engraved view of the Hortus Palatinus at Heidelberg: the building at the far right of the garden is probably a cabinet and laboratory.

end of the famous garden created at Heidelberg by Salomon de Caus for the Elector Palatine in the 1610s was a building that (it has been convincingly argued) was a combined cabinet/museum *and* a laboratory [Fig.8] (see *Journal of Garden History* I/1, 1980). Leiden, too, had established a chemistry laboratory alongside the botanical garden by the mid-seventeenth century. In England *virtuosi* likewise experimented in their gardens: Evelyn's, for example, contained a transparent beehive given him by Dr Watkins of Wadham, another scientist/virtuoso whose garden in Oxford was the site of both botanical and hydraulic experiments. Evelyn's diary records many such alliances of garden and science in the houses of people he visited: Henry Winstanley, builder of the Eddystone Lighthouse, had a villa at Littlebury "with abundance of fine Curiosities all performed by clockwork" — these included both whimsical devices such as a chair that ran backwards into the garden on rails, taking an unsuspecting visitor with it, and more "practical" machines which served tea and coffee in cups to the company. At Sir Thomas Browne's in Norwich Evelyn found "the whole house and garden" was "a paradise and cabinet of rarities, and that of the best collection, especially medals, books, plants, and natural things". The role of the garden in these utopian endeavours is captured well by Abraham Cowley in the first book of his *Davideis*: with an eye perhaps on Eusebius, maybe More, but certainly on Salomon's House in Bacon's *New Atlantis*, Cowley describes library, hall, and synagogue (the utopian return of the Jews to England) grouped around choice gardens, with the walls of all units adorned with maps, stories, texts and Egyptian hieroglyphs.

But there inevitably came a time when the profusion of the world's riches seemed too large for any one cabinet. Peter Mundy visiting the Tradescants' Ark in London — a botanical garden and a museum which eventually became part of the Ashmolean Museum — found a "little garden with divers outlandish herbes and flowers"; and he was *"almost* persuaded a Man might in one day behold and collecte into one place more Curiosities than hee should see if he spent all his life in Travell". That was in 1634. Gardens and cabinets bulged more and more, as collectors increased their holdings: verses prefixed to the catalogue of the Tradescants' Museum claimed

Nor court, nor shop-crafts were THINE arts, but those
Which Adam studied ere he did transgresse,
The wonders of the Creatures, and to dress
The worlds great Garden.

But while the Tradescant catalogue of 1634 listed some seven hundred and fifty species and varieties, by that of 1656 these holdings had doubled. We are again indebted to Keith Thomas for drawing attention to the "dozens of now forgotten amateur helpers and correspondents" who from Tudor times onwards helped more prominent collectors by bringing items to their notice and therefore into the many botanical gardens up and down the country where local and foreign plants were grown and studied. Their efforts and the efforts of explorers meant that in the end the botanical garden of however generous dimensions could not hope to include all of the world's great garden let alone its prelapsarian profusion.

The true and full utopian dimension of the Renaissance garden probably died with the idea that one botanical garden could recover Paradise. Specialization, for one thing, intervened: when the Tradescants' collections were transferred to what would become the Ashmolean Museum, their garden was not included; since 1621 a separate botanical garden had existed at Oxford where the proper care due to plants could be given. Both Evelyn and Aubrey voiced their opinion that different materials needed different curatorial attention and expertise.

At the same time princely gardens also came under suspicion. Not the least reason for this was the frequent identification of Stuart absolutism with the garden — had not Inigo Jones often imaged the ideal world of kingly creation and power in terms of fine gardens? Indeed, all over sixteenth and seventeenth-century Europe royal entertainments — ballets, *intermezzi*, masques, entries, progresses — used the garden as the apt metaphor for the ruler's beneficial and creative régime. The political claims implicitly made for such gardens inevitably lost them their utopian attraction when the political ideology with which they were associated came into question: Louis XIV's exercise of garden imagery at Versailles or Marly did not help the universal claims for a garden as utopia, at least in England.

The garden necessarily retained something of the ideal: if only as the perfect alliance of art and nature it could preserve its paradisical reputation. Yet the history of English gardens after the Civil Wars and the Interregnum suggest that they became personal retreats from far more than attacks upon a fallen and postlapsarian world. Utopiary rather than utopia was the order of the day (the pun is not, alas, mine, but Glenn Lewis's: see *Paradise/Le Paradis*, The Photo Gallery, Ottawa, 1981, p. 31). For this new and reduced vision of gardens Evelyn speaks well:

> they are a place of all terrestriall enjoyments the most resembling Heaven and the best representation of our lost felicity. It is the common term and the pit from whence we were dug; we all came out of the parsley-bed — at least according to the creed of a poet (Lucretius, V, 807-10). As no man can be very miserable that is master of a garden here; so will no man ever be happy who is not sure of a garden hereafter. From thence we came, and thither we tend; where the first Adam fell, the second arose. Kings, philosophers, and wise men spent their choicest hours in them; and when they would frame a type of Heaven, because there is nothing in nature more worthy and illustrious, they describe a garden, and call it Elysium.

What that declares is that each man has the opportunity to make his garden as perfect a model of his own felicity as he can, but that the garden no longer stands for any universal ambition to bring the whole world into shape and form before one's eyes.

Yet the rhetoric of admiration for gardens continues to be used throughout the first half of the eighteenth century. It is often inert cliché; but it can also be capable of sustaining a vision of garden art as a *feasible* utopian world, subject however to more constraints, to more "natural" eventualities, than would have been admitted before. Beneath continuing claims for the garden as utopia, arcady or the *locus amoenus* were clear recognitions of other, competing energies, disruptive and sceptical. One example will have to serve: the Elysian Fields at Stowe, in Buckinghamshire.

Here a carefully contrived cluster of temples, facing each other over the waters of what came to be called the "River Styx", suggests that the present cannot achieve the perfections of the past. A perfect and classical circular Temple of Ancient Virtue confronts a somewhat dumpy, even Gothick Temple of British

Worthies across the river of death. The pagan temple contains full-length statues of a poet, a philosopher, a general and a lawgiver (Lycurgus, this last, a creator supposedly of institutions to make Spartans austere, morally upright, simple, self-sacrificing, brave, hardy and happy); British Worthies only has busts in niches and a larger selection must now stand for the diversity of national achievement. Behind the Temple of Ancient Virtue is a specially created heap of rubble, the Temple of Modern Virtue. Behind the Temple of British Worthies is a monument to a dog, eulogized with such solemn celebration that it calls into question the notable figures on its other side. It has the air, this *ensemble*, of a three-dimensional satire in the mode of Pope's *Dunciad*, and its irony finally defeats any hope that the garden can fully achieve any ideal status.

There is much in the history of the English landscape garden that suggests a prevalent scepticism with any garden's claim to be utopian. The elegiac quality of the very idea of a garden or arcadia or Elysian Fields or world of the Golden Age is never far from the surface. We are often invited to remember that *a* garden is no substitute for *the* Garden and that each garden since the first must fade (even though, as Pope said of Stowe, "time shall make it grow"). Pope made his own garden at Twickenham a coherent antidote to Grub Street and the City; it became, as Maynard Mack has shown, a base for his career as satirist. But he was forever aware that it was only his until he died (having no immediate heirs and, being a catholic, unable to *own* property). And from 1735 its termination point was a memorial to his dead mother. This elegiac emphasis found itself echoed in many other gardens far from Twickenham, among them Shenstone's The Leasowes, created as a veritable *memento mori* to friends and poetic predecessors. Doubtless with some support from Poussin's *Et in Arcadia Ego* the landscape garden readily adopted the tomb in the landscape as a characteristic feature until, with the establishment of the cemetery of Père Lachaise in Paris after the Revolution, the cemetery itself became a garden (see Richard Etlin, *The Architecture of Death*, MIT Press, 1984).

I want to end this garden excursion with a few remarks on the relationships of cemetery, garden, city and utopia. It seems perfectly apt that the new cemetery movement of the nineteenth century took its inspiration from English landscape parks and removed burial grounds from crowded and unhealthy inner cities. But these new cemeteries became in their turn as densely packed as the urban centres from which they had been removed: gardens of death became cities of the dead. All this is (as I said) apt, because man's progress has also been plotted along a route that leads from the Garden of Eden at one end of time to the City of God at the other. (There are exceptions, such as the Apocalypse of Peter to whom the Lord revealed "a very great country outside of this world ... blooming with unfading flowers and incorruptible and bearing blessed fruit". But it is essentially St Augustine's imagery of the City of God that has prospered.)

What are the implications of man's choosing his utopian imagery from either of these termini? If he takes it from the original garden it will or should be unbounded, all nature, without the need of protection. But as William McClung has recently argued in a fascinating book on *The Architecture of Paradise* man has consistently opted for the urban imagery of a ring of walls and other protective buildings. The *hortus conclusus* already compromises the Edenic Garden with architectural components. Many representations of paradise equally hedge their bets. In Fra Angelico's *Last Judgement* the blest celebrate in a celestial garden beneath the ramparts of a city: as McClung says, "the bastioned city satisfies as a representation of triumph, power and security, the garden as a representation of innocent delights." So too in the Utrecht codex of St Augustine the imagery of divine urbanization exists alongside that of a fine garden [Fig.9].

What may explain the ascendency of an architecture over a horticulture of Paradise is the essential vulnerability of the unenclosed garden. As Bunyan put it in *The Holy City*:

> Adam, you know, was once so rich and wealthy, that he had the garden of Eden, the paradise of pleasure, yea, and also the whole world to boot, for his inheritance; but mark, in all his glory he was without a wall: wherefore presently, even at the very first assault of the adversary, he was not only worsted as touching his person and standing, but even stripped of all his treasures, his paradise taken from him....

It was not only for protection that Bunyan recommended a city for

136

Figure 9. St Augustine preaches of the City of God, Utrecht Codex.

his utopia; he also considered that the diversity and multitude of
the blessed urged their being housed in a city. A celestial highrise.
To protect a garden with a wall, then, or to provide it with
buildings, is to acknowledge that Eden in its pure form is
irrecoverable; St Augustine denied that the garden would be
restored on earth. Furthermore the walled or claustral garden, the
garden of architectural forms, satisfies because instead of
reminding us elegiacally or ironically of a lost Eden it anticipates
and celebrates our eventual arrival at the City of God. It secures
us, too, from our fear of the unpathed wood and the unstructured
wilderness, which are for Gaston Bachelard the primal dystopia.
Maybe — it is something about which I have long puzzled — these
configurations of conscious and unconscious attitudes towards the
architectural garden explain the outcry when Capability Brown
tried to eliminate all buildings, all fences, all urban traces, from
his landscapes; certainly, the reaction to his work was a speedy
reversion to the architectural garden by Humphry Repton, J.C.
Loudon and others.

But as the names of nineteenth-century garden history must

remind us there were reactions also to the architectural garden. Gertrude Jekyll and William Robinson promoted the horticultural paradise, whose walls — though they were necessary for social and legal reasons — were not insisted upon; not considered to be confining. A nineteenth-century fear and horror of urban crowding, of architecture used often to cramp and constrain the population, led to utopian visions of green worlds and wondrous gardens. No romance of William Morris is without its hortulan paradise; and other utopians like Carlyle and Ruskin also invoke the world of flowers and cultivation as an antidote to the dystopia of the city. Interestingly, the place in Orwell's *1984* where Winston and Julia can recover the satisfactions of love-making is outside the regimented city in a pastoral landscape of bluebells and the "droning of ring-doves".

There are, then, two rival imageries of gardens as utopias. One is controlled by the ultimate satisfactions of the City of God. The other recalls the pristine openness of Eden. One is architectural, the other natural, even wild (Robinson's famous book is *The Wild Garden*). Between them there is historically and ideologically a basic conflict. But in practice they have learned to compromise with each other. The paradigm of that collaboration is the garden city; but before its invention there were the gardens in the cities of More's Utopia, the nineteenth-century establishment of city parks, all of which are somehow summarized in Frank Lloyd Wright's dreams of a cityscape with intermingled gardens or in the utopian cities projects of Henry Dreyfuss's *Democracity* at the 1939 New York World's Fair (these and other examples are illustrated in *Dreams and Nightmares. Utopian Visions in Modern Art* by Valerie J. Fletcher, a catalogue for the exhibition at the Hirshhorn Museum, Washington, D.C., 1963).

The city is under threat once again, of course — the prime target of thermonuclear attacks: in those conditions gardens, walled or unwalled, will yield no protection. A few years ago Robert Morris envisaged his sculpture, *Tomb Garden Outside the City* (illustrated in the catalogue mentioned above), as the mechanized burial ground after atomic disaster. Those who see either hope or the paramount need for there to be space for hope are today identified with the garden's primordial colour: green. They are the Green Party or Greenpeace. Their imagery is gardenesque and they perpetuate the strong instinct of mankind to project utopias in traditional forms. We may hang representations of gardens on the walls (the marvellous Stoke Edith tapestries); we may wear fantastical head-dresses in the shape of gardens to the fleshpots of Vauxhall or Ranelegh, the green retreats of eighteenth and early-nineteenth-century Londoners; we are seduced by coloured ads which promise us immaculate lawns if we use their special fertilizer. These — and others — are the continuing expression of our wish for an impossible, nonsensical, healing, perfect, nowhere world.

Norwich   John Dixon Hunt

"A PARADISE UNLOST": EDWARD YOUNG AMONG THE STARS

Moreover, so boundless are the bold excursions of the
human mind, that in the vast void beyond real existence,
it can call forth shadowy beings, and unknown worlds,
as numerous, as bright, and, perhaps, as lasting, as the
stars; such quite-original beauties we may call
Paradisaical,

Natos sine semine flores.　　　OVID.[1]

Can one legitimately smuggle Edward Young into a conference (or
a book) on Utopia? Well, in one of the more easily available
nineteenth-century editions of *Young's Night Thoughts* (by 1853 the
inclusion of the author's name in the abbreviated title seems to
have been already traditional), we find the editor, the Rev. George
Gilfillan, a friend of De Quincey and Carlyle, proclaiming
enthusiastically that "Young deserves praise for the following
things":

1*st*, He has nobly sung the magnitude and unutterable glory of
the starry hosts. His soul kindles, triumphs, exults under the
midnight canopy .... in the last part of the poem. Escaped from
dark and mournful contemplations on Man, Death, Infidelity,
and Earth's "melancholy map," he sees the stars like bright
milestones on the way to heaven, and his spirit is glad within
him, and tumultuous is the grandeur, and fierce and rapid the
torrent, of his song.

2*dly*, He has brought out, better than any other poet, the
religion of the stars .... Young, we need scarcely say, finds in the

---

1. Edward Young, *Conjectures on Original Composition* (1759), Scolar
Press facsimile of the 1st edn, Leeds, 1966, p. 70.

nocturnal heavens lessons neither of Atheism nor of Superstition, but of Religion, and reads in the face of Old Night her divine origin, the witness she bears to the existence of God, her dependence upon her Author, and her subordination to His purposes. He had magnified, as Newton himself could not so eloquently have done, the extent of the universe; and yet his loyalty to Scripture compels him to intimate that this system, so far from being God, or infinite, or, strictly speaking, Divine, is to perish and pass away.[2]

It is important to record that this extreme, and undoubtedly at the time already old-fashioned, view was expressed only four years before the appearance, in January 1857, of the essay which is said to have finally exploded Young's reputation — George Eliot's aptly titled examination of his all too evident "Worldliness" which, in the wake of worldly failure, his rhetorically effusive "Other-Worldliness" sought to disguise or to distract attention from.[3]

But it is as a (possibly *the*) poet of the stars,[4] as a poet of genuine "other worldliness" that, even allowing for the persuasive force of George Eliot's charges, one feels justified in linking Young and his "night thoughts", in particular those of "Night the Ninth and Last", the lengthy and apt culmination of the work, to the utopian theme. Even the blank verse form of *The Complaint: Or, Night-Thoughts on Life, Death, and Immortality* (to give Young's poem its full, proper title[5]) is not without its other-worldly implications.

2. *Young's Night Thoughts*, with Life, Critical Dissertation, and Explanatory Notes, by the Rev. George Gilfillan, Edinburgh, 1853, xxi-xxii.

3. "Worldliness and Other-Worldliness: The Poet Young" in *Essays of George Eliot*, ed. Thomas Pinney, London, 1963, pp. 335-85.

4. As distinct from Dante or Milton, who might be more truly considered poets of Heaven and Hell, and the regions between.

5. Young's *Complaint: Or, Night-Thoughts* was published for the first time in its complete form in 1750, although individual "Nights" had been appearing since 1742 (I, II & III in 1742, IV & V in 1743, VI & VII in 1744, VIII in 1745, and IX in 1746). All the quotations in this article are taken from a copy of 1768, which apart from minor details on the title page conforms to the issue of 1755, described as "A NEW EDITION,

The greater part of Young's other poetry is in rhyme, a great deal of it, as one might expect, in rhyming couplets: for instance, his very first published poem, *The Last Day* (1713) — a significant early choice considering his later achievement in *Night Thoughts* — and his first real success, *Love of Fame, The Universal Passion* "In Seven Characteristical Satires" (1725-8). Critics commenting upon Young's choice of blank verse in *Night Thoughts* have commonly pointed to the success of Thomson's *The Seasons* (1730), which so impressed the older poet. But at least after his own success with *Night Thoughts*, Young could afford to directly imply another reason for his choice of blank verse, "a term of diminution" which he objected to, since "what we mean by blank verse, is verse unfallen, uncurst; verse reclaim'd, reinthron'd in the true *language of the Gods*; who never thunder'd, nor suffer'd their *Homer* to thunder, in Rhime"[6] — in fact, the verse form of "Paradise unlost", of which the culminating section of *Night Thoughts* attempts, with some accomplishment, to give us a glimpse.

Paradise, lost or unlost, has evident associations with the Golden Age, and with its traditions before Saturn fell, which led to the fall of man more irrevocable than the fall of Adam and Eve, which was itself a consequence of Satan's fall. In popular imagining at least, and even in common academic use (as books

---

Corrected by the Author" (see Henry Pettit, *A Bibliography of Young's Night Thoughts*, Boulder, Colorado, 1954, p. 41). All capitals and italics in the quotations are as in this edition. However all line numbers are from Gilfillan's edition.

6. *Conjectures*, p. 60. Since later in this article a comparison is to be made with Blake, it is perhaps worth reminding ourselves of his comments on the freedom of verse in what amounts to his "Preface" to *Jerusalem* (Plate 3: "To the Public"): "When this Verse was first dictated to me, I consider'd a Monotonous Cadence, like that used by Milton & Shakespeare & all writers of English Blank Verse, derived from the modern bondage of Rhyming, to be a necessary and indispensible part of Verse. But I soon found that in the mouth of a true Orator such monotony was not only awkward, but as much a bondage as rhyme itself. I therefore have produced a variety in every line, both of cadences & number of syllables .... Poetry Fetter'd Fetters the Human Race" (Blake, *Complete Writings*, ed. Geoffrey Keynes, Oxford, 1969, p. 621).

and conferences reveal), "Utopia", "Paradise", the "Golden Age" tend to bear comparable resonances and similar connotations: "Aurea prima sata est aetas, quae vindice nullo,/sponte sua, sine lege fidem rectumque colebat" ("Golden was that first age, which, with no one to compel, without a law, of its own will, kept faith and did the right").[7] This is not really Utopia, of course — at least, not More's Utopia, nor the Paradise of either the Bible or Milton. However, there are resemblances between the three places of a perfected, if vulnerable, style of living, both in their physical and moral geography and in their literary provenance and uses. "Utopia", "Paradise", the "Golden Age" all indicate places that are insular or isolated (for obvious mythical, fictional and moral advantages). The men of the Golden Age knew only their own shores and had dipped no pine tree "into the watery plain to visit other lands" (*Met* I 95-6). More's Utopia is a crescent shaped island (although it had not always been "compassed about with the sea" — a state which had been achieved by King Utopus' engineering work[8]). According to Milton "this mount/Of Paradise" only became "an island" ("salt and bare,/The haunt of seals and orcs, and sea-mews' clang" — in Alastair Fowler's brisk summary "a bare island in the Persian Gulf"[9]) after the Flood. But before that, of course, it had had its "verdurous wall" (*PL* IV 143), which failed to keep Satan out, but which later, after the expulsion of Adam and Eve, was strengthened with extra angelic guards to prevent anybody ever getting in again. It is notable that when Britain has been extolled patriotically, its island status has been exploited as a means to forge a link between the Golden Age, Utopia and Paradise, as in John of Gaunt's famous speech in *Richard II* (II i 39-50) or the Queen's speech in *Cymbeline* (III i 17-23).[10]

7. Ovid, *Metamorphosis*, I, 89-90, Loeb Classical Library edn and trans., 1977.

8. *Sir Thomas More's Utopia* (in Robynson's translation), ed. J. Churton Collins, Oxford, 1904, p. 49 (cf. Penguin Classics edn, pp. 69-70).

9. Milton, *Paradise Lost*, XI 834-5, and n. 829-38 in Longman Annotated English Poets edition, ed. Alastair Fowler, London, 1971.

10. For the traditions of patriotic praise that associated Britain with various forms of paradise, see commentary on John of Gaunt's speech in

Edward Young's starry night is clearly no simple island nor even a walled retreat; but self-evidently it is remote, and physically it is out of the reach of man or any other earthly creature whose soul has not been parted from the flesh. Although partly visible through a telescope, it can only be "read" in a style analogous to the way that More's *Utopia* can be literally read, by someone fired with the appropriate imaginative propulsion. Young offers support to our more particular analogy by calling the firmament or the skies "the Garden of the DEITY,/ Blossom'd with Stars, redundant in the Growth/Of Fruit ambrosial" (IX 1042-4) and by attributing to the furthest reach of God's "mighty Building" and "The Suburbs of Creation" a "Wall/Whose Battlements look o'er into the Vale/Of Non-Existence" (IX 1510-22). Moreover Young is carried away at one moment of speculation to wonder if the "One Universe" is "too small":

> in the Map
> Of universal *Nature*, as a Speck,
> Like fair BRITANNIA in our little Ball;
> Exceeding fair, and glorious, for its Size,
> But, elsewhere, far out-measur'd, far outshone?
> In *Fancy* (for the *Fact* beyond us lies)
> Canst thou not figure it, an *Isle*, almost
> Too small for Notice, in the *Vast* of Being;
> Sever'd by mighty Seas of *unbuilt* Space,
> From other *Realms*; from ample *Continents*
> Of higher Life, where nobler Natives dwell;
> Less *Northern*, less remote from DEITY,
> Glowing beneath the *Line* of the SUPREME;
> Where Souls in Excellence make Haste, put forth
> Luxuriant Growths; nor the late Autumn wait
> Of *Human* Worth, but ripen soon to Gods?
>
> (IX 1594-1612)

---

the New Arden edition of *Richard II*, ed. Peter Ure, London, 5th edn, 1961, esp. on II i 42; and note the passage from Sylvester's Du Bartas given in Appendix IV of that edition (p. 207) and the article by Josephine Waters Bennett, "Britain among the Fortunate Isles", *SP*, LIII (1956), 114-40, cited and summarized on p. 208.

In such a passage as this Young's fantasy anticipates some of the gawdy of science-fiction, as well as echoing Renaissance arguments about the plurality of worlds, and justifies the use as an epigraph to this paper that passage from his *Conjectures on Original Composition* which associates such flights of fancy with the ability to contemplate Paradise. That particular quotation from *Conjectures* ends with a quotation from Ovid, "Natos sine semine flores" ("the flowers that sprang unplanted"), from that same paragraph of the first book of the *Metamorphoses* describing the Golden Age from which we have already quoted the opening lines.[11]

The writers, the poets, who describe the Golden Age, or Paradise, or Utopia, share more than a willingness to indulge in what Young calls "the bold excursions of the human mind". They also usually share a desire to teach by a description of their little state or garden or landscape how things really ought to be. The Golden Age, or Paradise, or Utopia is a measure of how far man has fallen, of the extent of his decline, of the distance from the origin which he so disturbingly fails to live up to. The didactic or even the satiric frame and basis of More's *Utopia* is self-evident and is made particularly clear in the opening conversation of Raphael Hythloday and his account of his experiences at Cardinal Morton's table. Equally clear is the reforming context and purpose of Young's "*Moral* Survey of the *Nocturnal* Heavens", as he announces the section on the title page of "NIGHT the NINTH and LAST": "THE/CONSOLATION./Containing, among other Things,/I. A *Moral* Survey of the *Nocturnal* Heavens./II. A *Night*-ADDRESS to the DEITY." ("among other Things" referring to an effective account of the Apocalypse and the Last Judgement in some 200 lines preceding the "*Moral Survey*" of the heavens).

Edward Young's first great success had been a set of satires (published before those of Pope), and in *Night Thoughts* he follows the precedent of Milton in "Lycidas" and in *Paradise Lost* of mixing with the elevated lyrical or epic vein an amount of abusive

---

11. In "Night 9" there is one reference to the Golden Age: "Enjoy your happy Realms their golden Age?/And had your EDEN an abstemious Eve" (1773-4) in the same passage from which I quote on p. 145.

satirical writing: for instance, in "NIGHT the EIGHTH" ("VIRTUE's APOLOGY;/OR,/The Man *of the* WORLD *Answered*"):

> In foreign Realms (for thou hast travell'd far)
> How curious to contemplate two State-Rooks,
> Studious their Nests to feather in a Trice,
> With all the *Necromantics* of their Art,
> Playing the Game of *Faces* on each other,
> Making Court Sweet-meats of their latent Gall,
> In foolish Hope, to steal each other's Trust;
> Both cheating, both exulting, both deceiv'd;
> And, sometimes, both (let Earth rejoice) undone!
>
> (VIII 343-51)

There is less of this kind of vituperation in the last book, but such a passage as the following (in which Young addresses the "Bord'rers on the Coast of Bliss", the inhabitants "Of this so foreign, unterrestrial Sphere,/Where Mortal, *untranslated*, never stray'd") may well be compared in content and tone with the outrage expressed by Hythloday or More himself in *Utopia*:

> "With War, This fatal Hour,
> "EUROPA groans (so call we a small Field,
> "Where Kings run mad). In *Our* World, DEATH deputes
> "*Intemperance* to do the Work of *Age*!
> "And, hanging up the Quiver *Nature* gave him,
> "As slow of Execution, for Dispatch
> "Sends forth *Imperial* Butchers; bids they slay
> "Their Sheep (the silly Sheep they fleec'd before),
> "And toss him twice Ten thousand at a Meal.
> "Sit all *your* Executioners on Thrones?
> "With *you*, can Rage for Plunder make a *God*?
> "And *Bloodshed* wash out ev'ry other Stain?—
> "But You, perhaps, can't bleed: From Matter gross
> "Your *Spirits* clean, are delicately clad
> "In fine-spun Æther, privileg'd to soar,
> "Unloaded, uninfected; How unlike
> "The Lot of Man! How few of human Race
> "By their own *Mud* unmurder'd!..."
>
> (IX 1782-97)

The abuse of political, social and spiritual evils, which are not at all to be distinguished, is part of the didactic purpose that More's and Young's work share: both are sermons presented in the guise of imaginative excursions. In a significant sense *Night Thoughts*, the last Night especially, like *Utopia* is also a traveller's tale of a purely imaginative kind: "Loose me from *Earth's* Inclosure, from the *Sun's/Contracted* Circle set my Heart at large", Young proclaims, "Eliminate my Spirit, give it Range/Thro' Provinces of Thought yet unexplor'd" (IX 589-92); "Above our Atmosphere's intestine Wars,/... /Above the Northern Nests of feather'd Snows,/... /Above misconstru'd Omens of the Sky,/... /Elance thy Thought" (launch thy thought, rather like a rocket: IX 620-30). "In Mid-way Flight Imagination tires;/Yet soon re-prunes her Wing to soar again" (1220-1): true, by the middle of the eighteenth century this kind of inspirational imagery and ecstatic rhetoric was a convention, even a cliché, of "the sublime poem"; but in Young's case, in its thematic and dramatic placing in the context of scanning the skies, the language sustains a conviction and its rhythms an energetic buoyancy that carry the reader:

In ardent *Contemplation's* rapid Car,
From *Earth*, as from my Barrier, I set out.
How swift I mount! Diminish'd *Earth* recedes;
I pass the *Moon*; and, from her farther Side,
Pierce Heav'n's blue Curtain; strike into *Remote*;
Where, with his lifted Tube, the subtil Sage
His artificial, airy Journey takes,
And to *Celestial* lengthens *Human* Sight.
I pause at ev'ry *Planet* on my Road,
And ask for HIM who gives their Orbs to roll,
Their Foreheads fair to shine. From SATURN's Ring,
In which, of *Earth's* an Army might be lost,
With the bold *Comet*, take my bolder Flight,
Amid those *sov'reign* Glories of the Skies,
Of independent, native Lustre, proud;
The Souls of Systems! and the Lords of Life,
Thro' their wide Empires! — What behold I *now*?
A Wilderness of Wonders burning round;
Where *larger* Suns inhabit *higher* Spheres;
Perhaps the *Villas* of descending Gods!

Nor halt I here; my Toil is but begun;
'Tis but the Threshold of the DEITY;
Or, far beneath it, I am grovelling still.

(IX 1715-37)

The reminder that this is but an imaginary journey through space is neatly conveyed in the reference to "the subtil Sage" 's "lifted Tube" — which has the double effect of indicating how distances in the universe are normally perceived and taken in and, at the same time, of suggesting (for a moment at least through the perspective that we are given of the telescope) that we are experiencing an unusual and superior voyage of discovery which passes and surpasses the usual method of the astronomer. This passage, like many in the "Ninth Night" reminds us that this poem is indeed inspired by the achievements of Sir Isaac Newton, but there is also an element of fantasy and the fantastic in such a description which aligns it with many another traveller's tale, including those of Raphael Hythloday, and nearer at hand, in time at least, of Lemuel Gulliver. The element of futuristic science fiction even extends to the imagining of lost empires and hidden realms. References to "the *Villas* of descending Gods" risks, and probably does not avoid, bathos; but at the same time it may equally well be regarded as a credibilizing detail that persuades the reader of the verisimilitude of the mental flight and indicates even to an unsympathetic critic how firmly the actual experience is lodged in Young's imagination: the very banality of imaginative detail helps to secure the excitable rhetoric.

But like Utopia itself this is a place to learn from: "This Prospect vast, what is it? — Weigh'd aright,/'Tis Nature's System of Divinity,/..../'Tis *elder* Scripture, writ by GOD's own Hand;/Scripture authentic! Uncorrupt by Man" (IX 643-7). Young claims that his "Mind, op'ning at this Scene, imbibes/The moral Emanations of the Skies" (IX 847-8), since man has been given the build ("A Make to Man directive of his Thought;/A Make set upright, pointing to the Stars"IX 870-1) "to read this Manuscript of Heaven" (IX 873), to "read the Stars" (IX 1304): a metaphor extended with, perhaps, over-expansive enthusiasm some 300 lines later:

DIVINE INSTRUCTOR! Thy *first* Volume, *This*,
For *Man's* Perusal; All in CAPITALS!
In *Moon* and *Stars* (Heav'n's golden Alphabet!)
Emblaz'd to seize the Sight; who *runs*, may *read*;
Who *reads*, can *understand*. 'Tis Unconfin'd
To *Christian* Land, or *Jewry*; fairly writ,
In Language universal, to MANKIND:
A Language, Lofty to the Learn'd; yet Plain
To Those that feed the Flock, or guide the Plough,
Or, from its Husk, strike out the bounding Grain.
A Language, worthy the GREAT MIND, that speaks!
Preface, and *Comment*, to the *Sacred Page*!
Which oft refers its Reader to the Skies,
As pre-supposing his First Lesson *there*,
And Scripture self a *Fragment*, *That* unread.
Stupendous Book of Wisdom, to the Wise!
Stupendous Book! and open'd, NIGHT! by thee.

(IX 1659-75)

(And later Young claims that he has "half read o'er the Volume of the Skies" — IX 2020).

What we find in Young's *Night Thoughts*, especially in this last Night ("The Consolation") are three strands. In the first place, Young is an old-fashioned, although to his contemporaries a still fashionable and familiar, theologian, of no great originality. Young is seeking to convert the Deists, the Atheists, the current Infidels — rakes, wastrels, libertine gamblers and whoremongers, the commonplace list of enemies to respectable society and conventional belief in eighteenth-century sermons and moral essays — who are represented in this poem by Lorenzo. This much debated figure, who could not be Edward Young's son, may well be considered the poet's own *alter* (alternative, evil) *ego* whom he seeks to convert by the evidence of the universe and the planetary systems. This is "Physico" or "Astro-Theology" of the kind that the Boyle lectures established in 1692 tended to promote.[12] Newton

---

12. "According to the terms of [his] will ... a lecturer was to be chosen annually to preach eight sermons on the evidences of Christianity" (see Isabel St John Bliss, "Young's *Night Thoughts* in Relation to Contempor-

himself had corresponded with the first Boyle lecturer, Richard Bentley, supporting his teleological arguments.[13] And as Isabel Bliss demonstrates such astro-Christian apologetics abound, usually with the overt support of Newton and other scientists, so that in his own day Edward Young's popularity "may be found in the fact that he was giving poetical expression to the theories that were felt to be vital in the religious life of the time":[14]

> But, Miracles apart, who sees HIM not,
> *Nature's* CONTROULER, AUTHOR, GUIDE, and END?
> Who turns his eye on *Nature's* Midnight Face,
> But must inquire — "What Hand behind the Scene,
> "What Arm Almighty, put these wheeling Globes
> "In Motion, and wound up the vast Machine?
> "Who rounded in his Palm these spacious Orbs?
> "Who bowl'd them flaming thro' the dark Profound,
> "Num'rous as glitt'ring Gems of Morning-Dew,
> "Or Sparks from populous Cities in a Blaze,
> "And set the Bosom of *Old Night* on Fire?
> "Peopled her Desert, and made Horror *smile*?"
>
> (IX 1272-84)

But besides being a preacher, Young was also clearly one of those genuinely interested in and inspired by Newtonian astronomy — for instance, he was a subscriber to Henry Pemberton's *A View of Sir Isaac Newton's Philosophy* (1728) and was apparently abreast of contemporary knowledge of the subject.[15] He not only sees in the universe evidences of God, but

---

ary Christian Apologetics", *PMLA* XLIV (1934), 38). As a young man of 20, Robert Boyle had been a friend of Samuel Hartlib, who planned the utopian Christian kingdoms of "Antilia" and, later, "Macaria" (1641) — see W.H.G. Armytage, *Heavens Below: Utopian Experiments in England 1560-1960*, London, 1961, pp. 8-9.

13. See Bliss, 48-50. For the pervasive influence of Newton on Anglican theologians and in particular his association with the Boyle lectures, see Margaret C. Jacob, *The Newtonians and the English Revolution 1689-1720*, New York, 1976, esp. chs 4 & 5.

14. Bliss, 55.

15. Bliss, 58.

also implies that Sir Isaac Newton and his discoveries were part of
the Divine plan, which, he suggests in his ironical interrogatives,
has been revealed by a special scientific Providence:

"Then whence these glorious Forms
"And boundless Flights, from *Shapeless*, and *Repos'd?*
"Has Matter *more* than Motion? Has it Thought,
"Judgement, and Genius? Is it deeply learn'd
"In *Mathematics?* Has it fram'd *such* Laws.
"Which but to *guess*, a NEWTON made immortal? —
"If so, how each *sage* Atom laughs at me,
"Who think a *Clod* inferior to a *Man*!

(IX 1475-82)

And at one point he exclaims:

O for a Telescope His Throne to reach!
Tell me, ye Learn'd on *Earth*! or Blest *Above*!
Ye searching, ye *Newtonian* Angels! tell,
Where, your Great MASTER's Orb? His Planets, where?
Those *conscious* Satellites, those *Morning-Stars*,
First-born of DEITY! (IX 1834-9)

On a number of occasions he successfully combines an
admiring sense of Newtonian order with spiritual and religious
elevation:

Then mark
The *Mathematic* Glories of the Skies,
In Number, Weight, and Measure, all ordain'd.
. . . .
Orb above Orb ascending without End!
Circle in Circle, without End, inclos'd!
Wheel within Wheel; EZEKIAL! like to Thine!
Like Thine, it seems a Vision, or a Dream;
Tho' *seen*, we labour to believe it *true*! (IX 1079-1101)

This last passage with its stress on observation, on the act and
wonders of seeing is characteristic of the poets living at the time
when Newton's *Opticks* (1714) made its first impact.[16] As Young

16. The response of eighteenth-century poets to the *Opticks* is well
documented in Marjorie Hope Nicolson's *Newton Demands the Muse*,

says, "Who sees, but is confounded, or convinc'd?/... /Mankind was sent into the World to *see*" (IX 861-3); and the verb "to see" in its various forms and synonyms of seeing occurs regularly throughout the poem, as some of the passages already quoted demonstrate. But more significant is the extent to which the two visions meet: optical vision, the mysteries and mechanics of which much exercised the speculations of Newton and his contemporaries, and spiritual and mystical vision. One cannot miss the real millenarian, or millennial fervour — the second of the two terms being used by Young himself:

> The Planets of each System represent
> Kind Neighbours; mutual Amity prevails;
> Sweet Interchange of Rays, receiv'd, return'd;
> Enlight'ning, and enlighten'd! All, at once,
> Attracking, and attracted! Patriot-like,
> None sins against the Welfare of the Whole;
> But their reciprocal, unselfish Aid,
> Affords an Emblem of *Millennial* Love.   (IX 698-705)

And this is a vision that expands in scale and exultation so that Young has no doubt that man's mortal aspirations are to be fulfilled among the stars:

Princeton, 1946. However, despite his interest in the astronomical evidences of God, Young on occasions sounds the traditional Christian warning against overestimating the value of learning: "Humble *Love*/And not proud *Reason*, keeps the Door of Heav'n;/*Love* finds Admission, where proud *Science* fails./Man's Science is the Culture of his Heart;/And not to lose his Plumbet in the Depths/Of *Nature*, or the more Profound of GOD./Either to know, is an Attempt that sets/ The Wisest on a Level with the Fool./To fathom *Nature* (ill-attempted *Here!*)/Past Doubt is deep Philosophy *Above*;/Higher Degrees in Bliss Archangels take,/As deeper learn'd; the Deepest, learning still./For, what a *Thunder* of Omnipotence/(So might I dare to speak!) is *seen* in All!/In *Man!* in *Earth!* In more amazing *Skies!*/Teaching this Lesson, *Pride* is loth to learn—/'Not *deeply* to *Discern*, not *much* to *Know*,/Mankind was born to WONDER, and ADORE' " (IX 1858-75).

How Great,
How Glorious, *then*, appears the *Mind* of Man,
When in it All the Stars, and Planets, roll!
And what it *seems*, it *is: Great* Objects make
Great Minds, enlarging as their Views enlarge;
Those still more Godlike, as *These* more Divine.
      And *more* divine than *These*, thou canst not see.
Dazled, o'erpow'r'd, with the delicious Draught
Of miscellaneous Splendors, how I reel
From Thought to Thought, inebriate, without End!
An *Eden*, This! a PARADISE *unlost*!
I meet the DEITY in ev'ry View,
And tremble at my Nakedness before Him!
O that I could but reach the *Tree of Life*!
For *Here* it grows, unguarded from our Taste;
No *Flaming Sword* denies our Entrance *Here*;
Would Man but gather, he might *live for ever*.   (IX 1061-77)

Throughout most of "NIGHT the NINTH and LAST" all three aspects of Young—the Christian apologist, the student of Newtonian science and the millenarian—are combined in a heady mixture of exhortation and rapture. Convincingly he persuades one that he is truly consumed by his imaginative experience and that he himself is in the condition of that spiritual being ("With Aspect mild, and elevated Eye/... seated on a Mount serene") whom he describes with such admiration in "NIGHT the EIGHTH"; a figure who "longs, in Infinite, to lose all Bound" (VIII 1083-1140).[17] So I would want to

17. It is hardly surprising in view of the *élan* and expansive measures of the poem that "boundless" and "unbounded" are favourite words throughout *Night Thoughts*, and, as we have seen, the first of these words has even found an appropriate place in the prose of *Conjectures*. Conceptually the notion of "boundlessness", as I will attempt to show on another occasion, accounts for the attraction and the fascination of Newtonian cosmology for so many eighteenth-century poets, since it is both limitless in its implications and orderly in its account of the unbounded universe. See Marjorie Hope Nicolson's comment on Edward Young and the "aesthetics of the infinite" in her *Mountain Gloom and Mountain Glory*, Ithaca/New York, 1959 (a book which touches at several places many of the themes of this essay): "No poet was ever more 'space intoxicated' than Edward

argue that although, as many scholars have already shown, Young is not particularly original in his material, and might be said to be entirely derivative, nevertheless he transforms, one might even appropriately say, transfigures his sources perhaps through the very recklessness of his rhetoric and the risk he runs in attracting ridicule.[18]

Young, nor did any other eighteenth-century poet or aesthetician equal him in his obsession with the 'psychology of infinity' — the effect of vastness and the vast upon the soul of man .... His canvas is interstellar space, his technique that of the cosmic voyagers, the 'soaring souls that sail among the spheres' " (pp. 362-3). The phrase from Young at the end of that quotation comes from the following passage: "Thou *Stranger* to the *World!* thy Tour *begin;/*Thy Tour thro' *Nature's* universal Orb./*Nature* delineates her whole Chart at large,/On soaring Souls, that sail among the Spheres" (IX 608-611).

18. Such sources, for instance, as Addison's *Spectator* 565 (Friday, July 9, 1714 in Everyman Library edn, reset 1945, 4, pp. 279-83) which allows us to identify "the Sage" of Young's "So distant (says the Sage), 'twere not absurd/To doubt, if Beams, set out at *Nature's* Birth,/Are yet arrived at this so foreign World" (IX 1227-9) as "*Huygenius*" who "carries this Thought so far, that he does not think it impossible there may be Stars whose Light is not yet travelled down to us, since their first Creation" (280). In view of n. 17, the following sentence of Addison's is particularly interesting: "There is no Question but the Universe has certain Bounds set to it; but when we consider that is the Work of infinite Power, prompted by infinite Goodness, with an infinite Space to exert it self in, how can our Imagination set any Bounds to it?" Since both writers are to some extent dealing with period commonplaces and reveal enthusiasms and responses that were widespread, drawing their knowledge from the same popularizing accounts, it is difficult to prove the direct influence of one writer upon the other. However, it is also unnecessary, since what the comparison mainly reveals is shared knowledge and interests, and the similarities and differences in tone and rhetorical effect. The last *Spectator* of all (635: Monday, December 30, 1714, Everyman edn, pp. 463-7) by Henry Grove may have been of equal relevance to Young's concerns and touches upon several of the themes of "Night 9", and shares something of the same rapture.

In *The Story of Utopias*, Lewis Mumford claims that "there is a gap in the Utopian tradition between the seventeenth century and the nineteenth", and adds: "Utopia, the place that must be built, faded into no-man's land, the spot to which one might escape."[19] Following our own experiences in encounters with Young's *Night Thoughts*, especially the last Night, perhaps one should broaden Mumford's proposition to suggest that the vision of Utopia in the eighteenth century went not only with Robinson Crusoe to his tropical island (which is what Mumford argues) but into the Newtonian skies as well. The excitement generated by Newton's work created an intoxicating brew of science and theology which stimulated a fervent though rational and consequently passive millenarianism, which preferred to wait for the inevitable transformations of progressive enlightenment rather than become involved in active campaigning. Therefore, to a large extent the millennium was to be regarded as an aesthetic experience, just as progress itself had become an artistic idea.

In those passages which have been quoted as representing Young's millennial fervour, there is a sense of both having your pie in the sky, and still being able to consume it down on earth. The "PARADISE *unlost*" is clearly in the heavens, but at the same time the vision sustains one now — "the Firmament" is "The noble Pasture of the *Mind*" (IX 1036-9) and "Affords an Emblem of *Millennial* Love" (IX 705): an emblem of what might be realized on earth should the mind continue to feed on this vision of heavens

19. Lewis Mumford, *The Story of Utopias*, New York, 1922; Viking Press paperback, 1969, p. 113, although Mumford's statement must be to some extent qualified by Armytage's account of eighteenth-century Utopian ambitions in *Heavens Below*, chs 5-7. Frank E. and Fritzie P. Manuel in *Utopian Thought in the Western World*, Cambridge, Mass., 1979, confirm the conclusions that one derives from other studies of the period (e.g. Peter Gay's *The Enlightenment*, New York & London, 1966 & 1970 and Paul Hazard, *European Thought in the Eighteenth Century*, Penguin edn, 1965) that the issue of Utopianism in the eighteenth century is mainly confined to discussions of progress and perfectibility (see notes 34, 36 & 38 below).

that has become so universal that its moral effects are felt
throughout civilized society. That Newtonian astronomy supports
a notion of improvement in the spiritual condition of mankind
might be one of the implications of Pope's famous couplet:
"Nature, and Nature's Laws lay hid in Night./God said, *Let
Newton Be!* and All was *Light.*" (1730) and indicates an
ameliorative attitude to the human condition that displaced earlier
kinds of Utopianism. Science, and a belief in scientific progress,
the development of an historical outlook which began to measure
present gains against the literal and cultural "backwardness" of
the past, all contribute to the suggestion that Utopia or the
millennium would eventually arrive as a destination determined by
history.

As Norman Cohn reminds us in the Introduction to *The Pursuit
of the Millennium*, "Millenarian sects or movements always picture
salvation as (a) collective, in the sense that it is to be enjoyed by the
faithful as a collectivity; (b) terrestrial, in the sense that it is to be
realized on this earth and not in some other-worldly heaven; (c)
imminent ...; (d) total ...; (e) miraculous ..."[20] And in *Millennium
and Utopia: A Study in the Background of the Idea of Progress*,
Ernest Lee Tuveson has demonstrated the transformation of ideas
about the Apocalypse, an interest which revived in the
Renaissance, particularly among reformers, into a confidence in a
progressive view of religion and the world. This resulted in the
eighteenth century in a number of important and influential works
which were assured that the scientific, philosophical and
theological progress of recent years would before very long issue in
a perfected state of life on earth and the beginning of God's
promised millennium.[21] It is unlikely that Edward Young was

20. Norman Cohn, *The Pursuit of the Millennium*, London, 1957;
paperback rpt, 1970, p. 13. As far as "(e) miraculous" is concerned
Young acknowledges that miracles have been necessary — "When
Mankind falls asleep,/A *Miracle* is sent, as an Alarm" (IX 1248-9) — but
he implies that in an Age taught by Newton miracles are superfluous,
since they "do not, *can* not, more amaze the Mind,/Than This, *call'd*
un-miraculous Survey,/If *duly* weigh'd, if *rationally* seen,/If seen with
human Eyes" (IX 1263-6).
21. Ernest Lee Tuveson, *Millennium and Utopia: A Study in the*

not familiar with Thomas Burnet's *Theory of the Earth* (1684-1690) and later books it provoked and inspired. Indeed, in a striking paragraph in his *Conjectures on Original Composition*, Young reveals millenarium sympathies couched in terms very like some of those one finds among Tuveson's witnesses:

> *since* an impartial Providence scatters talents indifferently, as thro' all orders of persons, so thro' all periods of time; *since* a marvelous light, unenjoy'd of old, is pour'd on us by revelation, with larger prospects extending our Understanding, with brighter objects enriching our Imagination, with an inestimable prize setting our Passions on fire, thus strengthening every power that enables composition to shine; *since*, there has been no fall in man on this side *Adam*, who left no works, and the works of all other antients are our auxiliars against themselves, as being perpetual spurs to our ambition, and shining lamps in our path to fame; *since*, this world is a school, as well for intellectual, as moral, advance; and the longer human nature is

---

Background of the Idea of Progress, Berkeley, 1949; paperback rpt, New York, 1964, pp. 104-12 and ch. IV: "Nature's Simple Plot: the Credo of Progress". See ch. 3 of the study by Margaret C. Jacob cited in n. 13 above which develops Tuveson and qualifies his interpretation, since she believes that "Ideas of progress in Anglican circles during the eighteenth century owe their origin more to smugness than to a rethinking of the meaning of the millennium" and "millenarianism died with the older generation of latitudinarians whose religious sensibility had been forged by the seventeenth-century revolution": however, "if [the Newtonians] imagined any sort of utopia it would have been a state where stability and order predominated, where the principles of Newton ruled nature and presented a model for the ordering of society" (*op. cit.*, 139-40). The peculiar fervour of Young's work, especially of "Night 9", seems to suggest that in the mid-eighteenth century it was still possible to combine something close to millennial rapture with an excited faith in science as a means of progressive revelation — science working with nature to ensure an increasing spiritual ascent: "*Nature* delights in Progress; in Advance/ From Worse to Better: But, when *Minds* ascend,/ Progress, in Part, depends upon *Themselves*./Heav'n aids Exertion; Greater makes the Great;/The *voluntary* Little lessens more:/O be a *Man!* and thou shalt be a *God!*/And *Half Self-made!* — Ambition how Divine" (IX 1960-66).

at school, the better scholar it should be; *since*, as the moral world expects its glorious Milennium, the world intellectual may hope, by the rules of analogy for some superior degrees of excellence to crown her latter scenes .... All these particulars, I say, consider'd, why should it seem altogether impossible, that heaven's latest editions of the human mind may be the most correct, and fair; that the day may come, when the moderns may proudly look back on the comparative darkness of former ages, on the children of antiquity; reputing *Homer*, and *Demosthenes*, as the dawn of divine Genius; and on *Athens* as the cradle of infant Fame ....[22]

Although George Eliot mocked Edward Young's curious combination of "worldliness and other-worldliness", this combination is, perhaps, just what creates the millennial tone in his poem. Young's heavens can be seen as representing the "vertical Utopia"[23] that transcends Utopia — the presence in the Ninth Night of the vision of the Apocalypse would tend to support this, as would the final paragraph of the poem in which Young addresses both God and Night, welcoming a future "When TIME .../.... /In NATURE's ample Ruins lies intomb'd;/And MID-NIGHT, *Universal* Midnight! reigns" (IX 2431-4). Equally one can see in his work an example of Utopia being replaced by the City of God.[24] But, however vertical Young's vision of the millennium may be; however it may resemble the City of God, it is achieved essentially by bringing closer the vision of the stars, the celestial panorama visible to man and compassed within the scope of his imagination by virtue of Newtonian physics and teleological speculation inspired by the New Philosophy. This displaced Utopia, this eighteenth-century version of the millennium, is to be

22. *Conjectures*, 72-4.

23. On apocalyptic transcendence to the "vertical Utopia" see Paul Tillich, "Critique and Justification of Utopia" in *Utopias and Utopian Thought*, ed. Frank E. Manuel, Beacon paperback, Boston, 1967, pp. 296-309.

24. This particular displacement is discussed by Northrop Frye in "Varieties of Literary Utopias" (*Utopias and Utopian Thought*, p. 34ff.).

158

established by the power of the telescope and faith in mathematical demonstration.[25]

The last lines of *Night Thoughts* just quoted seem also to be a rejoinder to Pope's pessimistically apocalyptic conclusion to *The Dunciad*:

Lo! thy dread Empire, CHAOS! is restor'd;
Light dies before thy uncreating word:
Thy hand, great Anarch! lets the Curtain fall;
And Universal Darkness buries All.

Daniel W. Odell has already written about "Young's *Night Thoughts* as an Answer to Pope's *Essay on Man*",[26] but Young could be implying at the end of his poem that Pope's City of Dreadful Night, his Dystopia of *The Dunciad*, will be redeemed by the approaching night that is not a chaos but an orderly transfiguration of planets and stars indicating God's order and control; a "verklärte" rather than an "aufgeklärte Nacht" — "a *new* Creation .../The World's great Picture soften'd to the Sight" (IX 1679-80) — representing the power of the Deity who at various times is addressed as "glorious Architect" (IX 766), "mighty BUILDER" (IX 817), "Great OECONOMIST" (IX 1089), "Great ARTIST" (IX 1322), "DIVINE INSTRUCTOR"(IX 1659) and "Great PROPRIETOR" (IX 1887):

Devotion! Daughter of Astronomy!
An *undevout* Astronomer is *mad*.
True; All Things speak a GOD; but in the Small,
Man traces out *Him*; in Great, *He* seizes Man;
Seizes, and elevates, and raps, and fills

25. In view of what he claims about blank verse (see above p. 141), the lack of fluency in Young's own unrhymed iambic pentameter, which tends to fall into couplets or even single lines, suggests that same mixture of worldliness and other-worldliness. If "blank verse, is verse unfallen, uncurst; verse reclaim'd, reinthron'd in the true *language of the Gods*", then Young's verse is not entirely reclaimed from the rhyming couplet, and still shows signs of its fallen, curst origins. As we have already seen (n. 6) it was left to Blake to attempt to achieve the final liberation and redemption from the tyranny of the line.

26. *SEL* XII (1972), 481-501.

159

With new Inquiries, 'mid Associates new.
Tell me, ye Stars! ye Planets! tell me, all
Ye Starr'd, and Planeted, Inhabitants! What is it?
What are these Sons of Wonder? Say, proud Arch!
(Within whose azure Palaces they dwell)
Built with Divine Ambition! in Disdain
Of Limit built! built in the Taste of Heaven!
Vast Concave! Ample Dome! Wast thou design'd
A meet Apartment for the DEITY?   (IX 772-85)

3.

If one detects in Young a critical response to Pope, equally one can
see why Blake would have responded to *Night Thoughts*.
Undoubtedly Blake would hardly have shared Young's particular
theological outlook, and would have disapproved fiercely of his
admiration for Newton, whom Blake repudiated as the arch
apostle of Urizenic materialism. But they would have joined faith
in the transformation of Albion. The millenarianism we detect in
Night Thoughts touches the visionary transformations of Blake's
Jerusalem, which records an abysm in the history of mankind when
"the Starry Heavens are fled from the mighty limbs of Albion"
(Plate 75:27), but ends:

All Human Forms identified, even Tree, Metal, Earth & Stone:
                                                        all
Human Forms identified, living, going forth & returning
                                                    wearied
Into the Planetary lives of Years, Months, Days & Hours;
                                                    reposing,
And then Awakening into his Bosom in the Life of Immortality.

And I heard the Name of their Emanations: they are named
                                                Jerusalem.
                                                (Plate 99)
But it is not only "The moral Emanations of the Skies" (IX 848),
which in one form or another, Blake and Young have in common;
one recalls that one of the illustrations that Blake did for "NIGHT
the SECOND" illustrated the following lines:

Measuring his Motions by revolving Spheres;
That Horologe Machinery Divine.
Hours, Days, and Months, and Years, his Children, play,
Like num'rous Wings, around him, as he flies:
Or, rather, as unequal Plumes they shape
His ample Pinions, swift as darted Flame,
To gain his Goal, to reach his antient Rest,
And join anew *Eternity* his Sire;
In his *Immutability* to nest,
When Worlds, that count his Circles *now*, unhing'd,
(Fate the loud Signal sounding) headlong rush
To *timeless* Night and Chaos, whence they rose.

(II 211-22)[27]

A curious combination this of Pope and Young: both to be redeemed by Blake as earlier he had attempted to save Milton from his errors. In this way, millenniums and Utopias touch, and the nineteenth century, having lost faith in the redemptive values and power of Newtonian physics, strives to salvage what it can from the eighteenth. In literature such eschatological dramas may be necessary to rescue the imagination: chiliasm exploding the conventions and errors of outdated structures of feeling, thought and form.

Perhaps one way of describing the essentially passive Millenium of the eighteenth century is as the dissolution of the earthly in the heavenly or as the permeation of the celestial in the material. One of the arguments that emerges from this consideration of Edward Young, and the last Night of *Night Thoughts* especially, is that the Rector of Welwyn is an essential figure in the transformation of Milton's physically hard-edged universe created in *Paradise Lost*, where despite the poet's (and Raphael's) refusal to confirm the Copernican system, one experiences a material cosmography of solid bodies and precise locations and distances,

27. The first four Nights of *Night Thoughts* as published by Richard Edwards with Blake's illustrations in 1797 is available in a facsimile edition ("reproduced at 65% of the original size") from Dover Publications, New York, 1975. The illustration in question is p. 26; however, the text there has been normalized, and the one quoted here is from the 1768 issue of *Night Thoughts*.

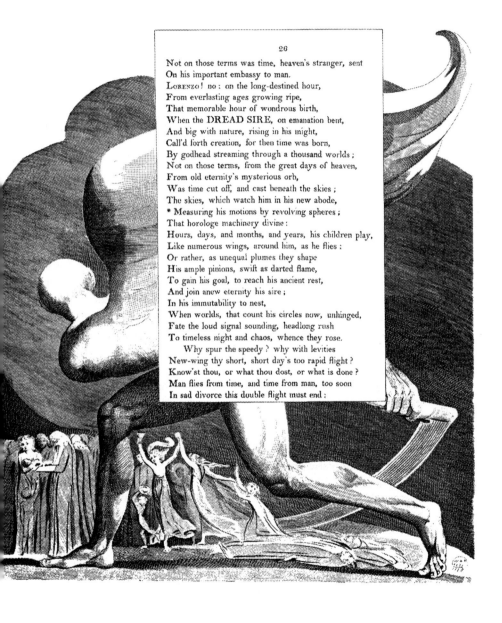

Not on those terms was time, heaven's stranger, sent
On his important embassy to man.
LORENZO! no : on the long-destined hour,
From everlasting ages growing ripe,
That memorable hour of wondrous birth,
When the DREAD SIRE, on emanation bent,
And big with nature, rising in his might,
Call'd forth creation, for then time was born,
By godhead streaming through a thousand worlds ;
Not on those terms, from the great days of heaven,
From old eternity's mysterious orb,
Was time cut off, and cast beneath the skies ;
The skies, which watch him in his new abode,
* Measuring his motions by revolving spheres ;
That horologe machinery divine :
Hours, days, and months, and years, his children play,
Like numerous wings, around him, as he flies :
Or rather, as unequal plumes they shape
His ample pinions, swift as darted flame,
To gain his goal, to reach his ancient rest,
And join anew eternity his sire ;
In his immutability to nest,
When worlds, that count his circles now, unhinged,
Fate the loud signal sounding, headlong rush
To timeless night and chaos, whence they rose.

    Why spur the speedy ? why with levities
New-wing thy short, short day's too rapid flight ?
Know'st thou, or what thou dost, or what is done ?
Man flies from time, and time from man, too soon
In sad divorce this double flight must end ;

into the spacially obliterated and temporally compressed world of Blake's Prophetic works. This may have been achieved by a switch, in the words of Josephine Miles's description of "The Sublime Poem", to the "vocabulary of cosmic passion and sense impression".[28] Milton, despite his doubts as to whether the sun or the earth is in the centre, takes the universe for granted as a stage for his epic narrative. Despite the gratitude and wonder which Raphael seeks to stir in Adam and Milton in the reader at the glories of God's creation, the tone of even the most exalted parts of *Paradise Lost* conveys a steady sense of this is how it was at the time of creation and, allowing for the deleterious consequences of the Fall, this is how on the whole it continues to be. In no way could one call the description of the creation of the sun and moon and the stars in Book VII (339ff.) matter of fact, but the poet's command of syntax and metre and the confidence of diction ensure a stability for the action that firmly locates it in space and time, as the Lord with "the golden compasses, prepared/In God's eternal store, to circumscribe/This universe and all created things..." (VII 225-7). Whether one believes that Milton gives an adequate visual account or not, the cosmos is evidently there, capacious but ruggedly furnished. This derives not so much from

28. Josephine Miles, *Eras and Modes in English Poetry*, Berkeley and Los Angeles, 1957, p. 57. This is her second distinguishing characteristic of the sublime poem. The first helps to account for the manner by which Edward Young hopes to escape the curse of fallen verse even though he is neither fluent in the blank verse styles of Shakespeare and Milton before him, nor able to anticipate the ease of Cowper and Wordsworth at their best. Professor Miles describes the "cumulative phrasal structure" of the sublime poem, "its piling up of nouns and epithets, participles and compounds, with a very minimum of clausal subordination and active verbs". The third characteristic she notes is an "internal rather than external patterning of sound, the interior tonal shadings and onomatopoeias of its unrhymed verse". Together with the strong visual reinforcement of Young's verse — the italics and capitals and exclamation marks which one finds in the eighteenth-century texts — one may agree that "these major traits make for an exceptionally panoramic and panegyric verse, emotional, pictorial, noble, universal, and tonal, rising to the height of heaven and of feeling in the style traditionally known as grand or sublime".

the visual description as such as from the confidence with which everyone from God the Father downwards assumes the existence of the material world which they have to negotiate and survive in.[29]

When we come to Blake and the other Romantics, this confidence in the physical has evaporated. Blake's work throughout represents an epic lament for the binding of man in a space and time from which only his threatened and endangered imagination can free him. Space and time are manifestations of the usurping power of Urizenic mathematics;[30] and with space and time go the chains and manacles, which are as inevitable as the transferring of God's golden compasses to Urizen and Newton.[31]

29. It is the very materiality of the War in Heaven in *Paradise Lost* VI which causes Milton and his readers particular problems: if spiritual beings cannot be irreparably damaged by material assault they cannot, in fact, be defeated either physically or morally. Therefore the battles are charades demonstrating a moral disposition, but otherwise inconsequential.

30. See Donald Ault, *Visionary Physics: Blake's Response to Newton*, Chicago and London, 1974. Ault suggests that it was the very imaginative appeal of Newton's system that inspired Blake to attempt to create "a new Imaginative countervision" (p.162). Indeed what needs to be investigated is the role that mathematics played in dissolving the physical universe that we find in Milton into the fluid world of Blake's prophetic poetry. Already one senses with Pope's depiction of "Mad *Mathesis*" who "alone was unconfin'd,/Too mad for mere material chains to bind,/Now to pure Space lifts her extatic stare,/Now running round the Circle, finds it square" (*The Dunciad* IV 31-4) the recognition of a world coming into existence in which abstraction and theory through the imagination threatened a man's faith in the secure nature of matter. In such a state it is no surprise that "*Mystery*" should "to *Mathematics* fly!" (IV 647).

31. In two of Blake's most famous designs, the print usually known as "The Ancient of Days" (also used as the frontispiece to *Europe*, 1794) and the large colour print of "Newton" (1795), the compasses that Milton derived for his account of the Creation from Proverbs (8:27), have been put into the hands of a Urizenic figure in the one print and of Newton at the bottom of the Sea of Time and Space in the other. Martin Butlin notes that "the composition of 'The Ancient of Days' is based on the frontispiece to the de luxe 1729 edition of Motte's translation of Newton's *Principia*" (*William Blake*, Tate Gallery Catalogue, 1978, pp. 52-53). So in both designs Newton is implicated.

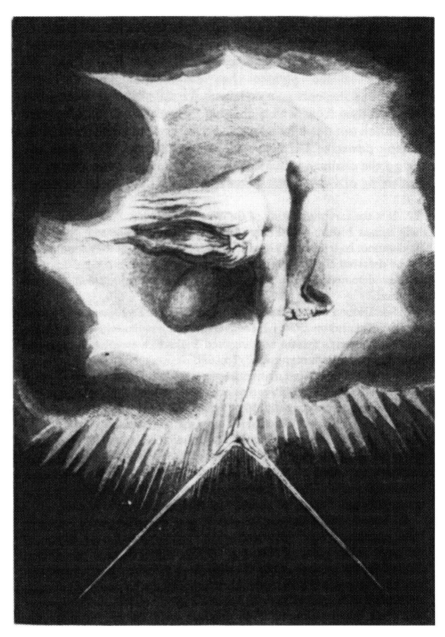

Frontispiece to Blake's *Europe*

Blake's Colour Print *Newton*

To Blake imprisonment and freedom are internal states of being; political repression is the outward sign of such "mind-forg'd manacles" ("London" in *Songs of Experience*). Eternity is also within; and Paradise is both lost and regained within the individual. Each man restores Albion for himself; were all men able to restore the Albion within him then Britain too, and the world, would be restored to Eternity.

Young, possibly with other eighteenth-century practitioners of the Sublime, represents a halfway stage between Milton and Blake. With him, we are not made aware so much of the cosmos itself as of the poet's exclamatory feelings being projected into boundless space: the universe with its celestial cycles and machinery of nicely calculated motions is rather like a cosmic gymnasium for the exercise of emotional muscles. Although the universe has not yet been interiorized, it is presented as an extension of Young's sensibility, an enlarged ego-chamber; one could equally say that it possesses him or he possesses it. In any event the universe "out there" does not seem to have an independent existence, as it still does have in Milton (despite attempts to show that *Paradise Lost*, too, is mainly designed to dramatize psychological space). Young's feelings about the universe that Newton has constructed for him are those of a colonist. Whereas Blake is constantly seeking to demonstrate how the fourfold vision of redeemed man is available within us if only we will cleanse "the doors of perception" (*The Marriage of Heaven and Hell*, Plate 14) and keep our Zoas in their places; Young is the first to imply that if a "PARADISE *unlost*" is in the heavens, at the end of a telescope, it is also ours to be gathered through the eye into the bosom of our feelings.[32] He is equally drawn to a millennium out of time or at the end of time and a perfected state of being within time, which may amount to the same thing, since "boundless *Space* .../... suggests the Sister-Thought/Of boundless *Time*" (IX 1174-6).

With the general assumption of the merging of the subjective

---

32. On Blake's use of Young's *Night Thoughts* as a parodic source for *The Four Zoas*, see John Howard, *Infernal Poetics: Poetic Structure in Blake's Lambeth Prophecies*, London and Toronto, 1984, pp. 217-19. Howard notes especially Blake's attack on Young's concern with "futurity" by identifying it as an obsession of Urizen's.

and the objective, in Romanticism it is difficult to judge to what extent we are to believe that the re-attainment of Paradise or the creation of Utopia has been achieved or is within sight of achievement in what we like to term "the real world", or is to be celebrated as a state of mind, symbolically, within. Wordsworth emphasizes how we should look to Nature to cultivate a "spontaneous wisdom" within us, to teach us "more of man,/Of moral evil and of good,/Than all the sages can" ("The Tables Turned" in *Lyrical Ballads*). The implication of Wordsworth's work is that each of us, through an attentive and receptive heart should cultivate an inner security able to withstand the loss of hope and eventually remove from society the tensions that promote revolution. This belief that the world will improve in accordance with the enlarged vision and hearts of individuals need not be seen only as an evasion of demands for social change, but also as an inevitable outcome of the Romantic poet's aspirations and his essential trust in the pre-eminence of the individual's sensibility, which so potently blends his perception of the external world with his empathic response.[33]

Even in the case of such a "poet of perfectibility" as Shelley,[34] it

33. Evidence for the merging of the objective and subjective is to be found throughout Wordsworth's *Prelude*, but one of the most directly graphic instances is to be found in "Tintern Abbey": "Once again/Do I behold these steep and lofty cliffs,/Which on a wild secluded scene impress/Thoughts of more deep seclusion" (4-7), where we find "cliffs" impressing "thoughts" on a "scene". It is in the same poem (105-6) that Wordsworth acknowledges "a close resemblance to an admirable line of Young, the exact expression of which I cannot recollect". It is particulary relevant in the present context that Wordsworth's lines — "of all the mighty world/Of eye and ear, both what they half create,/And what perceive" (the note is appended to the line ending with "create") — echo Young's lines from "NIGHT the SIXTH" of *Night Thoughts*, in which he describes "Our *Senses*, as our *Reason* ... divine" taking in "the landscape [*sic*] of the World,/At a small Inlet, which a Grain might close,/[to] half create the wond'rous World they see" (VI 425-7). It is not surprising that this phrase should lodge in the memory of a Romantic poet only too conscious of the collaboration of vision, consciousness, and the external object in creating our sense of material reality.

34. The description is from J.B. Bury, *The Idea of Progress*, London,

is difficult to see how his vision of the transformed universe in the last act of *Prometheus Unbound* could be conceived of as actually being effected in reality (one is drawn to say, "for real"). The ethereal lyricism is stirring enough to colour the mind and imagination of the reader, but how the love which Earth declares "interpenetrates my granite mass" (IV 370) might actually shift the balance of power in the world or help to reshape institutions could never be demonstrated. However, one should add, that it is Shelley, the acknowledged heir of Godwin, and the unconscious successor of Blake, who became the Romantic poet who actually inspired at least one utopian community in the nineteenth century.[35]

The other Romantic who had direct political influence was, of course, Coleridge. It is not clear whether the concept of Pantisocracy or its failure tells one most about the nature of Romantic utopianism. But it is not this early failure which is most significant in considering Coleridge's political influence, whatever its consequence might have been for his poetic career as the laureate who celebrated a "stately pleasure dome" that he himself

---

1932; paperback rpt, Dover Publications, New York, 1955, p. 233. William Godwin as an intermediary between eighteenth-century French ideas of perfectibility and Shelley is implied in Bury's discussion of "The Theory of Progress in England" (ch. XII). For a recent discussion of Rousseau's "concept of perfectibility" as coming "as close as possible to supplying a purely formal ... definition of man", and its ambiguous relationship to Romanticism and Romantic creation myths, see Paul A. Cantor, *Creature and Creator: Myth-making and English Romanticism*, Cambridge, 1984, pp. 4-25. In the Introduction to his translation of the *Discours sur l'origine de l'inégalité* (1754), Maurice Cranston reminds us that Rousseau's "'perfectibilité'... means not at all a potentiality for perfection, but simply a capacity for self-betterment" (A *Discourse on Inequality*, Penguin, 1984, p. 33).

35. See *Heavens Below*, p. 199. Art as a substitute for active Utopianism (see above p. 154) is reflected in Cantor's consideration of the third stage of Romantic myth-making: "the stage portrayed in the apocalyptic phase of Romantic myth, symbolizing some form of revolution, originally conceived as coming about through political means, but later thought of as a more purely spiritual liberation, accomplished through art itself" (p. 22).

could not build and voyages that ended disastrously. It is in his later prose writings that he expressed his faith in the progress which he identified with the hope that was one of the "positive ends" of the state.[36] Indeed Coleridge's later vision of the efficacious role of the clerisy suggests the possible translation of Utopia into every village of the land:

> That to every parish throughout the kingdom there is transplanted a germ of civilization; that in the remotest villages there is a nucleus, round which the capabilities of the place may crystallise and brighten; a model sufficiently superior to excite, yet sufficiently near to encourage and facilitate, imitation; *this* unobtrusive, continuous agency of a Protestant Church Establishment, *this* it is, which the patriot, and the philanthropist, who would fain unite the love of peace with the faith in the progressive amelioration of mankind, cannot estimate at too high a price...[37]

"The progressive amelioration of mankind" gives us the clue to the essential balanced attitude of the Romantics and their immediate successors to utopian notions. The eighteenth century had so effectively established, in theory and practice, a belief in progress

36. See *The Collected Works of Samuel Taylor Coleridge*, 6, *Lay Sermons*, ed. R.J. White, London, 1972, p. 216. Cf. n. 6 on p. 63 of the same volume, where one of Coleridge's annotations is quoted: "... for man is destined to be guided by higher principles, by universal views, which can never be fulfilled in this state of existence, — by a spirit of progressiveness which can never be accomplished, for then it would cease to be." The two works in this volume, *The Statesman's Manual* and *A Lay Sermon*, date respectively from 1816 and 1817.

37. *The Collected Works of Samuel Taylor Coleridge*, 10, *On the Constitution of the Church and State*, ed. John Colmer, London, 1976, p. 75. The work was first published in 1830. For Coleridge's earlier poetic feelings about Utopian schemes see his sonnet on "Pantisocracy" (1794), where in 11. 7-9 he sounds a note not so very different from the final paragraph of "Kubla Khan", which suggests a possible association between the underlying sentiments of the two texts. A second sonnet "On the Prospect of establishing a Pantisocracy in America" is only uncertainly attributed to Coleridge (Coleridge, *Poetical Works*, ed. Ernest Hartley Coleridge, Oxford Standard Authors edn, 1967 rpt, pp. 68-9).

and destroyed the "illusion of Finality",[38] that no imaginative man, let alone any poet, would wish to commit himself to some scheme of things that would actually seek to achieve a conclusive end. Romantic assumptions of organicism and vitalism involved the creed that life was continually renewing itself, remaking itself, even evolving. Constant change, perpetual improvement, evolution replaced utopianism as an image of a once-for-all perfected society. The dynamic model of change taken for granted in Romantic writing was later to be impersonalized as process, dialectical and determined, in later nineteenth-century thought. The Romantics interiorize Paradise (as Milton's Michael had predicted: *PL* XII 587); their successors (including Karl Marx) on occasions spoke of Utopia as an extremely distant end of historical process: a projection into historical space of the unlost Paradise within. Modern industrial society was not achieved without destructive and painful side effects which spawned all those many later nineteenth-century utopian communities and fictions that attempted to capture the benefits of technology without the traumas, leaving its citizens free to cultivate the sensibilities that poets like Edward Young had first begun to exercise.[39]

Leiden   C.C. Barfoot

---

38. Bury, p. 351. For another account of eighteenth-century considerations of perfectibility and the movement of the nineteenth century to social Darwinism, see Sidney Pollard, *The Idea of Progress*, London, 1968, chs II & III. Pollard notes that "Godwin has been called a Utopian rather than a believer in progress, but his state of perfection was a long way off, and required a slow process of evolution and amelioration"; and goes on to quote Godwin to demonstrate that it was he who "translated the French idea of 'perfectibility' most correctly in terms of evolution rather than Utopia" (pp. 70-71).

39. And later writers such as James Joyce continued to emulate in the first half at least of the twentieth century. Towards the end of Bloomsday (16th June 1904) Leopold Bloom and Stephen Dedalus emerging "from obscurity by a passage from the rere of the house into the penumbra of the garden" were confronted by the spectacle of "The heaventree of stars hung with humid nightblue fruit". Further contemplation and self-interrogation leads Bloom logically to conclude "That it was not a

heaventree, not a heavengrot, not a heavenbeast, not a heavenman. That it was a Utopia, there being no known method from the known to the unknown: an infinity, renderable equally finite by the suppositious probable apposition of one or more bodies equally of the same and of different magnitudes: a mobility of illusory forms immobilised in space, remobilised in air: a past which possibly had ceased to exist as the present before its future spectators had entered actual present existence" (*Ulysses*, Penguin edn, 1969, pp. 619-22). Cf. n. 18 above: does the spirit of Edward Young live on in Leopold Bloom and in Joyce, his creator?

WOMEN AND UTOPIA:
SOME REFLECTIONS AND EXPLORATIONS

Adopting one of the rhetorical stances of utopian writing, the enumeration of negatives, let me begin by stating that I am no specialist in utopian thought, that I am no dreamer or visionary, no philosopher, no social reformer, nor a radical feminist either. Yet, when the idea for a conference on "Utopia and Dystopia" was launched I felt impelled to try and offer a more or less feminist contribution. "Utopianism", after all, has been attracting a good deal of attention in contemporary Women's Studies, and the occasion of this conference created a welcome opportunity to address my own comparative ignorance of the field. This grew the more urgent as I encountered reactions to my topic which ranged from the polite raising of eyebrows to outright incredulity. And although honesty bids me to confess that such reactions were given by both men and women, male scepticism predominated: "Women and Utopia?" — slight pause - "But I thought you were a Richardsonian?" — pause — "Is there a connection between women and Utopia?" — and then a final most dramatic pause producing: "Did ever any woman conceive of a Utopia?"

None of these queries was altogether unexpected. Samuel Richardson, to whom I have given my best energies these past few years, may indeed seem very far removed from the subject. After all, being married to Mr B. would nowadays strike most of us as about the most limited woman's dream one could think of, even if it was Pamela's ambition, as perfect wife and mother, to set the world an example of all her domestic arrangements, and so improve the human lot.

Still, on second thoughts Richardson's works provide as useful a starting-point as any. His speciality is of course the world of women, and his explorations of that world guide the reader of his novels to a recognition of their utopian as well as dystopian domesticities. Moreover, in *Clarissa* and in *Sir Charles Grandison* the male protagonists briefly entertain specific utopian schemes in which women take up a central position. Although presented and described by the heroes of the novels, the two schemes focus on issues and preoccupations which, interestingly enough, have played an important role in the utopian dreams and speculations of women themselves, both before and after Richardson.[1] One of these projects involves the institution or, as Lovelace views it, the life-imprisonment of marriage, the other concerns the establishment of all-female societies — for educational purposes, as a refuge from the world of men, and as an ideally harmonious way of life.

Thus Grandison, amidst his company of admiring women, proposes the establishment of protestant nunneries, being well-organised societies of single women of unblemished reputation which might grow into: "a *national* good, and particularly a seminary for good wives, and the institution a stand for virtue, in an age given up to luxury, extravagance, and amusements little less than riotous."[2] Such a retreat would prove "a blessing to the Kingdom", for its inmates would always be allowed to leave it, continuing their good works in the less exclusive circles of society at large. Clearly, the ideas of Sir Charles and his mentor Dr Bartlett were to be commended and promoted by men and women alike. Rousseau, for one, would no doubt have supported them, as long as everyone remembered that the education and duties of women should "always be relative to men".[3]

On the other hand, Lovelace's scheme, the annual change of marriage partners "every Valentine's Day", ought to be condemned as the poisonous fruit of his hot fancy. The plan is devised on the day on which he rapes Clarissa, and he describes its larger benefits in some detail:

1. See below for a brief discussion of three such instances in the work of Mary Astell, Mary Wollstonecraft, and George Eliot.
2. *Sir Charles Grandison*, ed. Jocelyn Harris, London, 1972, Part II, p. 355.
3. From *l'Emile*, as cited by Eleanor Flexner, "Ideas in *A Vindication of the Rights of Woman*", in Mary Wollstonecraft, *A Vindication of the Rights of Woman*, ed. Carol H. Poston, New York, 1975, p. 233.

Such a change would be a means of annihilating, absolutely annihilating, four or five very atrocious and capital sins. *Rapes*, vulgarly so called; adultery, and fornication; nor would *polygamy* be panted after. Frequently it would prevent *murders* and *duelling*: hardly any such thing as *jealousy* (the cause of shocking violences) would be heard of: and hypocrisy between man and wife be banished from the bosoms of each.

In addition, domestic quarrels would decrease, for men and women would have to be on their best behaviour "either to reduce a renewal with the old love or to recommend themselves to a new". Always concerned about the interests of women, Lovelace notes that they "will have equal reason with the men to be pleased with [the arrangement]". No one could ever get bored, "the galant and generous last partings between man and wife" would form charming subjects for conversation, and the newspapers would be filled with equally charming gossip, "all the world their readers". Parsons and lawyers need never fear unemployment, and the only sufferers would be "the physical tribe", since "fresh health and fresh spirits ... would perpetually flow in, and the joys of *expectation*, the highest of all our joys, would invigorate and keep all alive". "In short", Lovelace concludes his fantasy, "a total alteration for the better, in the *morals* and *way of life* in both sexes, must, in a very few years, be the consequence of such a salutary law."[4]

Now it would be Charles Fourier who might have expressed his support and approval, since Lovelace's plan for the pursuit of happiness, if not exactly a system of free love, is akin to the nineteenth-century Frenchman's vision of future human bliss in what he called the "state of Harmony". Here the highest good consisted in the multiplication of amorous relations, in "satisfying and experiencing an immense quantity of passions".[5] The enemy, just as in Lovelace's case, was boredom, dullness, repression, and

4. *Clarissa*, introd. John Butt, Everyman's Library edn,1962, III, pp. 181-83.

5. As quoted by Frank E. Manuel and Fritzie P. Manuel, *Utopian Thought in the Western World*, Cambridge, Mass., 1979, p. 661.

these could only be defeated through being subversive, extravagant, and endlessly inventive.

The annual change of mates proposed by Richardson's hero, benefiting both sexes equally, and Fourier's vision of a "nouveau monde amoureux" are a far cry from classic utopian thinking. Love is hardly an issue in More's *Utopia*, where marriage relations appear sensible and dispassionate, perhaps a trifle dull, and where sexual transgression is severely punished. Women and their concerns play, of course, a subordinate role in Utopia's strictly patriarchal organisation. For although every Utopian, irrespective of sex, works at farming and is taught a special trade, and both sexes are given military training, authority within the household plainly resides with the man. Equality can only go so far, and so, before religious feasts "wives kneel down at home before their husbands ... to confess all their sins ... and ask to be forgiven", the husbands needing no such domestic cleansing before they enter into their religious devotions.[6]

Further reflections on "Women and Utopia" might at this point lead to the proposition that not until the eighteenth century do the special needs and concerns of women begin to gain prominence in the utopian dreams of men.[7] If we grant his works a utopian dimension, this could be said of Samuel Richardson. It certainly is true of several eighteenth-century French utopias. In their comprehensive survey of *Utopian Thought in the Western World* F.E. and F.P. Manuel discuss a number of these, drawing my attention in particular to Louis Rustaing de St Jory's *Les femmes militaires: Relation historique d'une isle nouvellement découverte*, published in Amsterdam in 1736. Here is depicted a society of total equality between the sexes, in education, in governance, in war, in love. Male and female alternate on the throne, the women electing the male, the male electing the female ruler. In the Isle of

6. *Utopia*, trans. and introd. Paul Turner, Penguin edn, 1965, p. 126.

7. Plato's *Republic* forms no exception really, despite its advocacy of the political and sexual equality of women, admitting them as members of the class of guardians (Book V). See for a brief but interesting discussion of this Elaine Hoffman Baruch, "Women in Men's Utopias", in *Women in Search of Utopia: Mavericks and Mythmakers*, eds Ruby Rohrlich and Elaine Hoffman Baruch, New York, 1984, pp. 209-18.

Manghalour everyone is gracious, wise, generous, and while love is taken very seriously, equality among the inhabitants has reached such a pitch that even right-left dominance has disappeared: everyone is ambidextrous. No man could possibly surpass St Jory in his desire to teach equality between the sexes in rights and privileges, in skills and capacities, and, not the least, in personal relations. Thus he attempted to enlighten the world, as the Manuels put it, about "the injustice of woman's subordination to the caprices of men and the legal order they have imposed"[8] — and all this some fifty years before the French Revolution.

But what about the women themselves? Did they or didn't they dream of better worlds, whether of the Cockaygne, arcadian, or millenarian type? Do they or don't they imagine ideal societies, perfect moral commonwealths, or utopias in the stricter sense, "total, perfect, ordered"?[9]

The question is a large one, and only a limited response can be provided here. Even so, when we consider present-day developments the answer must clearly be in the affirmative. As I have indicated in my opening remarks, "utopianism" is a major concern in recent feminist writing, especially in France and America, the approach varying greatly with respect to form and tone. France, as it has often done before, has taken the lead in radical theory, while American women seem to be more practically inclined, not only experimenting in sisterhood communities, but also producing numerous concrete utopian fictions. At the same time American critical and scholarly efforts are not only directed at "reconstructing" literary tradition, but also at disseminating the ideas and writings of the French avant-garde in feminist journals and publications. Thus we can read in more accessible if perhaps less elegantly playful English, the strange and provocative utterances of women such as Monique Wittig, Hélène Cixous, Anne Leclerc, Luce Irigaray — writing their "écriture féminine" as

8. Manuel and Manuel, p. 537.
9. These categories are discussed by J.C. Davis, *Utopia and the Ideal Society: A Study of English Utopian Writing 1516-1700*, Cambridge, 1981, pp. 11-40.

they explore the unknown, envision a new way of being, and desire a new way of writing.

"La femme trouvera l'inconnu!" Rimbaud prophesied as early as 1871, "Elle trouvera des choses étranges, insondables, repoussantes, délicieuses". It is a prediction quoted with some reservation by Simone de Beauvoir in *Le deuxieme sexe* in 1949. By the seventies, however, such reservations have been cast aside: "I think the future belongs to women", Marguerite Duras declared in an interview in 1975, "Men have been completely dethroned. Their rhetoric is stale, used up. We must move on to the rhetoric of women, one that is anchored in the organism, in the body."[10] Also in the mid-seventies Hélène Cixous published her influential "Le rire de la méduse" (1975) and "Le sexe ou la tête" (1976), in which she moves away from what are referred to as the "phallocentric values" of the patriarchal past and its institutions, including language itself with its treacherous signifiers and authoritarian signifieds. Proposing a female "elsewhere", a land of boundless "giving", Cixous affirms, explores, and practices the differences and unforeseeables of a "feminine textual body". It is a genuine temptation to surrender to the Siren song of this new rhetoric, through endless recitation, but I am afraid that really would lead us too far out of the way.

As has already been suggested, American feminists interested in utopianism appear less abstract, less extreme, less "flighty" shall we say, although not necessarily less imaginative. Their activities include the revealing of a hitherto obscured tradition through rediscovering and reissuing feminist utopias of the past. The three fictions of Charlotte Perkins Gilman are a case in point. *Herland*, originally published in 1915 and describing a peaceful, prosperous matriarchal society visited by three representative American males, has become by far the best known of these.[11] Similar scholarly interest in reconsidering the past and exploring its implications for particular developments in the current scene, has resulted in the publication of a volume entitled *Daring to Dream*

10. From an interview by Susan Husserl-Kapit in *Signs*, Winter 1975; repr. in *New French Feminisms: An Anthology*, eds Elaine Marks and Isabelle de Courtivron, New York, 1981, p. 238.
11. *Herland:* introd. Ann J. Lane, New York, 1979.

(1984). Chiefly an anthology of "Utopian Stories by United States Women: 1836-1919", the book includes an annotated bibliography that takes us to the present day and consists of no less than 137 Utopias written by American women since 1836. Forty per cent of these tales are defined as "feminist" by the editor, in that they "provide a critique of women's status, offer alternative ways of being female, recommend reforms benefiting women, place women centrally in the plot, [and] show either sex atypically". Closely reflecting developments in the women's movement, the earlier works address issues such as female education, marriage reform, and women's rights; more recently, according to the editor of the volume, the approach has become more "holistic", and the focus has shifted to "communitarian values, nature-awareness, and spiritual quest".[12] Several of these more recent works (as well as Gilman's *Herland*) present chaste, all-female societies where procreation is achieved through some form of parthenogenesis — curiously enough a development already envisioned by Auguste Comte in the 1850s. In his positivist polity, where altruism has replaced self-love, sensuous desires, the passions, will gradually weaken, "disposing man to appreciate woman more". And while "the participation of the female sex in human reproduction would continually increase", it would "ultimately reach a point where birth would emanate from woman alone".[13]

Whatever one's attitude towards contemporary feminism may be, it should be clear that Utopia has been a rich and fruitful land for many feminist writers and critics, hospitable not only to the wild dreams and theoretical projections of the French, but also to the literary ambitions and intellectual explorations of writers such as Ursula Le Guin, Joanna Russ, Marge Piercy, and, in England, Doris Lessing. The sheer profusion and variety are impressive. It certainly makes one wonder why none of this material is mentioned or even hinted at in the Manuels' large volume on *Utopian Thought*, not even in the "Epilogue", where the authors reflect on the present state of affairs.

12. *Daring to Dream*, ed. and introd. Carol Farley Kessler, Boston, 1984, pp. 1-25.
13. Cited by Manuel and Manuel, p. 732.

All the same, I cannot quite call myself a devotee of current feminist utopianism yet. One reason for this may be that I have internalized the ideas and values of my patriarchal environment to such an extent that it has rendered me incapable of fully accepting the radical implications of "écriture féminine", no matter how seductive. Another explanation may be my strong dislike of science-fiction. Many of the tales by Russ, Le Guin et al., heavily rely on the employment of elements such as time and space travel, sex change, and other phenomena which are either not yet of our world or too recent to have struck deep into our literature. And although, as a teacher of literature, I can have no objection to speculative and didactic discourse, I do prefer it in a less fanciful, less technological form.

This inevitably draws me back to the past and, as is only appropriate for a conference sponsored by the British Council, to three British women: Mary Astell, Mary Wollstonecraft, and Marian Evans, or, as she wished to be known, George Eliot. The convergence in my mind of these particular writers in relation to the theme of "Women and Utopia" — as personal touchstones in largely unfamiliar territory — was first of all inspired by Richardson. Several of the women with whom he conversed and corresponded and who influenced the debates on love and friendship, marriage and female education conducted in the pages of *Sir Charles Grandison*, knew Astell's work intimately. Thus Sir Charles's plan for the establishment of "protestant nunneries" may well have been derived, directly or indirectly, from Astell's *Serious Proposal*.[14] The vicissitudes of love and friendship, female education and the institution of marriage are also among Wollstonecraft's central concerns. And while George Eliot is of course by far the more complex thinker and writer, she nonetheless shares these same interests. In addition, a recent reading of her novels led me to the conviction that "utopianism" would be a rewarding topic to pursue in the study of Eliot.

I shall, then, briefly consider what could be called the "utopian propensity" in the two Mary's, and conclude this paper with the

14. Jocelyn Harris, "Samuel Richardson, Mary Astell, and the Protestant Nunnery", ASECS Convention, Atlanta, 1979.

beginnings of an exploration of the "utopian impulse" in George Eliot's writing, especially in *Romola*.[15]

2.

Mary Astell is chiefly known for two works. The first, *A Serious Proposal to Ladies for the Advancement of Their True and Greatest Interest* (1694), envisions the establishment of a "monastery", or "religious retirement" for women which, according to Astell, would be "the most probable method to amend the present, and improve the future age". Here, through study, prayer, and good works, women would develop their minds through substantial reading and intellectual conversation. "Happy Retreat!" we hear Astell exclaim at one point, simultaneously speaking to her female readers:

> Which will be the introducing you to such a *Paradise* as your Mother *Eve* forfeited, where you shall feast on pleasures that do not, like those of the world, disappoint your expectations, pall your appetites, and by the disgust they give you, put you on the fruitless search after new delights, which when obtained are as empty as the former; but such as will make you truly happy *now*, and prepare you to be *perfectly* so hereafter ... In fine, the place to which you are invited will be a type and antipast of Heaven.[16]

Nothing came of the project, but Astell did write several other tracts. *Some Reflections Upon Marriage* (1700), addresses the authorized abuses, the tyranny and degradation inherent in marriage. Even under the best of circumstances, Astell argues, wives are slaves and, like slaves, for their own comfort's sake, they would be wisest to exercise discretion and patience, to submit and to endure. This bitterly ironic pamphlet ends on a curious utopian note. Invoking the protection of the "great Queen", in the exalted terms of a mother-goddess, Astell bids adieu to "the Liberties ... of the Moiety of Mankind. To all the great Things that Women might

15. Both suggestive phrases have been carefully borrowed, one from Manuel and Manuel, the other from Keith Thomas.
16. As quoted in *Before Their Time: Six Women Writes of the Eighteenth Century*, ed. Katharine M. Rogers, New York, 1979, p. 30.

perform", if such protection were denied. In the event, her final adieu would be:

> To the Women's tracing a new Path to Honor, in which none shall walk but such as scorn to Cringe in order to Rise, and who are proof both against giving and receiving Flattery! In a Word, to those Halcyon, or, if you will, *Millennium* Days, in Which the Wolf and the Lamb shall feed together, and a Tyrannous Domination, which Nature never meant, shall no longer render useless, if not hurtful, the Industry and Understandings of Half Mankind![17]

About a century later Mary Wollstonecraft, both in her political writings and in her fictions, addresses essentially the same issues, female education and the miseries of marriage. Demanding freedom, equality, and independence, Wollstonecraft of course went a good deal further in her *Vindication* than Astell. Far from seeking any " happy retreat", she asserted with great stubbornness "the rights which women in common with men ought to contend for".[18] In her fictions she also went a good deal further, dramatizing the sanctioned, legalized oppression of women by men, both inside and outside marriage, and depicting her heroines' loveless isolation in bleak and sombre tones. "Was not the world a vast prison, and women born to be slaves?" we hear Maria muse in *The Wrongs of Woman*.[19] To be sure, an apt reflection when we have seen the heroine robbed of her child and thrown into an asylum by her drunken, gambling, revoltingly rapacious and unscrupulous husband. Mary, the heroine of Wollstonecraft's earlier (completed) novel, ends her adventures in a state of "solitary sadness". Bound to a man she cannot love, Mary finds temporary relief in charitable projects. She "retired to her house in the country, established manufactories, threw [her] estate into small farms ... She visited the sick, supported the old, and educated the young". The very last sentence of the book, however, informs

17. *Some Reflections Upon Marriage* (1700), rpt of the 1730 London edn, New York, 1970, pp. 126-8.
18. *A Vindication of the Rights of Woman*, ed. Poston, p. 194.
19. Mary Wollstonecraft, *Mary* and *The Wrongs of Woman*, ed. and introd. Gary Kelly, Oxford, 1976, p. 79.

us that the heroine will not be long for this world, and rejoices at the thought that "she was hastening to that world where there is neither marrying, nor giving in marriage."[20]

How like, and yet how deeply unlike the progress in George Eliot's *Romola* (1862-3), whose heroine starts out as a patient support to her blind old father. In the end, having ministered to the sick with passionate devotion, we see her at the head of a predominantly female household, past any thought of marriage, educating the young. Through loss and disillusionment, and the acceptance of human suffering, Romola has attained the serene yet active wisdom which enables her to transmit a hope for the future. In Eliot's moral universe such hope for a better world based on the slow growth of fellow-feeling could never be founded on what she referred to as "shifting theory". Wary of systematic abstraction, the novelist felt it could only reveal itself "clothed [in the] human figure and individual experience" of her fictional characters,[21] in this case that of the heroine herself.

Of *Romola*, her fourth novel, Eliot said that she "began it a young woman", and had finished it an old one, and that she "could swear by every sentence having been written with my best blood" (*Letters* VI, 335-6). The merging of intense vision with encyclopaedic knowledge clearly proved a huge and costly effort. Whether we regard the novel a "historical romance" (Lewes's puzzling phrase), whether we judge it a "literary hybrid" (Leslie Stephen's criticism), or whether, like Browning, we praise and admire it as "the noblest and most heroic prose-poem", *Romola* occupies a central position in George Eliot's *oeuvre* in more than the chronological sense.

The novel's setting, or rather its "medium" · is Florence, Renaissance Italy, and while its action opens with reports of the death of Lorenzo de' Medici in April 1492, it closes with the hanging and burning at the stake of Girolamo Savonarola. The two events, the natural and violent deaths of two great men, embrace a period of intense political and religious conflict, and they suggest the epic dimensions of the story. Aiming to explore no

20. *Mary*, pp. 67-8.
21. *The George Eliot Letters*, ed. G.S. Haight, New Haven, 1954-1978, VI, 217.

less than the History of Western culture, the progress of
civilization — this large theme is already sounded in the "Proem",
as the " angel of the dawn" travels over the Western world — Eliot
chose a time and a place where the pagan and Christian traditions
converged and collided.[22] Out of it might come, despite, or perhaps
because of "the broad sameness of the human lot",[23] a hope for the
future which is, we should realize, our continuing present.

Thus Romola, the "Florentine lily", evoking the figures of
Antigone, Ariadne, and the Holy Virgin, journeys from the pagan
world of classical antiquity to the Christian world of the Church
Militant. Her connection to the former is by way of her father,
godfather, and husband, all three men embodying aspects of
Renaissance Florence. Her connection to the latter is Savonarola,
spiritual guide and teacher to an ardent, inspired disciple. But
Romola does not, cannot stop here. Having passed through all her
trials she emerges, on her own at last, into the morning light of
what could be called her "high humanity", herself an inspiration
to the world around her, herself the guide and teacher. Indeed,
perhaps we should refer to Romola's achievement as a kind of
"utopian humanity".

As we follow the progress of this journey, we see it marked
throughout by numerous symbolic references to time and place.
The days of the religious festivals, carnivals, and processions form
a symbolic calendar for the action, while the city itself, with its
palaces and churches, plays an equally suggestive part. The
particular "experiment in life" named Romola — the phrase is a
crucial one in Eliot's aesthetic[24] — is as it were enshrined in a rich

22. From the earliest critical reactions to *Romola* onwards, this aspect
has been frequently commented on; more recently, Felicia Bonaparte has
traced the pagan and Christian motifs in great detail in her stimulating
full-length study of the novel, *The Triptych and the Cross: The Central
Myths of George Eliot's Poetic Imagination*, New York, 1979.

23. *Romola*, ed. and introd. Andrew Sanders, Penguin edn, 1980, p. 43.
Further references to this edition will be indicated by page numbers
following each quotation.

24. The phrase occurs in a letter to Dr Joseph Frank Payne, January
1876 (*Letters* VI, 216-17). See also Bernard J. Paris, *Experiments in Life:
George Eliot's Quest for Values*, Detroit, 1965.

texture of cultural, historical, and religious allusion.

We first encounter the daughter in her father's library, with its pale and sombre colours, its vellum bindings, and its "marble fragments of the past" (p. 93). Old Bardo's library is a monument to classical antiquity, the world of "the great dead". Still, despite his blind pedantry, the living Bardo bequeaths to his daughter a developed and cultured mind and, his own greatest virtue, integrity, "nobility of soul" (p. 100). Through Tito Melema, the beautiful and bright Greek stranger who becomes her husband, Romola briefly tastes the sensuous delights of Bacchic pleasure, symbolically represented in Tito's betrothal gift. The triptych is a pagan tabernacle painted by Piero di Cosimo, depicting:

> the triumphant Bacchus, with his clusters and his vine-clad spear, clasping the crowned Ariadne; the Loves showering roses, the wreathed vessel, the cunning-eyed dolphins, and the rippled sea: all encircled by a flowery border, like a bower of paradise (p. 397).

But Tito, having denied his father, his past, proves to be the living embodiment of amoral selfishness, the quintessential manipulator and shrewd political agent. From the outset, his bright hopefulness is associated with treachery, with the figures of Sinon and Judas. His selfish calculations and his betrayals of trust soon touch his young wife. Robbed of her love for Tito, overcome with a sense of utter desolation, Romola decides to leave her husband, to leave Florence. Dressed in nun's clothes, she carries with her the crucifix which had been thrust upon her by her dying brother, and which till her departure had been locked away inside the tabernacle of her marriage. Just outside the gates of Florence, however, Savonarola's voice arrests her, and it is the crucifix which inspires the Frate's greatest eloquence as he teaches Romola "a new fellowship with suffering" (p. 435), "not integrity only, but religion" (p. 431). Romola must not deny her parentage: she is a daughter of Florence and Florence needs her. She is a daughter of the church, a daughter of Savonarola. She cannot stay aloof, she must go back and live "for the great work by which Florence is to be regenerated and the world made holy" (p. 434).

Yet, her trust and belief in Savonarola are also betrayed: when she goes to him to plead for the life of her godfather, Savonarola chooses "not to meddle". Seated in his cell, at work on the sheets for his "Triumph of the Cross", he claims, ironically, to "stand aloof" from the affairs of the State, and tells Romola that "the death of five men ... is a light matter weighed against the withstanding of the vicious tyrannies which stifle the life of Italy, and foster the corruption of the Church; a light matter weighed against the furthering of God's kingdom upon earth" (pp. 577-8). We sense that Savonarola's millenarian hopes for Florence are doomed, for the man who once had been "an incarnation of the highest motives", is now caught, we are told, "in a tangle of egoistic demands, false ideas, and difficult outward conditions" (p. 576). Rejecting his disciple's plea for mercy and justice, Savonarola equates the interests of his own party with the cause of God's kingdom. Romola is appalled at such narrow, self-serving and tyrannical sophistry, and asserts with fiery indignation that "God's kingdom is something wider — else let me stand outside it" (p. 578). Aggrieved, and deeply disillusioned she exiles herself from Florence, from Savonarola's irrevocably failing utopia.

Alone at last, "standing on the brink of the Mediterranean", stripped of all her connections with love and hope and duty, as daughter, wife, and ardent proselyte — that is to say, of all her woman's connections with the world of men — Romola longs "to be freed from the burden of choice when all motive was bruised" (p. 589). She drifts away in her boat, feeling "orphaned" in the "wide spaces of sea and sky" (p. 590). However, as "the rays of the newly risen sun [fall] obliquely on the westward horn of [a] crescent-shaped nook", her boat lying still, Romola awakes to "a new life" (pp. 640-1). She is further aroused by the cry of a child, the cry of needy humanity, and proceeds to inspire new life into the plague-stricken village where she has landed. No longer entangled in a web of argument (a phrase which seems to define the world of men), Romola has finally found her true and natural self, and "simply" follows the "impulse to share the life around her" (p. 650). Her task of healing completed, she returns at last to her native city: "Her feelings could not go wandering after the possible and vague", the narrator tells us, "their living fibre was fed with the memory of familiar things" (p. 652).

Back in Florence Romola hears how her husband has met his

violent death at the hands of the mob and of the revenge-crazed Baldassarre; she also hears of Savonarola's impending execution. The men in her life gone, destroyed by their different ambitions, she now turns to the world of women, longing to take care of Tessa, Tito's "other wife" and their two children. Thus the two women in Tito's life, archetypically represented as Florentine madonna and peasant maiden, find themselves in the end strangely but happily united.

The epilogue of the novel, which takes us to the year 1509, shows Romola seated in a large room, looking out on the mountains beyond the city. She is a kind of matriarchal figure here, a secular Virgin Mother. Teaching young Lillo (the only boy in this female household) how "we can only have the highest happiness, such as goes along with being a great man, by having wide thoughts, and much feeling for the rest of the world as well as ourselves" (p. 674), she fills the child with awed wonder. Greatness must include goodness, large sympathy and fellow-feeling. Yet as we have seen, the arenas for potential greatness are fraught with the dangers of public and private corruption, and society, the man-established worlds of politics, religion, and learning will therefore not change for the better very rapidly. Man's nature, Eliot wrote late in her own life, "can only be wrought on by little and little" (*Letters* VII, 346). This, it would seem, is Romola's patient, unobtrusive, and very feminine contribution to the improvement of the world, as she leaves the reader with the hope that her lesson of humanity will make a difference in the life and career of Tito's illegitimate son, that it perhaps has made a difference.

As to feminism or utopianism, George Eliot was averse to schools and movements, to any form of doctrine or, as she puts it, "shifting theory" — even though she was deeply involved with ideas and ideals, actively concerned about the education of women (contributing for example to the founding of Girton College), and profoundly interested in the institution and meaning of marriage. "My function is that of the *aesthetic*, not the doctrinal teacher", she wrote to a feminist correspondent (*Letters* VII, 44). The utopian impulse in her writings is therefore best defined, in her own artistic terms, as "the rousing of the nobler emotions, which make mankind desire the social right" (*Letters* VII, 44). If in the perfect moral commonwealth the emphasis was on "duty, loyalty, charity and virtue practised by each individual as a precondition of society's regeneration"[25], in Eliot's world moral life rests, in addition, upon the individual's ability "to *imagine* and to *feel* the pains and the joys of those who differ from [one's self] in everything but the broad fact of being struggling, erring, human creatures" (*Letters* III, 111). It is Romola's greatest gift, shown to be specifically if not uniquely feminine.

Amsterdam   Marijke Rudnik-Smalbraak

25. Davis, p. 31.

AMERICAN APOCALYPTICISM: A READING OF
THE SCOFIELD REFERENCE BIBLE

On Jordan's stormy banks I stand,
And cast a wishful eye
To Canaan's fair and happy land,
Where my Possessions lie.[1]

1984 was celebrated as the year of the Apocalypse primarily
because of George Orwell's use of the year as the title for his
memorable novel and also because of our present preoccupation
with the deployment of nuclear armaments. For the first time in
several hundred years large numbers of people in the West are
prepared to entertain the possibility of "an end of time" or "a
termination of human life, as we know it, on this planet". To be
sure, the notion of such an end, of a violent conclusion to our
civilization, was not unknown among early Christians, but it has
been a very long time since the majority of Christian believers have
considered the possibility as a real option within their own
lifetimes. We know that the early Church wrestled with this belief
in a slightly different form, namely, that of Christ's immanent
bodily return, and their disappointment with his failure to
reappear filled them with dismay, as the Epistles of Paul reflect.
We know, too, that the year 1000 was seen as the year in which
Christ could be expected to return and that the Western Church
reacted accordingly. But to repeat, it has been a very long while
since the idea of an end, any kind of an end, has been taken very
seriously by large numbers of people.

---

1. "On Jordan's Stormy Banks", No. 179 in *Gospel Hymns: Nos. 1 to 6
Complete,* by Ira D. Sankey et al., New York/Chicago, 1894; rpt. New York,
1972, p. 124. This is a facsimile edition of the *Moody-Sankey Hymnal.*

With such reasons for anxiety, with thousands upon thousands of atomic warheads being stored across the world, utopian dreams have come to lose much of their credibility in the forty years since World War II. Where once socialism in various forms seemed attractive to many as a solution to man's problems, now the socialist movement throughout the West is in alarming disarray. Having achieved for the working classes the material security demanded by the excesses of nineteenth-century capitalism, having made unemployment compensation and an adequate health insurance a basic right of every citizen, contemporary socialist movements have come to trivialize their moral energies in an hypocritical involvement with the environment and a position on the problems of war and peace so cluttered with jargon and hasty gestures as to be useless, indeed dangerous, in the present situation.

Utopian dreams and apocalyptic visions are both convictions about some kind of an end of time which would transcend our experience of time were such an event ever to occur. Both conclusions contradict our sense of duration by seeking to move beyond it, by propelling man beyond all the reasonable expectations of his existence into a timelessness aptly described by Wallace Stevens in his "Sunday Morning". At this logical extreme both beliefs find one another in a self-destructive denial of the very foundation on which they were built, the moral inadequacy of experienced history.

Both these attitudes have found expression in Christian thinking from the first. There have always been those who have grasped the Kingdom of God through the image of the germinating and growing seed, as a divine structure which would gradually come to overwhelm the institutions of men and transform them finally and for the good. Other believers, equally convinced, have felt the Judgement of God more fiercely and have argued that the gulf between God and man is so great that growth is an inadequate image by means of which to grasp God's purposes for fallen man and fallen society. Only a complete break with the past is morally acceptable here, a break followed by "a new heaven and a new earth".

In the intellectual and moral fury we call the Reformation both of these attitudes toward the end of time received expression, and

in the early seventeenth century in England, church and sect mixed
the Kingdom and the Second Coming with an alacrity rarely found
in Christian history. From the realized eschatology of the
Commonwealth itself to the apocalyptic confusions of sects such as
the Diggers and Levellers the churches of England presented every
possible hope for the future of mankind, ideal democracies, divine
republics and a monarch who was annointed. Out of this
confusion of vision the Puritans and the Pilgrims sailed for North
America with a specific religious purpose in mind.

The settlement of New England, then, did not take place without
apocalyptic implications or intentions. Boston was, after all, the
city set upon a hill, a New Jerusalem, to which all men, and
particularly the Puritans who had remained behind in England,
could and must look for an example of a perfect commonwealth,
the true Kingdom of God among men. And we know with what
great disappointment the settlers of that colony greeted the
Restoration, for it indicated the end of their apocalyptic-utopian
hopes, a fact which turned them loose in a part of the world which
they had already associated with the Wilderness of the Old
Testament. It is no wonder, then, that these settlers attempted to
free themselves from the mother country one hundred years before
they finally succeeded in doing so, or that they sublimated their
disappointment in their failed apocalypse into the fury of settling
the continent. Perhaps, the fate of the Indians, too, should be seen
in this light, for they had long been associated with Satan, the
"Black Man".

Apocalyptic and utopian ideas, they are so mixed in this
instance, having once been part of the thinking of the new nation,
were never to leave it completely. One recalls the many utopian
communities along the western frontier, the Millerites and their
failed apocalypse as well as the strong millenarian strains in
Mormonism. There is, too, the presence in American thought of the
sense of being "a chosen people", one that is to lead mankind to a
better, more humane form of government. One recalls Lincoln's
description of the troubled Republic of his time, the last good hope
of mankind.

Within this general presence of apocalypse most American
churches have maintained, with varying enthusiasm, a belief in
Christ's bodily return, and over the past 150 years considerable

debate has taken place about the time of that marvellous reappearance, when and for how long the devil is to be chained and cast in the pit, and when finally believers are to be taken up with their Lord eternally. Such speculations did not become divisive in American Protestantism until the early part of this century when a great many other doctrines also became matters of serious dispute, especially that of the nature of biblical revelation, the question of how and in what way the Bible could be taken as God's word. Once this issue had been broached, not only was the idea of creation a matter of great concern, but, given the many prophetic books of the Old and New Testaments, the time and even the nature of Christ's return (did he only return in spirit?) was also the occasion for much argument, disagreement and even schism. The Great Argument that tore the American churches apart in the first third of the twentieth century had its beginning in the key issue of the nature and means of God's revelation, an issue still very much alive at the present time, and the discussion which arose as a result included all of the basic doctrines of the faith, of the Kingdom of God as well as the Day of Judgement.

In the late nineteenth century, before these matters had become polarized, most American Christians of a conservative orthodox persuasion appear to have been little concerned with the detail of doctrine; the great Moody, for example, seems hardly to have mentioned them.[2] During the same period the American churches expanded at a frightening pace while Sunday schools and YMCAs spread like wildfire across the land. The major problem, therefore, that the churches faced was not one of the purity of doctrine, but rather one of manpower: how do we fill our pulpits? And perhaps even more urgently, how can one clergyman do the work of a medium sized congregation? To answer this urgent need Moody established in Chicago his Institute, meant to train laymen to help in the work of the churches and thus to relieve the badly overworked clergy. And in the century that has followed, over a

---

2. On D.L. Moody, see my *D.L. Moody: The Chicago Years, 1856-1871*, Amsterdam, 1984, and "Longing for Home: Images of a Gentle Apocalypse" in *Nineteen Eighty Four and the Apocalyptic Imagination in America*, ed. R. Kroes, Amsterdam, 1985, pp. 158-165.

hundred similar institutions have been founded in North America alone.

The need, then, was to improve the efficiency of the work of the churches. In order to do so, the need, too, was to get religious information, for want of a better term, to the thousands upon thousands of dedicated people who were filling the tasks of the local church, as the leaders of study groups and prayer meetings, as Sunday school teachers who were being asked to cope with the needs of children of all ages. Cheaply printed manuals and Bible handbooks were distributed by the tens of thousands, national foundations supplied monthly magazines containing Sunday school lessons for all age groups, and so on. For once again, how could one expect a single clergyman to do the necessary work of the Church and, at the same time, train a staff to fill the new demands of an ever-expanding American Protestantism?

2.

Of all the many practical aids offered the laity at the beginning of this century, the best known and probably most interesting is *The Scofield Reference Bible* which first appeared in 1909 and has been in print ever since.[3] Its obvious purpose is to make the Bible "available" to the average layman (p. 1354), that is, to grant him entry into this most complex of holy texts with an eye to the layman's need to understand and then to explicate and to defend its basic doctrines. But it is precisely in the area of doctrines that the matter becomes most urgent, for, one may reasonably ask, what are the basic doctrines of the Bible?

Although Scofield repeatedly affirms that Christ is the centre of the Scriptures, he has no difficulty proclaiming the hard circularity of his commitment: the Bible is God's Word, therefore it must be true; the Bible is true, therefore it must be God's Word.[4] This

3. *The Scofield Reference Bible*, New York, 1909, 1917, renewed 1937, 1945. All references are to this book which has remained unchanged to this day. In a recent (1984) conversation with a representative of O.U.P. he gently and with a smile refused to reveal how much the Press still depended upon revenues from the Scofield Bible.

4. The back of the dust jacket, question number 17, "How do we know that the Bible is inspired? [pages] 1213, 1353".

unique version of the hermeneutic circle, one very common among American Fundamentalists, permits him in his commentary to avoid detailed questions of biblical accuracy and to move forward to what he takes to be the more central matter of Christian belief. The Bible consists, after all, of sixty-six books written over a considerable period of time, and if one is disposed to believe, as Scofield most certainly was, that these many books must reflect the acts and purposes of a single mind, God's, revealed literally to his many prophets, then the primary task of the commentator, and that is what Scofield in fact becomes, is to make unified "sense" out of this marvellous variety. The real question from our point of view will be, to be sure, what kind of sense is this "sense"?

Even a quick glance at what Scofield has done will reveal the detail of his intentions. Aside from offering the reader a variety of cross references for most verses in order to confirm the basic doctrines of scripture, he is also intent upon convincing the reader that the Bible contains a master plan for man's collective as well as individual life. To his mind history is naturally divided into vast periods which reflect the way in which God is dealing with man during that particular time. These "covenants", as he calls them, lead from Eden to the final consummation of God's purposes as revealed in the Revelation of St John the Divine. History is divided into eight periods during each of which God has made a particular agreement with men about the nature of their divine-human relation. And man who chose to disobey during the first covenant continues to writhe in his sin until the final Judgement is completed, though God offers him, time after time, a new basis for covenant, a new kind of relation. In this way the incredible variety of the Bible is reduced to a seemingly comprehensible structure in measured time, past and future, in which the present-day believing Christian has a clear and specific place with clear and specific expectations.

Although traces of such thinking can be found in the writings of St Paul and certainly in John's Revelation, even Augustine in his *City of God* did not presume to offer his readers a timetable of God's intentions. It was not until the Reformation, with its peculiar rediscovery of the text of the Bible that such speculation led to an attempt to specify the detail of God's time. The name of the Reformer Heinrich Bullinger has been traditionally associated

194

with this periodization of God's way with the world although the American concern with the question comes most likely from William Miller and his attempt to fix the return of Christ with precision. In any case, millenarianism has traditionally existed along the edges of Christian concern, and in the recent of history of American Protestantism it is significant only because it has been so very divisive.[5]

It is not my intention to enter into a theological discussion of the implications or merits of this kind of thinking for the religious life of the average believer, although the deleterious effects of such a reduction must be manifest, even to the most casual observer. Our problem is of a more literary nature, namely, what happens to the great biblical images of time and apocalypse when they have been dealt with in this way? In other words, what is the fate of the literary qualities of the holy text when it has been analyzed in this fashion? Indeed, is there anything left?

3.

The best example of Scofield's kind of interpretation and its effect upon one's reading of the Bible is his presentation of the Revelation of St John, together with his usage of particular passages in the books of Ezekiel and Daniel which are traditionally seen to be relevant to an understanding of "last things". This "mer à boire" of apocalyptic imagery has long been a severe stumbling block to biblical scholars, and at one time Revelation's right to be included in the canon was profoundly questioned for just this

5. For a description of the place of the millenarian influence in American Fundamentalism, see A. Sandeen, *The Roots of Fundamentalism: British and American Millenarianism, 1800-1930*, Chicago, 1970, and for a more moderate interpretation of the same history, see George M. Marsden, *Fundamentalism and American Culture: The Shaping of Twentieth Century Evangelicalism, 1870-1925*, New York/Oxford, 1980. On the basis of my own experience the millenarian element was always present in Fundamentalist circles but never a matter of great contention. There is still much to be said for Sidney E. Mead's distinction, however, between Fundamentalism and Conservative Orthodoxy, the former being a more aggressively defensive form of the latter.

reason. The life of the Church would be ill served by an invitation to speculate about the end of the world.

Scofield, however, appears to have very little difficulty with this most troublesome text. In his introduction to the book he outlines with great precision its contents, and not only that, he summarizes with equal ease the significance of its imagery. There is no question about the date of the book's composition, neither is there any doubt about the structure of its contents. Christ is presented by John "as to time", "as to relationships" and "in His Offices", while the theme is concluded to be "the bringing of the covenanted kingdom" (all references to p. 1330).

The book may, according to this commentator, be divided into three large parts in which the bulk of the text, eighteen chapters, deals with "things future". There are, aside from particular details presented in "six sevens" and "seven sevens", five important "parenthetical passages" containing matters concerning the Jewish Remnant, the Lamb and the gathering of the kings at Armageddon, to mention only three.

One must quote from Scofield, however, to obtain an adequate picture of the nature of his reasoning. The penultimate paragraph of his introduction to Revelation illustrates the mind of this commentary on the Bible clearly:

> The end of the church period (2.-3.) is left indeterminate. It will end only by the fulfilment of 1 Thes. 4. 14-17. Chapters 4.-19. are believed to synchronize [sic] with Daniel's Seventieth Week (Dan. 9. 24, note). The great tribulation begins at the middle of the "week" and continues three and a half years (Rev. 11. 3-19.21). The tribulation is brought to an end by the appearing of the Lord and the battle of Armageddon (Mt. 24. 29, 30, Rev. 20. 11-21). The kingdom follows (Rev. 20. 4, 5), after this the "little season" (Rev. 20. 7-15), and the eternity (p. 1330).

And he concludes his introduction: "Doubtless much which is designedly obscure to us will be clear to those for whom it was written as the time approaches" (Ibid.).

This quotation reflects most accurately the kind of reduction suggested above. There is, first of all, violent theological oversimplification to be found in this book as it attempts to summarize the contents of Scripture in this remarkable way. The doctrine of the Last Things is reduced to little more than a time-table of events to come in which the accent seems to fall upon clarity because that supposed virtue in matters of faith is what the believing Christian is presumed to need. Faith in this context is little more than the confidence one might be prepared to have in a railway, namely, that it is likely to run on time.

In the international conflicts of the twentieth century, great wars which were transformed into confrontations between good and evil with eschatological enemies such as the Hun, the Nazis and the godless Reds, English-speaking peoples have come to see their wars in apocalyptic terms, and as these wars have increased in magnitude and potential destruction, the apocalyptic vision has become increasingly appropriate. Such an interpretation of international conflicts has been current among fundamentalist Americans since World War I, and with the establishment of the state of Israel, in which these believers see the fulfilment of specific biblical prophecy, present conflicts take on an even more urgent character than before. In this context the many remarks in Isaiah and Jeremiah about evil coming from the North possess a most ominous tone, indeed.

Althought Scofield did not look upon biblical prophecy with the eyes of a late twentieth-century Christian, he did have a clear idea of the time and place of the battle of Armageddon, and he certainly believed that it would take place in all the detail given in the Bible. Commenting on Revelation 19: 17ff., he said:

> Armageddon (the ancient hill and valley of Mediggo, west of Jordan in the Plain of Jezreel) is the appointed place for the beginning of the great battle in which the Lord, at His coming in glory, will deliver the Jewish remnant besieged by the Gentile world-powers under the Beast and False Prophet (Rev. 16. 13-16; Zech. 12. 1-9). Apparently the besieging hosts whose approach to Jerusalem is described in Isa. 10. 28-32, alarmed by the signs which precede the Lord's coming (Mt. 24. 29, 30), have fallen back to Mediggo, after the events of Zech. 14. 2, where their destruction begins, a destruction consummated in Moab and the Plains of Idumea (Isa. 2. 12, *refs.*), and is the fulfilment of the smiting-stone prophecy of Dan. 2. 35. (p. 1348f.).

Again something has been lost. It is not upon which hill or in which valley Armageddon will be fought; it is, surely, that it will be fought and for most of us, still, in the rhetoric of the Authorised Version.

From a literary point of view the matter is also quite serious. The great images, indeed the basic metaphors of the Bible, and in this instance those pertaining to the end of time, cease to be images at all. They are now confused with simple historical events presented in the atmosphere of oversimplified nineteenth-century historiography. Armageddon loses its terrifying resonance and becomes just another conflict, like the Battle of the Bulge or Anteitam. The "weeks" of Daniel, though not reduced to periods of seven days, are removed from their Old Testament context and then split up to make them fit into a particular schedule for the ending of our world.

In other words, the Kingdom of Heaven is no longer within us, it is just around the corner. It has become another naive utopia among many, an unsecular city inevitably coming. In this context, then, it is most important to recall that it can be otherwise:

At the round earths imagin'd corners, blow
Your trumpets, Angells, and arise, arise,
From death, your numberlesse infinities
Of soules, and to your scattred bodies goe
All of whom the flood did, and fire shall o'erthrow,
All whom warre, dearth, age, agues, tyrannies,
Despaire, law, chance, hath slaine, and you whose eyes,
Shall behold God, and never tast deaths woe.

And one must add: "But let them sleepe, Lord, and mee mourne a space"(Donne, "The Holy Sonnets" IV).

Amsterdam   A.J. Fry

SHAW'S OWN UTOPIA

"The trouble with Bernard Shaw is that we always believe what he says. Whether the topic is war, wool or women, his assertions strike us with the force of commandments", in the view of Margot Peters, the expert on Shaw's relations with women. "And so the contradictions in Shaw's nature tend to be ignored, although they are many", she continues.[1] It is a relief to read these last words, because the preceding statement causes an uneasy feeling that Margot Peters and some of us live in different worlds.

One does not normally meet people who have the problem of believing everything that Shaw says. The reader or playgoer who believes little of it is surely a far more common type. One can phrase this disbelief in a variety of ways, sometimes quite subtly, like Alfred Turco who says that Shaw's "ideas are today less germane to those who believe in a radical restructuring of society than to those interested in making intelligent modifications of traditional value systems."[2] That was probably as true yesterday as it is today. Shaw was always more admired as a contradictor of conventional notions than as an adviser of the revolution. He was good at contradicting not only because his brain moved so swiftly that by the time his opponents or victims had thought of a reply he might well be several points of discussion away; also because he had a reputation, which was sometimes deserved, of knowing what he was talking about, with more facts and figures and well-tested ideas at his disposal than the others; and beyond that, because he was able to go on talking longer than most people. "It is positively because he is quick-witted that he is long-winded", as G.K. Chesterton said of him.[3]

His intellectual delivery remains rapid; but always to be believed

1. Margot Peters, "As Lonely as God", in Michael Holroyd, ed., *The Genius of Shaw*, London, 1979, p. 185.
2. Alfred Turco, *Shaw's Moral Vision*, London, 1976, p. 38.
3. G.K. Chesterton, *George Bernard Shaw*, London, 1910, p. 7.

he was not, and is not now. It may be unfair to trip him up with an oral statement he made to Stephen Winsten towards the end of his life, to the effect that "The world will never be the same again because I have educated four generations to see things as they are, and not what they imagine them to be or want them to be".[4] If the fourth of these generations was still given to seeing things as they imagined or wanted them, the difference Shaw made could not have been very marked; but perhaps this is indeed unfair because these words were doubtless spoken more casually than the prefaces and the plays were written.

The assertions that Margot Peters cannot help believing in, then, would rather be those made in *Man and Superman* and *Major Barbara* and *Saint Joan*. We should accept, for instance, that a modern Don Juan would necessarily be a man with his thoughts consistently turned away from the subject of sex because the essence of him had always been the rebellion against existing institutions, which in the early sixteenth century, but not in the twentieth, could be carried out through one's girl friends. We should be ready to believe that an arms manufacturer who like Major Barbara's father started out as a poor and dangerous man will become a kindly and beneficent person once he has made his first million. Also, we must be expected to know what Shaw was talking about when he stimulated our understanding of Joan of Arc's times by writing that "Today, when the doctor has succeeded to the priest, and can do practically what he likes with parliament and the press through the blind faith in him which has succeeded the far more critical faith in the parson, legal compulsion to take the doctor's prescription, however poisonous, is carried to an extent that would have horrified the Inquisition and staggered Archbishop Laud."[5]

In fact these pronouncements fail to convince us, or most of us, of their truth. One has no great difficulty in understanding those who find Shaw too loud in proportion to the amount of insight he

4. Robert E. Whitman, *Shaw and the Play of Ideas*, Ithaca/London, 1977, p. 39.
5. *The Bodley Head Shaw*, London, 1970-74, VI, 58. References to this edition will be referred to in the text by Volume number.

has to offer, and who are reluctant to put up with him. Yet it is not as if the last word about him had been said. He is more controversial than that. There is more discussion of his significance now than there was thirty years ago, when the dominant opinion was that his work had grown stale. He provides loud and clear subjects for academic treatment, and he has found many devotees who are not noticeably disturbed by the overemphasis or the wilfulness of his sweeping statements.

Those of us who are put off by him when he lets himself go have a more difficult task accounting for their continued interest. He would be much easier to ignore if it were not for his comic dialogue. There is a crucial dispute possible about Shaw's merits starting from his own view that that the first three scenes of *Saint Joan* form only an appetizer to introduce the meat of the play in the next three. The dispute arises when one observes that the first three are better: not richer in ideas or more complex in characterization, but better as fragments of drama in their own right, catching the attention and surprising and delighting it. Not all Shavians will agree; but a case can be made out. Similarly, one may prefer *Arms and the Man*, with its mock knowledge of what war is really about, to *Major Barbara* which has views not only on war but many other subjects besides, and gets quite entangled in them. Again, *Too True to be Good* is a more engaging play than its reputation suggests, not because of the importance of its views on unearned wealth, but because of its dialogue, and the comic figures of Corporal Meek and Colonel Tallboys.

"Go and send the interpreter to me", says Tallboys, loosely modelled on General Allenby, to Meek who is loosely modelled on T.E. Lawrence and whom he finds an irritating little man. "And dont come back with him", he adds: "Keep out of my sight."Meek hesitates and says "Er —", and Tallboys repeats his order, peremptorily. "The fact is, Colonel", replies Meek, and Tallboys is outraged: "How dare you say Colonel and tell me what the fact is? Obey your order and hold your tongue", to which Meek has to answer "Yessir. Sorry sir. I *am* the interpreter", — for he has in fact been acting in several capacities at the same time. — "Tallboys bounds to his feet; towers over Meek who looks smaller than ever; and folds his arms to give emphasis to a terrible rejoinder. On the point of delivering it he suddenly unfolds them again and sits down resignedly" (VI, 460).

Excellent comedy, this, just like the scene it is reminiscent of in *Arms and the Man* when Captain Bluntschli has told Raina the Bulgarian officer's daughter that the two lies in her whole life so far to which she admits seems too little and he does not believe her, at which she rises to her full height and gasps indignantly; and then suddenly sits down to ask him "How did you find me out?" (I, 446).

Such scenes are most satisfying; but then come the weightier passages. "That is the history of Catholicism and Protestantism, Church and Empire, Liberalism and Democracy, up to date", says the Preface to *Too True to be Good*, having named disorder, indiscipline, breakdown and disappointment: "Clearly a ghastly failure, both positively as an attempt to solve the problem of government and negatively as an attempt to secure freedom of thought and facility of change to keep pace with the thought" (VI, 421). It is a common Shavian note, as familiar as the comic dialogue: the image of the failure and collapse of the conditions we live under as well as of the good sense we should have used to do better, contrasted with a quick view of the simple tasks that were all history asked us to perform. The Preface to *Major Barbara* ends on a memorable complaint about the need for creeds to become intellectually honest: "At present there is not a single credible established religion in the world. That is perhaps the most stupendous fact in the whole world situation" (III, 63). One single credible established religion, is even that too much to ask? we are meant to exclaim: stupendous! And how is it possible that such a reasonable requirement should have proved too heavy for us? Surely somebody could have done something!

Judging by many of the prefaces there would in fact be little hope of remedying any of the conditions described in them now that they had fallen so deeply below any tolerable standard. Here I am, Shaw said: originally a quiet respectable man, yet now a revolutionary writer "because our laws make law impossible; our liberties destroy all freedom; our property is organized robbery; our morality is an impudent hypocrisy; ... and our honor is false in all its points" (III, 59). If the "we" this refers to included the writer and the reader there was no chance of improvement, one might suggest; even preface-readers were bound to be false and impotent — unless we were not meant to take the argument seriously, just to pick the bits out of it that suited us personally and throw the rest away. But we *were meant to* take it seriously: "The real joke is that I am in earnest."[6]

Yet Shaw did think improvement possible. He proposed images of a better world, not just to provide standards for his denunciations in the Swiftian manner but as projects to be realized in the continuation of history. His reforming zeal survived the moods of contempt and despair that marked the prefaces; he just recommended increasingly drastic means to bring about the necessary improvements, and allowed longer and longer terms for them to take effect.

It began in 1880 when he attended a lecture by Henry George and followed it up by reading Marx. From then on he was a socialist: mostly, except in his more excitable pronouncements, of a revisionist rather than a revolutionary type. "Poverty is a crime", as he said in *Major Barbara*, and he occasionally went on record as a champion of absolute equality of incomes. *Major Barbara* was not a smooth vehicle of socialist thought, however. For one thing, the curious formulation of that central economic idea suggested that the crime was committed not so much by the rich as by the poor themselves, who lacked the guts to improve their lot.

Although this was not necessarily the whole of Shaw's thought on the subject, it did fit in with a part of his philosophy that had been revealed together with his preceding play, *Man and Superman*. Only under despotism and oligarchies, said Shaw disguised as John Tanner in *The Revolutionist's Handbook*, has the radical faith in universal suffrage been able to maintain itself. "It withers the moment it is exposed to practical trial, because Democracy cannot rise above the level of the human material of which its voters are made", and this material was not in Shaw's estimation of prime quality. "We must therefore frankly give up the notion that Man as he exists is capable of net progress" (II, 754 and 764). Our only hope, in this perspective, lies in the Superman, to be bred in

6. Quoted in Eric Bentley, *Bernard Shaw, the Darker Side*, Stanford, 1982, p. 172.

increasing numbers by eugenic methods. If only people would give up combining the idea of living together with that of having children together, we could arrange for the conception of large numbers of superchildren, and democracy might pick up.

What the distinguishing characteristics of the Superman were to be was also beginning to be revealed by this play. One component was the Don Juan unobsessed by sex; the other was the religion of the Life Force, intended to remedy the stupendous absence of a credible established one. The Superman was seen in action in Act III, in the dream scene in hell, where he explained to the devil that eternity as one long round of pleasure, which was what hell had to offer, seemed to him unbearable: he left for heaven where he would be allowed to devote his existence to his research projects, undisturbed by pretty and demanding women.

The role of the Life Force in the development of supermanhood remained ambiguous at this stage. In the scene in hell, although logically he had to be presumed dead, Don Juan has no difficulty in harnessing the Force for his purpose. In Life, John Tanner was defeated by Ann Whitefield who represented the same Force in its basic form, in which it was only concerned to perpetuate the human race. He was not strong enough to use the top end of the Life Force that would have enabled him to become an eternal philosopher like his dead predecessor. He had to make babies first, some of whom would perhaps succeed in becoming super — like gentlemen not being created in a single generation.

The superman went on to dominate Shaw's views of the better world of the future in the twenties and into the thirties, when he seemed to split apart into two types. On the one hand there were the strong men of real life in the thirties, Mussolini and Stalin and Hitler, for whom Shaw developed an often deplored tolerance, which in some views seems the continuation of a road he took by mistake on his way to a better version of humanity — although he was in no great hurry to return from it. "It should be noted that Shaw never believed in a cult of isolated great men", says Turco, but that he considered that "the proper role of the extraordinary individual ... is not to dominate and exploit other people, but to use his gifts to raise the level of the mass of men."[7]

7. Turco, pp. 49-50.

For Turco, Shaw was betrayed into short-term reactionary politics by his long-term humanitarianism. That is the forgiving view. In the eyes of Arnold Silver, who has written an unusually severe book for a Shavian, he found a "sinister attraction" in the limitless power of the superman.[8] It must be admitted that some of his pronouncements of the 1930s sound frightening. "There is nothing that can be changed more completely than human nature when the job is taken in hand early enough", he wrote in the Preface to *On the Rocks* in 1934 (VI, 602); and at various points in his work of the time he suggests that it might be a good idea to eliminate people who cannot justify their existence as a contribution to the general welfare.

That was Shaw as a crusty old gentleman, expressing himself more drastically than some. It was his temper rather than his philosophy speaking. Where his philosophy led him had in the meantime been set out just after the First World War in *Back to Methuselah*, which in its last part brings the future up to 31,920 A.D. "A sunlit glade at the southern foot of a thickly wooded hill ... A dance of youths and maidens is in progress ... music provided by a few flutes ... perfect balance and remarkable grace ... a strange figure appears on the path ... his eyes and mouth show no signs of age; but his face ... bears a network of lines ... Except for his eyelashes he is quite hairless ... He is unconscious of his surroundings, and walks straight into one of the dancing couples" (V, 564).

Now this looks like a society that has divested itself of the violent tendencies of ours, and is at peace; and after twenty years, in 1944, Shaw offered *Back to Methuselah* when he was asked which of his works he would like included in a World's Classics series. Even if he did not think it was his best play, he thought it summed up the main points of his thinking. It was what a proper response to the Life Force would achieve; it was where Creative Evolution would lead, and it has a proper utopian look about it.

Nonetheless even *Back to Methuselah* ends on a note of restlessness. The youths and maidens and the self-absorbed old man have not achieved a final balance and peace. "Best of all, they

8. Arnold Silver, *Bernard Shaw, the Darker Side*, Stanford, 1982, p. 172.

are still not satisfied", says Lilith about mankind at the end of the play: "the impulse I gave them in that day when I sundered myself in twain and launched Man and Woman on the earth still urges them: after passing a million goals they press on to the goal of redemption from the flesh, ... to the whirlpool in pure force" (V, 630). So we are still where we were with John Tanner when he was pressing on from hell to heaven so as to have some work to do, and when the letter to A.B. Walkley asserted that "This is the true joy in life, the being used for a purpose recognized by yourself as a mighty one; the being thoroughly worn out before you are thrown on the scrap heap; the being a force of Nature instead of a feverish selfish little clod of ailments and grievances complaining that the world will not devote itself to making you happy" (II, 523). "Of life only there is no end", says Lilith: "And for what may be beyond, the eyesight of Lilith is too short" (V, 631).

In other words, it is going to be trouble and strife forever, and our best hope is to learn to enjoy it. The prospect is comparable to that of permanent revolution as opposed to that of a more agreeable world waiting round a few awkward corners. Equality of incomes and selective breeding of human beings, and general exposure to Shavian enlightenment, were not after all going to be enough for at least the next thirty thousand years. We were going to have to content ourselves with the being a force of Nature: embodying the Life Force in a process to be known as Creative Evolution. The idea of creative evolution, which was developed fully in the Preface to *Back to Methuselah*, sounded as if it might have been taken from Bergson, but Shaw considered it, like all his ideas, rather more his own. "My dear fellow, I understand your philosophy much better than you do", he said to Bergson, who was not amused, at a lunch.[9]

It is true that Shaw lent an inspiring quality to his own version of creative evolution. It was meant to be the opposite of what the Darwinists had made of Darwin, arguing that natural selection had to be a mechanical process uninfluenced by conscious purpose, and in Samuel Butler's term, "banishing mind from the universe". Shaw preferred Lamarck's ideas: the giraffe's long neck

---

9. J. Percy Smith, *The Unrepentant Pilgrim*, London, 1966, pp. 146-7.

was the result of that animal's desire to get at the higher leaves near the top of the tree — not just of the long-necked ones surviving the shorter ones in times of scarcity. It was not due to mere Circumstantial Selection, as he liked to call it rather than Natural; it was the giraffe creating its own future.

A similar process could be seen at work in men, moving in the direction not of higher leaves but, like Tanner, out of the biological into the spiritual field, thinking of their new religion as a "science of metabiology". There is something evasive and pedantic about Shaw's urge to get away from the physical life, whether in the form of sex or gastronomy or sickness and death. Few of us have the opportunity or desire to live as largely as he did on carrots and words and fame, and the hygienically unerotic quality of his imagination appeals to most of us some but not most of the time. His spiritual ambition strikes one as a private thing before it can be seen as the continuation of a Christian tradition, and as the expression of a universal need.

Yet it has an exhilarating quality about it if we are prepared to go along with him for a while at least. Creative Evolution means us — us realizing the purpose of history in the world, if at least we are prepared to let ourselves be used for it. There are several warnings to the effect that "If Man will not serve, Nature will try another experiment" (V, 269); but if we do serve, we will be the form the Life Force takes, and more: we will be God's attempt to create himself. In a letter to Tolstoy in 1910 Shaw wrote: "To me God does not yet exist, but there is a creative force constantly struggling to evolve an executive organ of godlike knowledge and power: that is, to achieve omnipotence and omniscience: and every man and woman born is a fresh attempt to achieve this object."[10]

Tolstoy did not believe Shaw was right, and few others will, but truth is not the best criterion to judge this vision by; what matters more is whether we can occasionally live in it sufficiently to have a fleeting impression of what it would feel like to be divine instruments. It depends on one's condition, and the circumstances of the day. Maurice Valency, who sets Shaw's identification of

10. Maurice Valency, *The Cart and the Trumpet*, New York, 1973, p. 291.

man with the divine purpose beside that of Gabriel Marcel, points out that in existentialist philosophy it takes place "in anguish, for the honest action can never, in the nature of things, occur in an atmosphere of certainty".[11] As it is, one can only keep in touch with his creative evolution as long as one feels sure of one's place in the world. It is a philosophy for confident times.

Even then one will have difficulty adopting it completely, or seeing it as what Shaw represents most vitally in our imagination. Few people if any derive their ideas of what should be done with the world from his works. In 1932, in the Malvern Festival Book, he reminded his readers that "extremely practical and precise remedies, including a complete political reconstitution, a credible and scientific religion, and a satisfactory economic scheme, are discoverable by anyone under thirty (the older ones are past praying for) who will take the trouble to bring his or her education up to date by ... reading my works carefully through from beginning to end" (VI, 529-30). From somebody else's pen there might be a dominant note of self-mockery in such an inflated pronouncement; not from Shaw, whose sense of humour did not run to acknowledging a distance between his aspirations and his achievements.

Whatever he thought, or pretended so hard to think that no one could tell the difference, his political reconstitution and his credible religion do not influence public affairs today. Yet he no longer threatens to be relegated to the second rank among playwrights. He is played, discussed, written about — not because of his philosophy or his immortal characters (when one has mentioned Candida and Eliza Doolittle and possibly Saint Joan it is hard to think of any others), nor because of his witty sayings few of which survive well in isolation. It almost looks as if we will have to concentrate on his gift for comic dialogue after all.

But there is more. One clear definition of what Shaw's importance consists in has come from Colin Wilson in his *Reassessment*. He thinks Shaw will be seen as standing at the beginning of a development of a scientific evolutionary psychology which will reveal to us new human powers just as unforeseen as

11. ibid.

aircraft and television were a hundred years ago.[12] That is the sort of position in history Shaw would have chosen: but until his claim to it becomes unmistakable his spirit will have to content itself with a smaller role, which is still quite a distinctive one.

There is a distantly utopian quality about the scene with the youths and the maidens and the old man in *Back to Methuselah*. Unfortunately for those who might hope to approach it, it is a receding utopia: even 30,000 years ahead, the best Shaw can offer us is a happier world that will withdraw further and further into the future as we roll forward in generation after generation. Like the heaven of *Man and Superman*, it is not a place to rest in peace and justice, but to work in; and as Lilith makes clear, once you get back to work there is no telling where you may end up.

The world of *Back to Methuselah* is not one that we can use as a guide for our own ambition, nor as one that we could expect to live in if we were better people. Its curious appeal comes from the similarity to the worlds of Shaw's other plays, set in the past, or in the present. It resembles the beach in a mountainous country of *Too True to be Good* as much as the edge of the quay in front of the palace, looking out over the east harbour of Alexandria to Pharos Island, in *Caesar and Cleopatra*. It recalls the garden of a villa in Grenada with a fine view of the town up the valley, of *Man and Superman*, as much as a patch of ground on the south bank of the silver Loire in *Saint Joan*. It is also like the cloudless summer night, where nothing disturbs the stillness except from time to time the long trajectory of a distant train, of *The Doctor's Dilemma*; and it is not unlike the lawn of a stately house on the north coast of a tropical island in the Pacific, in *The Simpleton of the Unexpected Isles*.

Moreover, we find the same sort of characters in all these places: all of them, whether statesmen or burglars, bluestockings or flower girls, corporals or colonels, able to express clearly their motivations and their preferences; all expert in lively repartee, and stimulated rather than irritated by each other's brilliance; no one, or hardly anyone, tortured or obsessed, by sickness or lust or neuroses, or tempted to acts of violence or low cunning; all breezy

12. Colin Wilson, *Bernard Shaw, a Reassessment*, London, 1969, p. 217.

and mentally alert, convinced that although there may be occasional setbacks, you never lose definitively.

One is led to conclude that in the plays we saw utopia all the time, with the oppressive hazards of life removed, and only the stimulating ones remaining. Not that Shaw thought the world he described in his prefaces was like that — with its inhabitants who, as Don Juan said, were not beautiful, only decorated; not moral, only conventional; not considerate, only polite, and on top of many other shortcomings, liars every one of them (see II, 651). There was nothing utopian about *them*; but they were the inhabitants of the outer world, quite unlike the sort of characters who appear in the plays. The ones who appear are not the types who are ruining the world; they are the sort who people Shaw's imagination, which is an entirely different place. They are the privileged, or even the blessed. In the words of Maurice Valency, Shaw "in his moments of exaltation felt not merely that he was godlike, but actually that he was God".[13] At such moments he would also be aware that utopia was the world of his imagination; and certainly the characters in the plays, so unlike the deplorable people who trudge down the long sentences of the prefaces, have an air of freedom from common faults. Why this is utopia, they might well say: nor are we out of it.

This state of being limits them; it leaves them superior in an incomplete way, but it also determines their significance for us. They live in a world where there is no condition that a few minutes bright dialogue won't cure; they are untroubled by rancour, dislike, envy, suspicion and estrangement. They are unlike us, whose lives are beset by these ills, in acuter or milder forms but mostly strong enough to cut us off from each other and to complicate simple exchanges. Perhaps these barriers, in ourselves and others, help to define us and to build up our aggressive energy; but they make us feel incompetent at the same time, locked in an isolation that we should be able but never quite manage to break out of.

Shaw's characters do manage it. Their true joy in life is the talking to each other, not because it makes them all friends, but because

13. Valency, p. 429.

they enjoy the things that occur to them, and do not begrudge each other their brilliance, feeling rightly confident that the aptness of their own phrasing is as good as anybody's. It is an activated and relaxed state of being that could be an essential part of a better life in a better world; and while we remain unable to attain it, one notices that it is an element in our poor natures that Shaw more than anyone else can call up out of its somnolence and inspire if not to sustained, at least to incidental action.

Defining the untortured and clear-eyed world that Shaw evoked as soon as he started writing dialogue helps both to put the plays in perspective and to account for all those sweeping condemnations in the prefaces: reality was full of stupendous omissions and ghastly failures compared not to any historic situation, but to his private world. The definition helps, but it leads to only half a critical view. It deals with the *pièce rose* quality that his plays possess; it leaves the *pièce noire* element out of consideration.

This black element is less in evidence, but it should be brought into focus before Shaw can be considered entirely human. There are dabs of it all over *Heartbreak House*; various shades of it are more subtly recognizable in a favourite of quite a number of Shavians, *John Bull's Other Island*. Arnold Silver, in *Shaw: the Darker Side*, has gone fearlessly into the blackness; and he has seen Shaw taking revenge on his wife, on Charlotte, in *Man and Superman*, and turning the knife again and again in Mrs Patrick Campbell with successive additions to *Pygmalion*.

Shaw was so successful in imposing his public image that he is still often judged by it, and sounds tiresomely positive: all intelligence and verve and confidence. When we get closer to his secret private world he becomes visible in more dramatic terms — in the tension between the bright talker and the dark avenger. We will have to look at his cloudless and his black sides at the same time before we can finally hope that we are seeing the true Shaw.

Amsterdam   J.J. Pereeboom

NINETEEN EIGHTY-FOUR AND THE LITERARY IMAGINATION

George Orwell's *Nineteen Eighty-Four* is a rich text, but in this year, when the title on the book and the date on the calendar finally coincide, the book has been discussed so fully and from so many angles that one wonders, at this late date, whether there is much more that can be said about it. I believe there is; *Nineteen Eighty-Four* is not exhausted yet. Certainly, there are aspects of the book which have been very fully debated, though not resolved: the nature of its politics and its satire; is it primarily an attack on Stalinism in particular, or totalitarianism in general? Does it represent Orwell's disillusionment with the British Labour Party, or a continuing commitment to democratic socialism? All these are interesting questions which I shall pass by. My interest in *Nineteen Eighty-Four* is literary rather than political. In saying this, I am aware of the current radical insistence that *all* questions, including literary ones, are really political. This is not what I believe myself and I remain unabashed. If anything, I would be inclined to toss the ball back and assert that many supposedly political questions are really literary ones, concerning rhetoric and myths and images.

Nineteen Eighty-Four is a kind of utopia; or more precisely, a "dystopia", showing not an ideal future society but a nightmarish one. English literature has been rich in works, from Thomas More's *Utopia* onwards, which present imagined societies, whether attractive or horrific. The late nineteenth century saw many such books. There were Samuel Butler's *Erewhon*, Edward Bulwer-Lytton's *The Coming Race*, and in America, Edward Bellamy's *Looking Backward*. William Morris replied to Bellamy in *News from Nowhere*, and in the last years of the century H.G. Wells wrote *The Time Machine* and *The Sleeper Awakes*. And when Orwell was beginning his career as a writer, in 1932, Aldous Huxley published one of the most celebrated of all dystopias, *Brave New World*. The book of this kind which most directly influenced Orwell, though, was by a Russian, Evgeny Zamyatin's

We, which he read in a French translation in 1946 and wrote an appreciative review of. Seen as an example of the dystopian genre, or even a kind of science fiction, *Nineteen Eighty-Four* has a distinguished ancestry. All such works, one can say, are at least as much about the age in which they were written as about the remote futures they purport to describe. They form palimpsests in which the present is frequently visible through the imagined forms of the future. Thus, in Wells's early dystopias the styles and preoccupations of the *fin de siècle* are apparent, while even such a work of bold technological speculation as *Brave New World* seems to me to reflect much of the quality of life of England in the early 1930s. Zamyatin's *We*, written in a present which is now very remote from us — Russia in 1920 — suggests to me the political excitements of the Russian Revolution, and the aesthetic excitements generated by Constructivism, particularly in the description of the space-ship called the Integral. Nevertheless, all these novels are set well in the future; no less than 800,000 years ahead in the case of Wells's *The Time Machine*. In *The Sleeper Awakes* he reduced the time to a couple of centuries; Zamyatin and Huxley set their futures several hundred years on. *Nineteen Eighty-Four* portrays a future only a few decades ahead, which Orwell, born in 1903, might have expected to survive to see, given a not exceptionally long life-span. Since the book came out "1984" has been used as a shorthand term for a horrendous future, but there is a question about how far Orwell thought of himself as writing about the future at all. It has been pointed out that "1984" is no more than a rearrangement of the digits composing "1948", the year in which Orwell wrote the novel. This is a suggestive idea, though in the drafts Orwell first proposed "1980" and then "1982" before settling for "1984". It is certainly true that in the book we are faced not so much with the present being more-or-less visible through the outlines of the future, as in earlier utopias and dystopias, as with the future being little more than a pretext for writing about the present. Compared with Huxley and Zamyatin, Orwell is uninterested in scientific and technological speculation. Helicopters and two-way television sets are about as far as he goes in that direction. This is in contrast to the gleeful ingenuity shown by Huxley in depicting the elaborate forms of genetic and biochemical control which will keep the population of his utopia happy. *Brave New World* is set several hundred years in the future, but more of its speculations have been realized than those of Orwell's dystopia, whose notional year we have now reached.

But to say this is to do no more than reinforce the point, often made and generally accepted, that the setting of *Nineteen Eighty-Four* is an exaggerated version of the London of the mid-1940s, not a freely imagined dystopia. The towering Ministry of Truth for instance, seems to have been based on the Senate House of London University, which in the 1940s was one of the tallest buildings in London. Much of Winston Smith's life as a minor bureaucrat in the Ministry of Truth is drawn from Orwell's experience of working for the World Service of the BBC during the Second World War: the institutional regimentation, the confined conditions of work, the dimly lit corridors, the bad meals in squalid, crowded canteens. There are many things in *Nineteen Eighty-Four* which recall the last year of the war, which I am old enough to remember. There is, for instance, the shabby dilapidated condition of London, the shortages of food and other necessities of life, the inferior cigarettes. There are, too, the sudden descents, without warning, of rocket bombs, a direct reflection of the bombardment of London in 1944-45, first by the German V-1 weapons, or flying bombs, and then by their much more powerful and destructive successors, the V-2 rockets. It is interesting to note in passing that two of the most celebrated works of modern fictional fantasy should refer to this bombardment: Orwell's *Nineteen Eighty-Four* from the author's actual experience, and Thomas Pynchon's *Gravity's Rainbow* from an extravagantly obsessive imagination.

In many respects, then, *Nineteen Eighty-Four* draws directly on Orwell's life in the mid-1940s. We are frequently reminded of something evident in his discursive books, such as *Down and Out in Paris and London* and *The Road to Wigan Pier*, which is that Orwell was capable at one and the same time of fastidiously recoiling from physical squalor and of showing a curiously intense interest in it. The wartime atmosphere is captured in the omnipresent official propaganda and the shrill communiqués put out by the Ministry of Truth. I found a disconcerting but fortunately short-lived reminder of all that in the presentation of news in the Falklands campaign of 1982. During the Second World War Britain was, in effect, a mildly totalitarian country; Orwell reluctantly accepted this state of affairs as necessary for the successful prosecution of the war, but he was troubled by it. I believe that *Nineteen Eighty-Four* reflects this particular perturbation, reinforced by anxieties about the general spread of totalitarian systems in the world at large. Soviet communism had proved much more enduring than the Nazi and fascist systems, which had been defeated in war. There were further worries, too, about the emergence of a different form of totalitarianism in the West, in the wake of what the political theorist James Burnham called the Managerial Revolution. As I remarked at the beginning, I am not dealing directly with the political implications of *Nineteen Eighty-Four*. But I mention these questions simply as instances of the kind of preoccupation that found their way into the book.

Can we conclude, then, that *Nineteen Eighty-Four*, a book about the present lightly disguised as a fantasy about the future, is no more than a fictional presentation of what Orwell had experienced and observed and thought about between 1944 and 1948? That would be an altogether inadequate response. *Nineteen Eighty-Four* is rich enough to resist such simplifying treatment. It is Orwell's last novel and his most famous. *Nineteen Eighty-Four* and *Animal Farm*, the books of the forties, brought Orwell celebrity; they were works of fabular fiction and seemed to indicate his true line of development, after his earlier, not particularly successful phase as a writer of realistic novels in the 1930s. But there were interesting continuities between the earlier Orwell and the later, and I would like to compare *Nineteen Eighty-Four* with the last of his prewar novels, *Coming Up for Air*, which was published in 1939, ten years earlier. There is no need to spell out what had happened in the intervening decade. The greatest, most destructive war in history had been fought; tens of millions were dead, whether killed in battle or simply exterminated, much of Europe was in ruins, the balance of global power had totally changed, and the atlas had been redrawn. Nevertheless, despite these cataclysmic changes, the forms of Orwell's imagination showed considerable persistence.

Coming Up for Air was written in 1938 and is set in the spring of that year. The novel is the first-person narrative of George Bowling, a fat, cheerful insurance salesman of forty-five. He unexpectedly wins some money on a horse and decides to take a little secret holiday away from his poky suburban home, his nagging wife and noisy children. He wants to rediscover his past by returning to the village of Lower Binfield, where he had spent his boyhood around the turn of the century. Dates are important in this novel: George was twenty-one in 1914 and joined the army. He was sent to France and was wounded; after he recovered he was fortunate enough to spend the rest of the war in a remote, neglected outpost in England. Having fought in one war, he bitterly resents the imminence of another.

In *Coming Up for Air* Orwell the novelist is frequently edged aside by Orwell the essayist and memorialist. A large part of the novel is taken up by George Bowling's intensely nostalgic but precise recreation of his early life, before the outbreak of war in 1914 changed everything. His naive attempt to recapture that lost world by returning to Lower Binfield, grotesquely modernised and transformed as he finds it to be, is sadly and predictably unsuccessful. Everything has changed, and for the worse. This discovery is partly the adult's perennial realization that the visionary gleam of childhood has always fled and cannot be recaptured. But it also implies a judgment on English society in the 1930s. George Bowling, like George Orwell, strongly dislikes the modern world: the factories, the new suburbia, the cheap and shoddy consumer goods in the shop windows, the American-style milk-bars selling disgusting synthetic foods. And above all, the aeroplane. The bombing plane forms a recurrent motif in *Coming Up for Air*, a noisy reminder of a disagreeable present and a threatening future. At the end of the novel, in a piece of rather clumsy symbolism, an RAF plane accidentally drops a bomb on Lower Binfield; it is quite a small bomb by later standards, but it causes damage and loss of life. *Coming Up for Air*, though a fairly minor novel, is of considerable interest in reflecting a particular state of historical feeling; it belongs with a number of other literary works written or set in England at the end of the 1930s, which are preoccupied with the looming threat of a new war. I am thinking, for instance, of Louis MacNeice's long autobiographical poem, *Autumn Journal*, Patrick Hamilton's novel, *Hangover Square*, and Virginia Woolf's last, posthumously published novel, *Between the Acts*.

At the same time, we cannot regard *Coming Up for Air* as in any sense a detached or objective account. George Bowling's irritation and fear and dismay, underlying his day-to-day cheerfulness, colour the whole narrative, reminding us that this is fiction, not history. And as I have suggested, many of Bowling's attitudes and convictions are not easily distinguished from those of Orwell himself, as expressed in his essays and autobiographical writings. In this novel George Bowling tries to discover the past; he dislikes the present and fears the future. And the future that he anticipates and dreads is described in terms that are curiously similar to those in which Winston Smith recalls his early life in *Nineteen Eighty-Four*. Here, first, is a passage from *Coming Up for Air*:

It's all going to happen. All the things you've got at the back of your mind, the things you're terrified of, the things that you tell yourself are just a nightmare or only happen in foreign countries. The bombs, the food-queues, the rubber truncheons, the barbed wire, the coloured shirts, the slogans, the enormous faces, the machine-guns squirting out of bedroom windows.

And now, from *Nineteen Eighty-Four*, Winston Smith looking back to his childhood:

His father had disappeared some time earlier, how much earlier he could not remember. He remembered better the rackety, uneasy circumstances of the time: the periodical panics about air-raids and the sheltering in Tube stations, the piles of rubble everywhere, the unintelligible proclamations posted at street corners, the gangs of youths in shirts all the same colour, the enormous queues outside the bakeries, the intermittent machine-gun fire in the distance — above all, the fact that there was never enough to eat.

The coloured shirts would have seemed somewhat anachronistic even by 1939, as a memory of the fascist uniforms of the 1920s and early 30s, which had been illegal in Britain for several years. By the outbreak of war they were being superseded by more military attire. But they were evidently a detail that lodged deeply in Orwell's consciousness. There are many embryonic anticipations of *Nineteen Eighty-Four* in *Coming Up for Air*. Here is an earlier moment from George Bowling's reflections on the future:

But it isn't the war that matters, it's the after-war. The world we're going down into, the kind of hate-world, slogan-world. The coloured shirts, the barbed wire, the rubber truncheons. The secret cells where the electric light burns night and day, and the detectives watching you while you sleep. And the processions and the posters with enormous faces, and the crowds of a million people all cheering the Leader till they deafen themselves into thinking that they really worship him, and all the time, underneath, they hate him so they want to puke.

This is preceded by a passage which anticipates the institutionalized Two Minute Hates of *Nineteen Eighty-Four*. George Bowling has been to an anti-fascist political meeting:

It's a ghastly thing, really to have a sort of human barrel-organ shooting propaganda at you by the hour. The same thing over and over again. Hate, hate, hate. Let's all get together and have a good hate. Over and over. It gives you the feeling that something has got inside your skull and is hammering down on your brain.

There are hints, too in the earlier novel of the social divisions of *Nineteen Eighty-Four*. George Bowling refers to "the proles" in a combination of resentment and middle-class idealization: "I'm not so sorry for the proles myself. Did you ever know a navvy who lay awake thinking about the sack? The prole suffers physically, but he's a free man when he isn't working."

The differences between the prewar and postwar novels are manifest, and I am not trying to minimize them. But there is, I believe, a significant relationship between the two books. In order to understand it we need to distinguish between the empirical reality of everyday experiences, and the imaginative and conceptual paradigms or models by which we select and shape and make sense of that experience. The distinction has been explored by a number of influential recent thinkers, such as Sir Ernst Gombrich on art and illusion, and Thomas Kuhn on the structure of scientific revolutions. It is obvious that in *Nineteen Eighty-Four* Orwell responds intensely to his personal, physical and ideological experience of the Second World War and its aftermath; but he does so in particular ways which were very personal to him, and which were already implicit in his prewar writing.

I want to quote one final passage from *Coming Up for Air* before I move on to a more detailed discussion of *Nineteen Eighty-Four*. Early on in the novel, George Bowling, who has something of the ruminative curiosity of Joyce's Leopold Bloom, reflects:

The past is a curious thing. It's with you all the time, I suppose an hour never passes without your thinking of things that happened ten or twenty years ago, and yet most of the time it's got no reality, it's just a set of facts that you've learned, like a lot of stuff in a history book. Then some chance sight or sound or smell, especially smell, sets you going, and the past doesn't merely come back to you, you're actually *in* the past.

This is an interestingly suggestive passage. It may remind us of the opening sentence of L.P. Hartley's *The Go-Between*, which has acquired a kind of proverbial status: "The past is a foreign country: they do things differently there." And inevitably it recalls Proust, in its account of how casual sights and sounds and smells can vividly recreate the past. Curiously enough, Orwell seems to have had no particular interest in Proust — there is only one fleeting reference to him in the four volumes of his collected essays and letters — but much of his writing is a "recherche du temps perdu". At the same time, this passage from *Coming Up for Air* also looks forward to the central conception of *Nineteen Eighty-Four*. There the Inner Party which governs Oceania is convinced that the past is no more than a lot of facts that can be learned and unlearned, or a series of entries in history books that can be constantly revised and rewritten. The past, in short, is always under the control of those who exercise power in the present, and has no independent existence. This is the burden of the exchanges late in the book between the triumphant O'Brien and the tortured, defeated Winston Smith.

In *Coming Up for Air* George Bowling undertakes a literal, physical *recherche*, in a spirit both Wordsworthian and Proustian, as he tries to recapture his early life by returning to Lower Binfield. In *Nineteen Eighty-Four* Winston Smith is engaged in a comparable but far more desperate and problematical attempt to recover the past. This attempt provides the essential action of the novel. In his official employment at the Ministry of Truth Winston rewrites old newspaper stories so that the current versions of the past are the only accessible ones. But in his private revolt against the Party he tries to rely on his own faulty memories and on the empirical reality of his own senses to provide him with the truth of things, as against the Party's continual manipulations of past and present. Winston Smith's attempt to find out about the past culminates in Chapter 8 of Part 1. He buys an old man a drink in a pub in a prole quarter of London and asks him what he can remember about the early years of the twentieth century, "before the revolution". He does not succeed; the old man rambles on but cannot provide any coherent picture to set against the Party's propaganda histories.

A sense of helplessness took hold of Winston. The old man's memory was nothing but a rubbish-heap of details. One could question him all day without getting any real information. The Party histories might still be true after a fashion: they might even be completely true. He made a last attempt.

But he can get no more sense out of the old man and he wanders out into the street again:

Within twenty years at the most, he reflected, the huge and simple question, "Was life better before the Revolution than it is now?" would have ceased once and for all to be answerable. But in effect it was unanswerable even now, since the few scattered survivors from the ancient world were incapable of comparing one age with another. They remembered a million useless things, a quarrel with a workmate, a hunt for a lost bicycle pump, the expression on a long-dead sister's face, the swirls of dust on a windy morning seventy years ago: but all the relevant facts were outside the range of their vision. They were like the ant, which can see small objects but not large ones. And when memory failed and written records were falsified — when that happened, the claim of the Party to have improved the conditions of human life had got to be accepted, because there did not exist, and never again could exist, any standard against which it could be tested.

Winston has to admit defeat in his larger design of establishing the truth of history, as against the Party's versions of it. But he persists in trying at least to record *his* memories and experiences in the illicit diary, as a gesture against the Party's claim to control all memory. Winston retreats to a basic sense of himself and his own senses, in a spirit of existential assertion and defiance. In this he is aided by his love affair with Julia, whose unashamed sexuality is another form of defiance, and an atavistic return to earlier and more basic forms of human existence.

Soon after he leaves the pub where he met the old man Winston finds a material manifestation of the past. Wandering through the slum streets he comes upon the junk shop where he bought the beautifully produced old writing book in which he keeps his diary. The shop's contents are mostly rubbish, but Winston buys a fine glass paperweight with coral embedded in it, that the owner of the shop tells him must be at least a hundred years old; it provides a beautiful if mute fragment of the past that he is trying to capture. The shopkeeper is an amiable Dickensian figure of about sixty, frail and bowed, wearing thick spectacles on a long nose, with almost white hair and a velvet jacket. He shows Winston a room upstairs which contains a large bed and other old-fashioned furniture, and no telescreen. It occurs to Winston that he could rent the room and ensure himself a truly private retreat:

the room had awakened in him a sort of nostalgia, a sort of ancestral memory. It seemed to him that he knew exactly what it felt like to sit in a room like this, in an arm-chair beside an open fire with your feet in the fender and a kettle on the hob; utterly alone, utterly secure, with nobody watching you, no voice pursuing you, no sound except the singing of the kettle and the friendly ticking of the clock.

And this is the room that Winston does rent before long, as a place where he and Julia can make love. Later he describes it in these words: "The room was a world, a pocket of the past where extinct animals could walk." On the level of plot everything in *Nineteen Eighty-Four* ends in betrayal, and so it proves with this "pocket of the past"; Winston and Julia are arrested there, and in a melo-dramatic revelation the Dickensian shopkeeper is shown to be an agent of the Thought Police in disguise.

But the sheer plot of *Nineteen Eighty-Four* seems to me one of the least interesting things about it. I am much more interested in the underlying attitudes and assumptions just below the overt surface, and to which there are many clues in the book; or, to pick up a convenient distinction made by Frank Kermode, in pursuing its "secrets" rather than its "sequence". You may have noticed in the passages I have quoted how frequently the words "memory" and "remember" occur in them, and indeed they are scattered thickly throughout the book. On the level of story this is what one might expect, as Winston Smith tries to assert his concept of memory against the Party's. But Winston in a sense remembers mor things than he could ever remember. He acknowledges this when he first sees the room which is to be for a time his secret "pocket of the past". It awakes in him what he calls "a sort of nostalgia, a sort of ancestral memory". He has a sense of things which he has never experienced, like sitting snugly in an arm-chair by an open fire, listening to the singing of the kettle and the ticking of the clock. Winston has to invoke an idea of "ancestral memory" to explain his familiarity with these things. But George Orwell knew about them at first hand, and there are passages in his essays and autobiographical writings which express a nostalgic longing for the open fire and the cosy interior of a working-class home. Here and elsewhere in *Nineteen Eighty-Four* Orwell is projecting his own experiences and fears and desires on to Winston Smith, just as ten years earlier he had done on to George Bowling. There is an interesting example of direct authorial intervention into Winston's narrative early in the book, in the description of O'Brien. "He had a trick of resettling his spectacles on his nose which was curiously disarming — in some indefinable way, curiously civilized. It was a gesture which, if anyone had still thought in such terms, might have recalled an eighteenth-century nobleman offering his snuffbox." It is a curious phrase, "if anyone had still thought in such terms". Winston is hardly in a position to think in such terms, for he is not familiar with the idea of eighteenth-century noblemen and snuffboxes. Orwell has taken over from the consciousness of his character. We sense the difficulty of portraying realistically an intelligent person whose understanding of the past is as limited as Winston's is supposed to be.

Orwell was very attached to the past, both to the Edwardian years of his own childhood, and to the longer past preserved in history and literature. In *Nineteen Eighty-Four* he makes a horrified but fascinated exploration of the possibility that the past could be abolished by the power of the state. As many critics have remarked, the central paradox of Orwell's literary personality arises form the tension between his backward-looking, conservative imagination and his radical political convictions. Literature is one of the major ways in which the past is re-enacted in the present, and George Orwell was a very literary writer. Born in 1903, he was part of what I regard as the best-read generation in history. He grew up in an age of general literacy, when the whole of English Literature was available in inexpensive editions or second-hand copies, or from public libraries; at the same time, reading had not yet been challenged and to some extent undermined by the spread of radio, cinema and television. I believe that the shaping categories or paradigms of Orwell's imagination were largely drawn from literature, and that *Nineteen Eighty-Four* is a very literary book. I have already touched on its literariness in referring to its relations to the earlier dystopias of Wells, Zamyatin and Huxley, though I think that these generic affinities are at best limited.

I now want to turn to a different aspect of *Nineteen Eighty-Four* and consider its image of London. For British writers London has several different dimensions: it is the vast, sprawling capital city, the centre of so many aspects of national life; it is the place where many writers live and set their fictions; and it is a deeply literary idea, as when we speak of the London of the Sherlock Holmes stories, or of *The Waste Land*, or the London of Dickens or Blake. Orwell had used London in his earlier books, such as *Down and Out in Paris and London* and *A Clergyman's Daughter* and *Keep the Aspidistra Flying*, and the process culminates in the shabby, run-down city portrayed in his last novel. As I have remarked, there is much in that portrayal that directly recalls the London of the end of the Second World War. And yet, as in an archaelogical site, there is another, earlier London a little below the surface of *Nineteen Eighty-Four*. On the second page Winston Smith reflects on the London where he lives and works:

> He tried to squeeze out some childhood memory that should tell him whether London had always been quite like this. Were there always these vistas of rotting nineteenth-century houses, their sides shored up with baulks of timber, their windows patched with cardboard and their roofs with corrugated iron, their crazy garden walls sagging in all directions? And the bombed sites where the plaster dust swirled in the air and the willow-herb straggled over the heaps of rubble; and the places where the bombs had cleared a larger patch and there had sprung up sordid colonies of wooden dwellings like chicken-houses.

Now as I can confirm from my own memories, quite a lot of London did look like that at the end of the Second World War, and for several years afterward. But as we read on we find that the London of *Nineteen Eighty-Four* is not merely a matter of a large number of surviving nineteenth-century houses, which was certainly the case in the 1940s, and is still so today to a lesser extent, but of the survival of a nineteenth-century way of life in the prole quarters. In Chapter 7 of Part 1 Winston has a comprehensive negative vision of London: "He seemed to see a vision of London, vast and ruinous, city of a million dustbins." Within this dismal expanse several different kinds of life are carried on. The apparatchiks of the Inner Party like O'Brien live in great luxury, while the operatives of the Outer Party, like Winston and Julia, exist in conditions of despondent shabbiness and deprivation that stop short of outright squalor. Below them are the teeming millions of the proles, 85% of the population we are told, whose lives resemble those of the Victorian urban poor:

> Even the civil police interfered with them very little. There was a vast amount of criminality in London, a whole world-within-a-world of thieves, bandits, prostitutes, drug-peddlars, and racketeers of every description; but since it all happened among the proles themselves, it was of no importance. In all questions of morals they were allowed to follow their ancestral code. The sexual puritanism of the Party was not imposed upon them.

This is certainly not the London of the 1940s, which was a remarkably law-abiding city, nor the London of the 1980s, which is more violent and lawless than it once was. The description directly recalls accounts of the Victorian underworld, where the high achievements of bourgeois culture were literally superimposed on a mass of crime and vice and exploitation. John Fowles has given vivid fictional expression of this dichotomy in Victorian society in *The French Lieutenant's Woman*. When Winston makes an expedition "somewhere in the vague, brown-coloured slums to the north and east of what had once been Saint Pancras Station", he seems to be taking a time-trip back to Victorian London. There, in the heart of the slums, he finds the junk shop which is briefly to provide him with a haven and a "pocket of the past". I described the owner as a Dickensian figure, and the shop itself embodies the archetype of the Old Curiosity Shop. In general, though, Winston's, or Orwell's, presentation of the slum world reminds me not so much of Dickens as of a later Victorian novelist whom Orwell much admired, George Gissing, and particularly Gissing's treatment of the London slums in *The Nether World*. In 1948, at about the time he was completing *Nineteen Eighty-Four*, Orwell wrote an admiring essay on Gissing, which gave an impressionistic picture of his London: "It is the fog-bound, gas-lit London of the eighties, a city of drunken puritans, where clothes, architecture and furniture had reached their rock-bottom of ugliness, and where it was almost normal for a working-class family of ten persons to inhabit a single room." The London of Gissing provides a literal and extensive underworld in *Nineteen Eighty-Four*; an important aspect of the novel looks back to the 1880s rather than forward to the 1980s. The importance of the proles is that they embody the past, albeit seen in a very literary way. In *Coming Up for Air* George Bowling remarked that the proles are freer than the middle classes, and in *Nineteen Eighty-Four* a Party slogan proclaims that "Proles and animals are free". Winston cherishes the desperate hope that the proles might provide the basis for a revolution against the Party, though he scarcely believes it in rational terms. But, for all their ignorance and even brutishness, the proles provide for Winston an almost aesthetic image of freedom and spontaneity. This is exemplified in the fat prole woman whom Winston sees from the window of the room above the junk shop, continually hanging out washing and singing a sentimental song. *Nineteen Eighty-Four* reflects Orwell's own complex and ambiguous attitude to the working class.

In several ways *Nineteen Eighty-Four* is a backward-looking book. As a dystopia it is indebted to Zamyatin's *We* and Wells's *The Sleeper Awakes*. And in its seemingly realistic accounts of London it has affinities with Dickens and Gissing. At the same time, the image of London in *Nineteen Eighty-Four* has provided a *topos* for much subsequent English fiction of a futurological or dystopian kind. There is a recurring picture of London, usually in the near future, as a somewhat nightmarish city: technologically advanced yet shabby, heavily policed yet violent and dangerous. This picture seems to me to be derived from *Nineteen Eighty-Four*. One finds it in Anthony Burgess' *1985*, which was written as a deliberate challenge to Orwell, though it appears more effectively in the same author's earlier *A Clockwork Orange*. It dominates Zoe Fairbairns' feminist dystopia *Benefits*. Other versions appear in Martin Amis's novel *Dead Babies* and Ian McEwan's story "Two Fragments: March 199-", and in J.G. Ballard's novels *High Rise* and *Concrete Island*. I am not, of course, saying that these writers copied Orwell; literary influence works in more complex ways than that. There are many differences between them and the ways in which they portray a dystopian London. But I believe the Orwellian image did provide a shaping model for their imaginations. One of the salutary lessons of recent criticism in the structuralist tradition is that literature is in certain important senses made out of other literature. Texts incorporate other texts, in the process known as intertextuality. Literature is made out of life, as well, of course. But in drawing on life writers, like painters, use categories and models and paradigms derived from earlier practitioners. This was always true of Orwell, I believe, even in his realistic novels of the 30s, which seem to be directly drawn from experience and observation. *Keep the Aspidistra Flying*, for instance, contains many autobiographical elements, but it also reads like a transposition of Gissing's *New Grub Street* to the London of the mid-1930s; while in *Coming Up for Air* Wells's *History of Mr. Polly* is a distinct intertextual presence. *Nineteen Eighty-Four* exemplifies the process in more interesting and complex ways. It draws on earlier literature, and at the same time has provided a potent example to subsequent writers.

I want finally to consider some of the ways in which literature has not only shaped *Nineteen Eighty-Four*, but how it works within the novel. Early on in the story Winston has a dream:

Suddenly he was standing on short springy turf, on a summer evening when the slanting rays of the sun gilded the ground. The landscape that he was looking at recurred so often in his dreams that he was never fully certain whether or not he had seen it in the real world. In his waking thoughts he called it the Golden Country. It was an old, rabbit-bitten pasture, with a foot-track wandering across it and a molehill here and there. In the ragged hedge on the opposite side of the field the boughs of the elm trees were swaying very faintly in the breeze, their leaves just stirring in dense masses like women's hair. Somewhere near at hand, thought out of sight, there was a clear, slow-moving stream where dace were swimming in the pools under the willow trees.

Julia appears in the dream and removes her clothes in a single forceful gesture. Winston's response is not so much sexual as aesthetic admiration of the gesture itself:

With its grace and carelessness it seemed to annihilate a whole culture, a whole system of thought, as though Big Brother and the Party and the Thought Police could all be swept into nothingness by a single splendid movement of the arm. That too was a gesture belonging to the ancient time. Winston woke up

226

with the word "Shakespeare" on his lips.

In Winston's consciousness, "Shakespeare", so unexpectedly invoked, is something else belonging to the "ancient time", along with the beauties of nature and of women, sexuality and free, spontaneous action. For Winston the Golden Country is a nostalgic image of perfection, rather as Lower Binfield had been for George Bowling. Eventually he discovers it in reality when he and Julia leave London and go into the country to make love; the landscape seems to correspond with his dream. The name "Golden Country" inevitably recalls the "Golden Age", that mythical age of perfection at the beginning of human history, the reign of Saturn, celebrated by Greek and Roman poets. But "Golden" was also a popular literary adjective at the end of the nineteenth century and the beginning of the twentieth. There were such titles as Kenneth Grahame's *Golden Days*, Sir James Frazer's *The Golden Bough*, Henry James's *The Golden Bowl* and James Elroy Flecker's *The Golden Journey to Samarkand*. Winston's brief rural idyll with Julia has richly literary implications, as does his later urban one in the "pocket of the past" above the junk shop.

The name of "Shakespeare", associated with the Golden Country in Winston's dream, is not directly followed up. But it recalls Huxley's *Brave New World*, where John, the "savage" from the New Mexico reservation, has devised a whole traditional world of culture and value, in opposition to the dominant one, from his study of a tattered volume of Shakespeare's collected works. The name of Shakespeare occurs later in *Nineteen Eighty-Four* when Winston is discussing with his colleague Syme, a Newspeak expert, the problems of turning the literature of the past into Newspeak. Syme, whom Winston thinks of as being too intelligent for his own good and who is eventually liquidated, says, "Chaucer, Shakespeare, Milton, Byron — they'll exist only in Newspeak versions, not merely changed into something different, but actually changed into something contradictory of what they used to be". It is not clear why the governing Party want to go to the trouble of laboriously rewriting the literature of the past when it would be much simpler to delete it *in toto*, but the effort is taken seriously. It is referred to again in significant terms on the last page of *Nineteen Eighty-Four*. There is a sense in which the book has more than one ending. Read as the human story of Winston and Julia it ends in unbearable defeat and betrayal — finally, Winston loves Big Brother. Yet the end of Winston is not quite the end of the book, considered as an Orwellian text. It is followed by the Appendix on Newspeak. In its final paragraph we read:

> Considerations of prestige made it desirable to preserve the memory of certain historical figures, while at the same time bringing their achievements in line with the philosophy of Ingsoc. Various writers, such as Shakespeare, Milton, Swift, Byron, Dickens, and some others were therefore in process of translation: when the task had been completed, their original writings, with all else that survived of the literature of the past, would be destroyed. These translations were a slow and difficult business, and it was not expected that they would be finished before the first or second decade of the twenty-first century.

"A slow and difficult business". It is evident that the literature of the past resists the ultimate totalitarian transformation, which is likely to take another twenty or thirty years to complete. It is not a very substantial hope, but it is more of a hope than anything in the sad story of Winston Smith's attempt at one-man resistance. Shakespeare, Milton, Swift, seem to have more resilience. As I have remarked, Orwell took literature very seriously.

Now that *Nineteen Eighty-Four* the book and 1984 the year have finally coincided I believe that the meaning of Orwell's text has changed decisively. The words on the page remain the same; but literary meaning, as I understand it, arises from the interaction between what an author wrote at a particular time and place in history, and the interests and expectations and knowledge that readers bring to it at successively different times and places. Literary meaning, in short, is never fixed or static. For thirty-five years Orwell's *Nineteen Eighty-Four* has been read mainly as a book about the future, even though his interest was very much in the present in which he wrote. Now its notional future has become our present; and one way of discussing the novel — taking its futurological speculations at face value — is now no longer feasible. For a brief twelve-month period the two 1984s — the book and the year — have been running parallel, like two trains on adjacent tracks. And now like passengers in one of the trains we can look across with mild curiosity at the passengers in the other train. Much recent discussion of the book has been in this spirit, comparing our present reality with Orwell's imagined one, and being grateful that however bad things are with us now they are not as bad as in Orwell's vision, or at least not bad in the same way.

Very soon the year "1984" will signify not the future but the past. And this will inevitably change our ways of reading and responding to the book. In the minor literature, or sub-literature, of the genres of science fiction and futurological writing there have been a good many books with dates in their titles, indicating an imagined future, usually involving wars or other disasters which never came to pass. Two examples which come to my mind are called *The Invasion of England in 1897* and *The Gas War of 1930*, and there are many others. It would be a misfortune if Orwell's book dwindled to this level of quasi-antiquarian historical interest. To avoid that, it will require different modes of reading. We shall have to read it as a book written at one point in history, 1948, notionally about another, later point in history, 1984. It will have become a book about the past, not the future. But as I have been suggesting, a good deal of *Nineteen Eighty-Four* is in any event about the past, in its evocation of Gissing's London, or the nostalgic Edwardian pastoral of Winston Smith's dream of a Golden Country. *Nineteen Eighty-Four* is not just about the past, however. It is about something subtler and less easy to grasp, which is memory, and the innumerable ways in which past and present interact. As George Bowling observed, "the past is a curious thing". The effort to recapture it and truly to understand it has been a major theme of the literature of the past two hundred years. As examples I need do no more than recall two names I have already mentioned in passing: Wordsworth, Proust. It was a great preoccupation of Orwell's, and I believe that *Nineteen Eighty-Four* is his most searching exploration of the nature of memory, both personal and collective.

Warwick   Bernard Bergonzi

Lightning Source UK Ltd.
Milton Keynes UK
UKOW050816240312

189499UK00001B/58/A